S. S. R.

Yakutsk

RIVER ALDAN

RIVER

STANOVOI

MTS.

SEA
of
OKHOTSK

KAMCHATKA
SOV.

KURILE ISLANDS
JAP.

SAKHALIN (SOV.)

Alexandrovsk

Komsomolsk

Khabarovsk

Blagoveshchensk

YABLONOVOI MTS.

RWY.

AMUR RIVER

Aigun

Amur River

Sungari River

Ussuri River

Chita

TRANS SIBERIAN

Hailar

CHINESE EASTERN

Tsitsihar

Harbin

RWY.

Vladivostok

Manchouli

MANCHURIA

SOUTH MANCHURIAN RWY.

Changchun

SEA
of
JAPAN

Tokyo

Yokohama

Mukden

Heijo

Nagoya

Kyoto

Jehol

Seoul

Kobe

Osaka

OLIA

Peking

Port Arthur

Dairen

Tientsin

YELLOW
SEA

Ningsia

YELLOW

Tsingtao

Tsinan

RIVER

Nanking

Shanghai

A

Books by the Same Author

SOVIET RUSSIA'S FOREIGN POLICY, 1939–1942
THE BIG THREE. THE UNITED STATES, BRITAIN, AND
RUSSIA
FORCED LABOR IN SOVIET RUSSIA
THE REAL SOVIET RUSSIA (REVISED EDITION)
RUSSIA AND POSTWAR EUROPE
SOVIET RUSSIA AND THE FAR EAST

THE
RISE OF RUSSIA
IN ASIA

BY

DAVID J. DALLIN

NEW HAVEN
YALE UNIVERSITY PRESS
1949

Preface

The founding of Vladivostok, the opening of Korea, the Kaiser inciting the Tsar to fight the "yellow peril," Theodore Roosevelt as Japan's friend and American delight at Russia's defeats in 1905, the first outline of a Russian "sphere" in China—are these not events that have long passed into ancient history, events that bear no relation to the manifold problems and troubles of today? Have not two great wars torn us away from these crises of yesteryear, and have not two great revolutions—in Russia and in China—opened a deep abyss between then and now?

The narrative of even the first phases of the Russian Revolution as it affected the Far East appears today as little more than a sequence of happenings long, long past. The Kuomintang's participation in the Comintern, Comrade Chiang Kai-shek as an admirer of Lenin, and Moscow proclaiming the seizure of Port Arthur by Russia to be "a base imperialist grab"—what relevance has all this to the realities of our days?

Yet there is an inherent, a close relation between that past and the present—a relation so intimate that no real understanding of current events is possible without an acquaintance with these seemingly obsolete theories and political trends. Before our eyes pre-revolutionary patterns are reviving; faded blueprints reacquire color. Often the similarity is so striking as to permit, on the basis of the experience of the past, predictions of imminent developments with a fair degree of accuracy.

What these chapters of history teach us is the basic element of all Russian policies once they become "dynamic," expansionist: opposition to the greatest naval world power—first, Britain and then its successor in international leadership, the United States. The Russian Far East was one venture in this relentless struggle and was developed into an anti-British base; to enlarge her possessions in the Far East Russia concluded alliances with other nations in the Orient whenever they stood ready to oppose Britain—except for those short periods when the greater German menace demanded a rapprochement with Britain or the United States (1907–17 and 1941–45), Russian Far Eastern policy, whenever subject to the over-all expansionism, was primarily and consistently directed against these two powers.

We further observe the pattern of a "Russian sphere in Asia"— China and Korea—emerging in the nineteenth century, and in the 60 years since its hesitant beginnings its confines have not substantially changed. The initial program from 1896 to 1904 called for the incorporation of Port Arthur and then the whole of Manchuria into the Russian Empire, just as they constitute the point of departure today. Even the political methods of our days call to mind the developments of the early 1900's: Russia's failure to evacuate Manchuria, contrary to signed agreements; the violation of treaties; the systematic weakening of China, aiming at her disintegration; and the proclamation of the "defense of China" against the West as the central slogan of Russian propaganda after the middle of the nineteenth century. Even the peopling of empty wastes like those of the Amur and Sakhalin with convict settlers is no innovation; it was resorted to as far back as 1860—with the difference, however, that it is now being practiced on a far larger scale.

"Dynamism" in Russia's Far Eastern policy has been the program of the extreme political elements since the 1890's: of extreme reactionaries before the Revolution; of extreme Communists today. Liberal and democratic elements have usually been opposed to Russian expansionism, as they are opposed today. Since the very outset there has been an adventurous element inherent in the Far Eastern extension of Russia. While the ensuing danger of war has always been great, the Russian people have invariably looked with indifference upon the acquisition of these unknown and distant lands and nationalities whose very names sound alien and whose conquest promises no benefit. This has been equally true before and after the Revolution.

In the initial Soviet period Russia's Far Eastern policy contained elements that did not attract general attention until recently. It was in Mongolia, not in Poland, that Moscow established its first "friendly government"—in 1921, not in 1945. There was a genuine prototype of the regimes later established in eastern Europe, with guarantees of "national sovereignty" and full power in the hands of Soviet envoys and representatives. Likewise the short-lived "sovereign" Far Eastern Republic, provided with a democratic constitution—without soviets—demonstrated how the substance of democracy could be dispensed with while the shell of nomenclature and propaganda slogans was meticulously preserved. If only the signatories of impressive documents guaranteeing democracy everywhere, in our own days, had been a little better informed of the lessons of the past . . . They might also have acquainted themselves with the history of Tannu Tuva, which shows how an independent People's Republic is but the first stage on the road to incorporation into the Soviet Union.

Yet despite these and a multitude of other similarities, analogies, and parallels between the prerevolutionary past and the present— particularly between the Russian *Drang nach Osten* from 1896 to 1904 and the Soviet drive in 1945–49—there are essential distinctions that belie the comfortable view of Soviet policy as a mere reverting to the patterns of Imperial Russia.

One distinction is ideological, the other is factual. The element of universality in Communist ideology, the product of its peculiar internationalism, serves as a basis for designs in foreign policy so great, so bold, so sweeping as never to have existed before in Russian history. Not even in the most fitful moments of expansionist fever did the old empire seriously consider blueprints encompassing the whole of the world. The other difference, since the end of the war, lies in the unique situation in which there is no other Asiatic power of equal or even comparable stature and might to Soviet Russia. The disappearance of an armed Japan and the utter impotence of China throw the gates to the East ajar for the only surviving power of the Eurasian continent. Thus an ideological inclination combined with the opportunity of the present merges into the most formidable expansionist drive in Russia's Far Eastern history.

But history also shows a way out of desperate situations. There is the lesson both of Russia's campaigns early in this century, and of Japan's bid for power in the thirties. The progressive isolation of each of these powers is the first consequence; the coalition of their adversaries is the second; and, finally, if nothing else is capable of stopping their relentless dynamism, an armed conflict ensues, in which the challenger invariably loses to the converging forces of the world.

This book is essentially a companion volume to my *Soviet Russia and the Far East*, published in 1948. The present book deals with Russia's Far Eastern policies from their genesis in the middle of the last century until 1931, where the previous volume takes up the story and carries it down to the present. The two volumes were initially meant to appear simultaneously; the manuscript of this part was, however, completed later than had been anticipated.

The dates throughout follow the Western calendar, and not the Russian "old style" in use before the Revolution.

Contents

Maps

Russia's Place in Asia

Three fundamental factors make up the framework of Russian policy in Asia: first, the great political vacuum in the vicinity of Russia's eastern borders; second, the peculiar configuration of Russia proper; and third, the basic divergence in the recent evolution of China and Japan.

The outline of Asia is determined by four great nations: Russia in the west; India in the south; China in the east; and Japan in the northeast. These four countries embrace roughly half of the world's population—over a billion human beings. Their population is, however, heavily concentrated at the extremities of the Asiatic continent, while the enormous spaces in its center constitute a sort of vacuum (see Map I). Mountain ranges and deserts, unfavorable climatic conditions and difficulties in communication make these focal areas all but uninhabitable. Only a few small, culturally backward nationalities live in these wide spaces of central Asia.

The area of the whole of continental Asia, exclusive of Siberia, is 8.9 million square miles. Of this large area, approximately 3 million square miles—or 34 per cent—constitute the central Asian vacuum. Of Asia's estimated population of 1,150,000,000 only 35 million—or 3 per cent—live in the 34 per cent of Asia that makes up this hub of the giant continent.[1] Of Greater China's 4.2 million square miles, China proper occupies but one third—1.5 million.

Russia proper covers one third of the surface of the Russian state. In Asia, the great bulk of people of Russia proper extends only as far as western Siberia. Russian-held central Asia is inhabited by non-Russian nationalities; only in the second half of the last century was this area conquered and incorporated into the Russian Empire. Essentially it remains a part of the central Asian vacuum.

---

1. Russia is now in possession of the western edge of the vacuum; of the 35 million mentioned above, about 20 million live in Soviet central Asia, the rest in Mongol, Chinese, and Tibetan territory.

I. The Power Vacuum in Asia

Natural barriers—the Himalayas—have limited the expansion of multinational India into the neighboring regions to the north, and the contested areas between British possessions and China were therefore confined to those parts of the vacuum which lie between China and India—Tibet, Burma, and Nepal.

Japan, the smallest of the Big Four, ranged across a series of islands, was not able until the end of the nineteenth century to develop into a great power on the mainland. She entered the race by a bid for empire building in Korea and the establishment of a corridor toward the vacuum through Manchuria and Mongolia.

In a geographical sense Russia occupies one sixth of the world's dry surface, nearly 9 million square miles in Europe and Asia, of which about three fourths are in Asia. This is the largest contiguous national bloc of land anywhere in the world, far greater than the territorial expanse of China, India, or the United States. Yet the population of Russia proper is only 40 per cent that of China and 45 per cent that of India. Vast parts of European Russia and still vaster regions of Asia are either sparsely populated or not inhabited at all. For a long time to come the deserts around the Caspian Sea are bound to play a most unimportant historical role. The Russian territories on the northern ramparts of Europe and Asia above the 60th degree, while enormous in size, provide only limited opportunity for agriculture and industry. The region of the "permanently frozen" earth, where the soil never completely thaws, stretches from the White Sea in Europe through the whole of northern Siberia to the Pacific. Of Siberia's 5 million square miles, 3.75—or about 75 per cent—are in this dismal frozen wasteland. The climate and geography of this vast expanse precludes its playing an important role in economics and politics. Some promising experiments in agriculture have been carried out in recent decades, but it will take centuries before the Asiatic north and northeast acquire first-rate political significance.

Political Russia—for centuries the locus of almost all Russia's population and of Russia's traditional historical development—is not identical with geographic Russia, just as political Canada and geographic Canada are not identical, nor geographic and political Africa, in whose northern part economic, cultural, and political development is confined to the coastal areas due to the existence

II. POLITICAL AND

GEOGRAPHICAL RUSSIA

of the Sahara Desert. In the case of Russia, the difference between the geographic and political entity is most pronounced. Political Russia (as shown on Map II) comprises only 35 per cent of Russia's territory but includes over 90 per cent of her population. It is in this area that the course of Russia's history has been shaped.

In western Asia political Russia embraces fertile lands and industrial centers in an area narrowing down from the Urals to Lake Baikal. Farther to the east, the map shows the vast emptiness of eastern Siberia, socio-economically and politically reduced to a mere narrow corridor to the Pacific. Only at the extreme eastern end of this corridor, around and below the Amur River, does the political territory widen again. The gradual conquest of Siberia in the sixteenth, seventeenth, and eighteenth centuries was the most easily accomplished phase of Russia's expansion. The scanty native population, where it existed at all, could not and did not offer any serious resistance. By the same token, however, for the people of Russia the benefits derived from this acquisition were less significant than from other areas.

Less than a century has passed since Russia acquired her Far East, covering a comparatively small area to the east of the 130th degree and to the south of the 54th parallel. Possession of the lands to the north of it, including the long shore of the Pacific, as well as Alaska (as long as the latter was a Russian colony), would not have sufficed to enable Russia to develop into one of the leading powers of the Pacific. The newly acquired Russian Far East has been the key to her influence in the Orient.

The third fundamental factor in all Far Eastern problems, down to our days, has been the great difference in the reaction of the two great peoples of the Far East to the influence of the West. This fact, often described but never adequately explained, is an outstanding phenomenon of contemporary history. Until a century ago both China and Japan stagnated in medieval backwardness. Both, and particularly China, could boast of a long history full of brilliant cultural accomplishments. But in recent centuries, while Europe and America were making progress in virtually all fields of human endeavor, the colossi of the Far East were lagging behind, and the chasm between them and the countries of the West in scientific and technical matters kept growing ever greater.

The impact of the West upon the East began to make itself felt about a hundred years ago. The incubation period, as it were, in the westernization of the Orient lasted about 50 years, down to the startling developments of 1895–98. In the 1840's Britain began her penetration of China; during the 1850's the United States "opened up" Japan. These two events marked a defeat for both China and Japan. Communication and commercial relations between the Far East and the Western world began to develop. Now, however, China and Japan moved in different directions. China proceeded from defeat to defeat. She suffered humiliations, was compelled to accept "unequal treaties," and had to cede territory and leaseholds to foreign governments. Efforts to rejuvenate and unify the huge nation remained on paper. China was clearly unable to conjure forth the forces needed for national unity and a resumption of progress. For a hundred years now China, under both monarchy and republic, has been on the downgrade—a course in which faithless mandarins, covetous war lords, pro-Japanese puppets, and pro-Soviet Communists have all played their part.

This weakening of China became the dominant factor in Far Eastern affairs. The country seemed doomed. The outlying dependencies on her peripheries seemed to be but loosely attached to the body politic of the parent state. China appeared to be a conglomerate of provinces, nationalities, and religions—an amalgam so weakened, disorganized, and heterogeneous that a strong jolt from the outside might be able to dislodge what unity remained and perhaps put an end to the very existence of China as a state. And there was assuredly no lack of such jolts—from the east, north, and west.

Japan, on the contrary, was rising. The painful stings she had suffered in the fifties and sixties served as both a lesson and a challenge. Within a few decades her internal political structure was remodeled, and from a multitude of semiautonomous provinces a strongly centralized state emerged. European and American ways were studied and successfully imitated, industry and trade developed at an amazing pace, and an army and navy were reorganized on European models, trained, equipped, and soon brought into action. Universal education was introduced in 1872. Railways, of which there were 23 miles in 1873, grew to 1,800 miles in 1893 and 4,200 in 1902. A university was founded in

Tokyo in 1877. Civil and penal codes were established after French models. In 1872, the first newspaper, successor to the verbal announcement of official news, appeared in Japan. Japan enacted reforms and introduced new institutions which it had taken other countries centuries to accomplish. Japan's superiority over the other nations of Asia became evident in all walks of life.

The 70 years from the 1870's to the end of the 1930's were an almost uninterrupted period of successes for Japan, in diplomacy as well as in war. Not once in the multitude of armed conflicts in which Japan was involved prior to the second World War did she suffer real defeat.

This divergence between China and Japan in their reaction to foreign pressure and influence has been an outstanding constant in the crosscurrents of the Far East. It is as significant and decisive today, even after Japan's defeat, as it was a century ago. Who knows what the fate of Asia—and of the whole of mankind—would have been had the positions of China and Japan been reversed: if China and not Japan had been rejuvenated, reorganized into a centralized state with considerable industrial potential, relatively high literacy, and, with her population of almost half a billion, had become the base of a modern army 5,000 divisions strong and of a navy five times as powerful as that of Japan?

Among Russia's problems in the Far East that of providing the vast vacuum with a population has been paramount now for wellnigh a century. This issue has acquired crucial importance as the Far Eastern areas figure increasingly in strategic calculations and as Russia wages defensive and offensive wars in the East.

The Russian Far East possesses considerable mineral resources; its seaports are excellent and can be enlarged at will; railways have been built, and new ones are constantly being added. The limitations to economic and cultural advance are set by the relatively low density of the population and by the great difficulties connected with its rapid increase. After 40 years of effort the Russian Far East in 1900 had a population of little over 300,000. Despite strenuous endeavors in the next 16 years, its population was still below the million mark at the time of the Revolution. Thereafter, the Soviet Government was certain that it could succeed where its predecessor had failed. The failures before 1917 were ascribed to tsarist policy and bureaucratic inefficiency; to the selfishness of the landlords, who were unwilling to release their cheap labor; and to the bad living conditions awaiting the settlers in the distant East. Now, with radical changes coming in all phases of Russian life, things were expected to progress more rapidly. Yet the movement of population to the East still continued at an exceedingly slow pace. It was not until 1925–26 that the Soviet Government was able to elaborate a consistent migration policy and to appropriate the necessary funds for its implementation. In spite of this more efficient program, the number of migrants to the Far East from 1925 to 1929 was only 109,000—fewer than in the prewar years.

Since 1927 the peopling and equipping of the Far East has been an important item in each of the all-encompassing Five-Year Plans. During the first plan, from 1928 to 1932, from 785,000 to 1,000,000 men were to settle in the Far East.[2] The plan was outspoken concerning the motivation of the development in the East. It pointed out that in Manchuria the grain crop had doubled since 1913, that the population there was growing by a million a year, and that, in general, that neighboring country was making rapid progress. Yet the Russian Far East, the authors of the plan stated, continued to lag. Cattle breeding, in fact, was slowing up, and even agricultural production was inadequate to supply the needs of the local population.

Under the First Five-Year Plan 2.5 per cent of new investments of the Soviet Union was to be allocated to the Far East. Since the population of that area was about 1 per cent of all of Russia, Russia proper was to expend a certain amount of its own national income on the Far East. The hundred million rubles—a very large sum for the Far East—were allocated for industrial investments in order to accelerate economic progress.

The Second Five-Year Plan was formulated after Japan had seized Manchuria.[3] In those years the importance of the Russian Far East enormously enhanced the attention paid by the Soviet Government to economic development in those provinces, as well

2. This figure, however, also included the anticipated migration to another region beyond the Baikal, which does not properly belong to the Far East. Cf., for instance, USSR Gosplan, *Pyatiletnii Plan* (3d ed., Moscow, 1930), III, 290–291.

3. Far Eastern events from 1931 on are treated in a companion volume, *Soviet Russia and the Far East* (Yale University Press, 1948).

as to the need of rapidly populating them. Of all capital investment for 1933–38, 4.14 per cent was assigned to the Far East.
The appropriations included the construction of new railroads of
a purely strategic nature; if, in case of war, the Trans-Siberian
Railway fell to the enemy, a second line—the Baikal-Amur Railway—far to the north of the old track would still connect the
Baikal region—and Europe—with the Pacific. The length of the
new railroad was to exceed 1,000 miles. Hundreds of millions of
rubles were to be spent for increasing the output of oil and coal
in the Far East and particularly for the creation of a so-called
machine-tool industry, a large segment of which, in Russia, serves
for armament production. The amount of Russian investments in
the Far East rose from year to year. In 1935–36 they came to almost a billion rubles.

The main difference between the character of the development
of the Far East during pre-revolutionary days and under the Soviets
was that under the latter it was industry, man power, and engineer-
ing that commanded attention, rather than agriculture and the
peasantry. This new form of development was costly. It was hard
for the people of Russia to provide billions for the Far East, but
now building and industrial expansion proceeded according to
plan. As far as augmenting the population of the regions was concerned, however, the results were less encouraging. The collective
farms of European Russia were almost the only source of additional
man power for urbanization and migration. Detailed plans had been
worked out as to the number of men to be drawn from the villages
for transfer to other regions. These plans fell short of fulfillment.
In 1938, for example, only 51 to 59 per cent of the planned amount
of man power was actually "transplanted" from the villages. Vol-
untary migration to the Far East was small. In contrast with the
optimistic forecasts, the overall increase of the Far East's population from 1926 to 1939 amounted to 1,097,000, of which immigration accounted for 899,000.[4]

On November 17, 1937, the government made available important facilities to encourage the migration of peasants to the Far
East. Travel expenses for them and their families were met by the

4. Frank Lorimer, *The Population of the Soviet Union* (Princeton, 1946), pp. 162, 164.

state. Their cattle, if delivered to the state's agencies before their departure, was replaced by equal herds upon their arrival in the new country. The state bore half the cost of building their new homes. A law was enacted exempting the migrants from payment of taxes and even, for a period of from five to ten years, from the duty of delivering their produce to the state. On June 27, 1939, the government decided to create a special Department of Migration, and large sums of money were put at its disposal. And yet, the results of the Soviet program in aid of migration were not satisfactory.

The possibility of a war conducted simultaneously by Germany and Japan against Russia became acute, and defense of the Far East became an urgent problem. In such a two-front war Russia would not be able to apply any part of her European resources toward the defense of the East. For its defense that area would have to rely on its own industry, railroads, and armament. Under these circumstances the low density of the Far Eastern population was a serious handicap. Therefore in the thirties, again, as in the days before the Revolution, the cry arose from the Far East for "more settlers" and "more material assistance"! Feeling ran high when the Third Five-Year Plan was discussed and announced in 1938–39, after the first serious clashes with Japan had occurred, and as new conflicts were expected.

The Third Five-Year Plan provided for the appropriation of 10 per cent of all industrial investments in the Far East. Commissar Molotov made a report on the new plan to the eighteenth Congress of the Communist party, which resolved in regard to the Far East:

An increase in coal output to 2.7 times the previous output;
The manufacture of synthetic liquid fuels by the process of hydrogenation of solid fuels;
The creation of a new metallurgical industry with all the equipment necessary to take care of all the needs of machine construction;
The speeding of new construction;
The acceleration of coal and cement output . . .

The most difficult Far Eastern problem, however, which this Congress took up continued to be the perennial population question. "The job of transplanting men into our region is not yet well organized," the commander of the Pacific Navy declared at the

Congress. "The question on which depends the solution of many problems in the Far East is the question of man power, of populating the region. This question is of economic as well as military importance." The situation was so difficult that Red Army men, having completed their military service in the Far East, had to remain there, settle, and have their families join them from Europe. One of the secretaries of the Central Committee of the Communist party, P. M. Pegov, wrote then in *Pravda:*

"The Third Five-Year Plan for the Maritime Provinces of the Far East must be a plan of colonization . . . there are not enough men in the region. The Ussuri area is likewise thinly populated. Sugar factories work at only half their capacity because an insufficient amount of sugar beets is sown. We must conduct a campaign for migration to the Soviet Maritime Provinces." Molotov, summarizing these discussions, then stated: "Settlement of the Far East has acquired great importance; it is time to pass from words to action."

Why is it, people asked, that so little success has been achieved in regard to settling the region? Why had the colossal efforts and the millions spent not converted the Far East into a densely populated country? The official explanation given was—acts of sabotage on the part of those Communist elements that were opposed to Stalin's government. "These internal enemies," the Far Eastern delegate, Donskoy, repeated at the Congress, "operated in the Far Eastern region; they intentionally created such conditions for workers and kolkhoz peasants that the new immigrants sometimes have had to go back."

The Third Five-Year Plan anticipated the immigration of 800,-000 people, but this goal proved difficult to achieve. The Central Planning Institute in Moscow analyzed the "reserves of man power" in the kolkhozes in the European part of Russia and demanded that part of the surplus move east. It assumed a theoretical surplus in Russian agriculture of no less than 2,600,000 able-bodied men and women. The efforts of the Institute, however, did not yield any important results.

"Comrade Stalin," the chief of the Planning Commission and member of the Politburo, Voznesensky, wrote in 1940, "stresses the fact that we have learned to distribute money and reserves of goods. But we have not learned to distribute man power according to plan, or to train it efficiently. Without such a distribution, the fulfillment of building and production plans is not assured." [5]

During the last 50 to 70 years several historically new regions in the Pacific have undergone spectacular development: Australia and New Zealand, the United States and Canada, Manchuria and the Russian Far East. Together with the ancient nations bordering on the Pacific—China, Korea, and Japan—they fill the main contours of the Pacific world of today. The Far Eastern picture of the future depends largely upon the evolution in the interrelationship of these regions.

It was during the middle of the nineteenth century that the new regions in the Pacific began to develop their economic resources and to attract settlers. At the beginning of that period none of them had more than a million inhabitants. In the subsequent colonial evolution which each of the regions experienced Australia's population rose to about 8 million, California's to 10 million, and Manchuria's to 40 million. The population growth of the Russian Far East as we have seen has been much slower. From the 1860's to the outbreak of the second World War it increased from 0.03 to 2.3 million.

A comparison of the Russian Far East with Manchuria is particularly to the point. One of the main arguments employed in favor of developing the Russian Far East used to be that of the "yellow peril." One of the chief aims of Russian demographic policy in the Far East prior to 1917 was the prevention of an influx of Chinese into Siberia and, in general, the stemming of "the expansion of the yellow races." This was the official reason given for the penetration into Manchuria early in the century and for making North Manchuria a Russian sphere of influence. The development of Manchuria was closely watched in the Russian capital.

Two provinces of North Manchuria, Heilungkiang and Kirin, which border on Russian soil, were and still are of special interest. Although no reliable statistics are available, the population of these two provinces in the 1860's and 1870's was estimated at about 1 million. At the end of the century, it had risen to 2 to 4 million, by 1920 to 10 million, and by 1940 to 18 million.

The differential rate of population growth in the new Pacific countries is evident from the following table.

5. *Planovoye Khozyaistvo* (1940), Nos. 4 and 12; and *Bolshevik* (1940), No. 1.

POPULATION (IN MILLIONS)

Area	1860–70	1895–1900	1920–21	1930–31	1939–40
Russian Far East	0.01	0.03	1.1	1.7	2.3
Manchuria: total	3.	9.	19.	31.	40.
Manchuria: two provinces, Kirin and Heilungkiang	1.	2–4	10.	15.	18.
Australia	1.4	3.6	5.4	7.	8.0
California	0.5	1.4	3.4	5.7	6.9

The Russian Far East has never attained a stage of self-sufficiency even in agriculture, while Manchuria's economy expanded and furnished Japan with important industrial products. The other new Pacific regions, too—for instance, California, Canada, Australia—had reached an economic level incomparably higher than that of the Russian Far East.

Today more than ever before, the political role of the Russian Far East is thus determined not so much by its own strength, its people, culture, and economy as by its backdrop, Russia in Europe, with her political mutations, social crises, and changing trends in international affairs.

I

The Rise of the Far East

That part of Asia that constitutes the heart of the Russian Far East was acquired by Russia about 90 years ago. By the middle of the nineteenth century Russia was in possession of eastern Siberia and Alaska, and bordered on the Asiatic shores of the Pacific from the Bering Straits to the vicinity of the Amur estuary. The vast spaces of northeastern Asia, virtually uninhabited, often inaccessible, and politically unimportant, did not constitute a base for either military or economic activity on the mainland or in the Pacific. Russia was in no position to participate in the great international ventures in the Far East which had begun to gain impetus in the 1840's and in which Great Britain was the leading power.

At that time Russo-British antagonism was at its peak. From the early days of the "Extreme Orient," as it was then called in Russia, down to the first Russo-Japanese war of 1904–5, this "cold war" of the nineteenth century was the determining element in Russia's Far Eastern policy. Russia's influence in Europe and Asia had grown immensely since the end of the Napoleonic Wars. It was strongly felt in Prussia and Austria-Hungary; it had increased as a result of Russian victories over Turkey and Persia; Russian penetration of central Asia was continuing successfully.

At the same time Britain, driving eastward from the Indian Ocean, approached China from the south. In 1842 China, defeated in the Opium Wars, signed a humiliating treaty ceding Hongkong to England. Five years later the British Navy took Canton. In 1854 the British took over the Shanghai customhouse. In 1860 a new war with Britain and France ended in a heavy defeat for China. The shadow of Britain lay over Russia's very first moves to acquire the new Far Eastern territories from China.

The Russian campaigns in the Far East in the middle of the nineteenth century were a departure from the age-old Russian movement to the east which had been a continuous move into the great vacuum of the northern Orient—to the wide and empty spaces of Siberia and beyond; on to the North Pacific and into the Western Hemisphere; into the wilderness, tundras, and unexplored mountain ranges; into immense spaces without cities and without roads, with native populations of a few thousand, nomads on the lowest level of civilization. Now Russia stopped this eastward expansion and contracted by withdrawing from America, and, in order not to have it fall into British hands, sold Alaska to the United States. Russia now turned south, toward Chinese Manchuria and Mongolia, against Korea, and closer to central Asia, into Chinese Turkestan.

Unlike the Russian expansion in Europe, this movement into eastern and central Asia pursued no strategic purpose, was not motivated by a need for resettlement of population nor by a desire for trade expansion. While encouragement of trade was part of the government's program, there was still a sort of aristocratic contempt of commerce in general as a guiding motive in foreign affairs; there was a marked feeling of superiority in St. Petersburg over the "merchant nations," like England and France, which occupied territories and built empires for the benefit of moneymakers. In a sense, this ideology was the forerunner of the contemptuous attitude toward capitalist colonialism in our days with which Soviet expansionism is contrasted as being motivated by loftier purposes.

It was axiomatic that the goal of Russian foreign policy was aggrandizement of Russia. No explanation was needed and the "ideology" of the policy could not be rationally explained. The aim was to enhance the grandeur of the empire, add to its glamor, and increase the glory of the Russian monarch. The tsar was the heir of a long line of leaders who in a chain of wars had enlarged their lands and pushed the borders of the once small principality farther and farther out to make it the greatest empire landmass of the world. The dominant view in Russia was that this process had not yet been completed. The unlimited autocratic power of the Russian sovereign over the life of each of his subjects and over the destinies of his country equaled that of a supreme military commander over the soldiers in his army. It was the tsar's duty and responsibility to work for the everlasting glory of Russia, for her continuous expansion, and toward making her superior in strength to other nations.

More than once in the history of the Far East a tsar acted boldly against the advice of his government. The Amur region down to the Sea of Japan was acquired on orders of Nicholas I. Fifty years later the second Nicholas dismissed some of his ministers and overruled others who opposed an aggressive course against Japan, and these steps led to Russia's first great war in the Far East.

The official philosophy made the Russian autocrat an instrument of divine power leading Russia toward victories and greatness. The old monarchy stood or fell with Russia's expansion. Once the expansion should reach its limits, the whole internal structure would collapse.

MURAVIEV, DEMOCRAT AND DESPOT

The outstanding personality of the first of the three great Russian drives into the Far East was the young Governor General of eastern Siberia, Nikolai Muraviev. In 1847 Muraviev was sent to the Far East by order of the Tsar, with the specific mission of starting a military and diplomatic campaign—one which would immediately affect China but which was, in the main, designed to counteract British and French activity at the other end of the Middle Empire. Muraviev's 14 years of activity in the Far East were marked by the first great push in a southerly direction in which Chinese possessions and a large number of uninhabited islands in the North Pacific were acquired.

Muraviev was on the one hand a devoted servant of his sovereign and on the other an ardent admirer of the United States, and was even interested in socialist and anarchist theories. Mikhail Bakunin, the father of modern anarchism, was a guest at his home. Another famous anarchist, Prince Peter Kropotkin, came to eastern Siberia soon after Muraviev's departure. In his memoirs he recalls that Muraviev "held advanced views and a democratic republic would not quite have satisfied him." In Muraviev's study, the young officers and Bakunin would discuss the possibility of establishing a United States of Siberia, federated across the Pacific with the United States of America.[1] In the words of Alexander Herzen,

1. P. Kropotkin, *Memoirs of a Revolutionist* (Houghton Mifflin Co., 1899), p. 169.

Muraviev "was an original man, a democrat and a tartar, a liberal, and a despot . . . He gave [the exiled] Bakunin a chance to breathe, an opportunity to live like a man, to read magazines and newspapers; and he himself dreamed with him about future cataclysms and wars." Bakunin himself wrote to Herzen in December, 1860: "Muraviev is the only man among all those who have power and influence in Russia who can and must fully and without the least reservations be considered *one of us*." [2]

Muraviev advocated the abolition of serfdom and was instrumental in easing the lot of political exiles in eastern Siberia. Anarchism and federation were more in the nature of dreams, however. His sympathies for the United States were, to a large extent, the product of his overwhelming emotional opposition to England and to British policy the world over. In 1853 he wrote the Tsar:

We have permitted the English to penetrate into this part of Asia—the same Englishmen who, quite naturally to the detriment and at the expense of all of Europe, prescribe their laws from their little island to all the continents of the world—except America—laws which tend not at all to benefit humanity but merely to serve the commercial interests of Great Britain, and to upset the tranquillity and welfare of other peoples. But this state of affairs will yet be remedied by *a close alliance between us and the North American States* . . . There can be no doubt that as part of the same scheme we must gain control of Sakhalin and the estuary of the Amur River . . .[3]

Muraviev predicted that the North Pacific would soon be dominated by only two nations: the United States in the east, and Russia in the west. The Russians were making a mistake, he maintained, in trying to penetrate the Western Hemisphere as far south as California in the expectation that the young United States would need a hundred years to expand from the Atlantic to the Pacific. The major task was the expulsion of Britain from the North Pacific, so that the two friendly nations—Russia and America—could divide the lands and the waters lying between them.

Since Muraviev was inclined to minimize the power of Britain, he saw no need to sell Alaska to the United States. He could see no reason for this diminution of the empire's colonial possessions.

2. Alexander Herzen, *Polnoye Sobraniye Sochinenii* (Lemke ed.), X, 402–403; XIV, 426.

3. I. Barsukov, *Muraviev-Amurski* (Moscow, 1891), I, 321–323.

Muraviev's chief aide in the operations in the Far East was Gennadi Nevelskoy, who later became Admiral of the Russian Navy. At the end of the forties Nevelskoy was ordered to sail from the Baltic to the Far East. It was Nevelskoy who explored the Amur estuary, Sakhalin Island, and North Pacific Oceania. It was he who found that, contrary to the prevailing assumption, the estuary of the Amur was navigable. Without Nevelskoy, Muraviev would have been able to achieve little. Both were animated by the same ideals and goals. Like Muraviev, Nevelskoy dreamed of great naviès and more ports for Russia—of everything Britain possessed and Russia wanted.

In 1848 Muraviev sent to his government a report concerning two Englishmen traveling in eastern Siberia of whom he was suspicious. One was an explorer, the other a geologist. "If they sail down the Amur," he wrote, "British ships will occupy Sakhalin next spring." In 1849 he again reported rumors of English intentions concerning the lower Amur and Sakhalin. "May the Lord have mercy on us, if they strengthen their positions there before we do!"

In 1850 the Chinese Emperor died, his heir at the time being only 18 years old. "The British will use this change," Muraviev wrote to the Tsar, "to seize control of not only the trade but also the policies of China."

In his address to China's envoys in 1855 Muraviev again returned to the subject of Britain: "Rapid conquests made by England in various parts of the world have brought her nearer to us. By means of her strong navy she had spread her influence in these countries. The perfidious roads traveled by Britain are well known to the Government of China." He was not being quite sincere, however, when he added: "But do not believe, gentlemen, that Russia is greedy for expansion of her frontiers. Such a plan is not within the scope of our intentions. All Russia cares for is the security of her boundaries."

Muraviev was appealing to the anti-British feelings of the Chinese, but he was of course glad to see how weakened China had become under the blows of war and internal disorders. This program of a pro-Chinese policy (that is, a policy opposed to encroachment by other great powers), coupled simultaneously with strong drives into China, was to become the pattern of Russian activity in the East for a hundred years. In a private letter, Muraviev said frankly, "I in no way regret that the British burned Canton, but of course I shall speak differently on meeting the Chinese." "If the defeat of China," he wrote in a memorandum, "should entail the fall of her dynasty, this outcome would of course be most favorable to Russia . . . Our neighbors, Manchuria and Mongolia, would become (in fact, if not in name) our possessions, and Russia would finally acquire all that she could here desire."

The military operations devoted to acquisition and occupation of territories in the Far East were simple. As a matter of fact, there was no war at all. Muraviev prepared ships and troops to sail down the Amur River, which at that time ran inside Chinese territory. When everything was ready he requested the Tsar's consent and obtained it in January, 1854. The Russian government believing, correctly, that England would consider the Far Eastern moves as operations directed against herself, was most reluctant. The Tsar, however, gave his order: "Sail down the Amur." But he added, "There must be no smell of powder."

It was easy for Muraviev to avoid the smell of powder. The Chinese Army, weakened by other conflicts, was far away, and the Chinese Government did not even attempt to oppose Muraviev's expedition. On reaching the mouth of the Amur River, he declared that all the territory on the left bank of the Amur must be ceded to Russia. The negotiations ended in 1858 in the Aigun Treaty, which declared the Amur to be the border between the two empires.

This was the first half of the operation. Muraviev soon demanded from China other territories to the east and south of the Amur along the Sea of Japan. His arguments during the negotiations with the Chinese in October, 1858, were all along the same line: "Protection of China" against England. "The pretext in our talks with the Chinese will be the same as before [he wrote], namely, not to let the English and the French seize any port between Korea and our possessions; it is therefore better that the whole shore, down to Korea, belong to us." [4]

Two years later China was compelled to yield to this demand. The so-called Ussuri region was ceded to Russia by the Peking treaty of 1860. To save face the Chinese Government, in truly oriental fashion, proclaimed to its people that the Emperor of China

4. Barsukov, *op. cit.*, II, 200–203 and 283 ff.

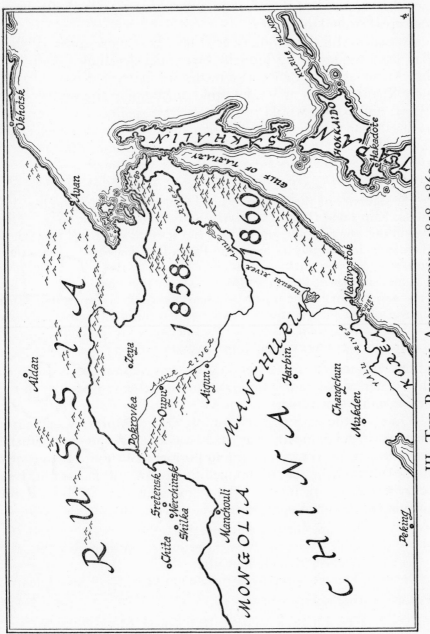

III. THE RUSSIAN ACQUISITIONS, 1858–1860

had pitied the poor Russians, who were in need of land for their population, and had therefore magnanimously granted them certain areas around the Amur.

Actually Muraviev took over from China more territory than had been requested by himself. His initial demands would have left Manchuria with an outlet to the sea between Korea and the new Russian border at Vladivostok; no common frontier between Russia and Korea would have been created. But then Muraviev realized that this short Manchurian shore line, with its excellent harbor facilities, might attract the British to establish footholds in the immediate vicinity of the new Russian territory.

We are leaving Posiet Bay to ourselves and are projecting the boundary to the estuaries of the Tumen River, which forms the boundary between Korea and China [Muraviev wrote home in July, 1859]. One would not want to take over more, but it turns out to be necessary: there is such a wonderful harbor in Posiet Bay that the English would certainly seize it at the first rift with China . . .

This entire shore line, from Posiet to Cape Povorotny for about 200 verst abounds in excellent bays and harbors which are so attractive for a naval power that, if this area were to remain in Chinese hands, the English would seize it all—especially since they saw and took notes in this area in 1855 and even published maps of it.[5]

Muraviev succeeded in extending the coveted territory down to the border of Korea by incorporating the area lying between the Suifun and Tumen rivers.

Thus was the Russian Far East established. Muraviev's achievement was hailed and he was made a count. Throughout Siberia receptions were arranged by the authorities to do honor to the hero. In the repetitious speeches and mellifluous poetry delivered at these festivities there are hints of the vague aims that lay behind the winning of this great new territory:

> Perhaps our two-headed eagle
> Will waken the dormant people [the Chinese]
> And call them to new life,
> Thus covering himself with glory.

Wrote another poet:

> Be still, thou Mongol! Be obedient, Chinese!
> For, to the Russians, Peking is not far!

5. Barsukov, *op. cit.*, I, 557–558.

A new city was to rise in the Far East on the bay where the British had landed in 1856, and which they had called Port May. The new outpost of Russian might, founded in 1860, was appropriately named Vladivostok—"Ruler of the East."

The attitude of the liberal opposition in Russia to the territorial acquisitions in the East was one of approval—but for peculiar reasons. The opposition saw in the new areas a bridge toward republican America, a springboard to a new and free world. They saw in the drive to the Pacific not so much of an extension of the empire's might as a harbinger of a decrease of autocracy and a turn toward political freedom. Alexander Herzen, the great spokesman of Russian liberalism, wrote in 1858 from London:

Russia has but one comrade in the future, one single companion: the Northern States . . . If Russia succeeds in freeing herself from the traditions of St. Petersburg, she will have an ally in the North American States.

The Pacific Ocean, he said,

. . . is the Mediterranean of the future. In this future the role of Siberia, as a country lying between the ocean, south Asia, and Russia, is of extreme importance. It is understood that Siberia must extend down to the border of China.

The names of Muraviev, Putyatin, and their comrades are indelibly inscribed in history. They have built the pillars for a long bridge across the ocean. While in Europe somber funerals are being held and everybody has something to grieve about, they at one end, and the Americans at the other, are hammering together a new cradle! [6]

A COUNTRY WITHOUT PEOPLE

What Russia had acquired in 1858–60 was a vast territory of about 400,000 square miles, the size of Germany and France combined. The population of the entire region, however, did not exceed 15,000. It was a huge emptiness, with no agriculture, no trade, no roads, and, of course, no industry. If the Maritime and Amur Provinces were to develop into an outpost of Russian power in the Pacific, armies must be stationed, ports erected, and a navy constructed and maintained in the Far East. These objectives entailed

6. Herzen, *op. cit.*, IX, 399–400; XII, 275.

hard work, large investments, and a consistent policy of support on the part of the Russian Government.

In the history of other empires, colonization often has proceeded from the economic to the political basis: economic pioneering opens new regions; subsequently, the political strength of a state advances along with its military force to protect its subjects. Such was the case, for instance, in Australia, Canada, California, Africa. In the history of the Russian Far East, the reverse has been true. The region was first occupied and annexed for political reasons; economic development occurred later.

To accomplish the political aim cities were needed to serve as centers of the administrative and military machine; ports were necessary, and a merchant marine; agriculture, villages, peasants were needed. Unless the Russian Far East became a well-populated country, the near-by Chinese population would settle in the Russian territory and thus lead to future demands of China for the return of her former possessions.

Transplantation of large numbers of Russians from Europe became more and more important. This was, however, almost impossible for Russia during the early decades of her occupation of the new Far East. Enormous funds were required which the state did not possess. The first Russian settlers were found among criminals from Siberia who had served sentences of hard labor for major offenses. There was difficulty in finding wives for these and the police therefore seized large numbers of prostitutes in the cities and hastily arranged marriages. Subsequently a semimilitary resettlement of the so-called "Cossack armies" (Amur and Ussuri Cossacks) took place. It was a compulsory resettlement and its results, when they became known in the European part of Russia, were anything but encouraging as far as further emigration was concerned. A great Russian explorer, Przhevalsky, visited the area at the end of the sixties and reported on the situation:

These settlers look upon the new region with animosity and consider themselves deportees. One hears bitter complaints about the hardships, and sad reminiscences of former habitations. Most of them lack even bread, and every year the state must feed a great part of the population, to save it from famine. The bread looks like dried clay and burns the mouth. As a result of poverty, there is terrible demoralization. It is difficult to believe the extent of the corruption among the population of the Ussuri region. Everywhere husbands sell their wives, and do it openly. Innocent girls, scarcely 15 years of age, are sold by their mothers for 25 rubles at the most, and often for less than that. Even transients acquire this cheap merchandise, never giving a thought to the future fate of their victim.

Obviously, with reports like these, everybody feared the new, uncultivated, faraway country.

The distance of the region from Russia proper was so enormous that it took the immigrants almost two years to travel from Europe, across Siberia, to the new Russian lands. Later, the travelers began to use the seaway, from the Baltic or the Black Sea, through the Mediterranean, around India and China, arriving at the port of Vladivostok.

Though in general it was opposed to the migration of peasants to Asia, the government had to make an exception in the case of the Far East. Since the very beginning of the Far Eastern settlement, in the 1860's, and increasingly since the 1880's, financial assistance to immigrants and settlers had been the government's policy. An acre of tillable land in the Far East was sold to new settlers for two rubles ($1.30), but even with state aid, the results, until the end of the century, were exceedingly poor.

The population of the Russian Far East which had amounted to 15,000 in 1860 grew to 65,000 in 1867, 108,000 in 1879, 310,000 in 1897. At the end of the century, when the great contest over Manchuria and Korea began, the entire population of the Russian Far East did not exceed one third of a million.

SAKHALIN AND THE KURILES

As Russia approached the Sea of Japan, new areas and peoples came in contact with her, and new international relationships began to be established. The island of Sakhalin lay only a few miles from the Amur estuary. Farther to the east there was the long belt of Kurile Islands. Japan was the nearest neighbor of Sakhalin. And Korea was contiguous to the new Russian Far East. These were the years when Commodore Perry opened the doors to firmly isolated Japan, proposing to establish trade relations with the Western Hemisphere; now Russia was striving to establish relations with Japan—not so much for trading purposes as for purposes of settling territorial differences.

During the preparations for the Amur expedition, years before China surrendered her northern territories to Russia, Captain Nevelskoy had explored the Kurile Islands and Sakhalin. Little was known about even the elementary facts of their geography. The Western world assumed that Sakhalin was a peninsula jutting out from the Asiatic mainland. In Japan, on the other hand, it was held that Sakhalin was a projection of the northernmost Japanese island of Yezo (Hokkaido). Japan learned the truth about Sakhalin's geography in 1808, but this knowledge was not imparted to Europe, and not until Nevelskoy circumnavigated Sakhalin in 1849 did it become known that it was separated from Asia by what later came to be called the Tartar Straits. Although only a few Japanese had settled at its southern tip, where they had engaged in fishing, Japan considered Sakhalin her own. The island remained almost uninhabited; the native Ainus, numbering less than 8,000, were slowly dying out.

Now a group of Russians was directed to land on Sakhalin, and in April, 1853, an edict of the Tsar ordered the government-sponsored Russian-American Company, which was often used as an instrument of policy, to take over the island and "not to tolerate any alien settlements on Sakhalin."

The first dispute with Japan over Sakhalin arose when the Russian envoy, Putyatin, reached Nagasaki in August, 1853, soon after Perry's first visit. The arrival of Russian vessels caused considerable confusion in Tokyo. Reiterating the main Russian contention, Putyatin sent the Japanese authorities a message stating that he "was not seeking small trading advantages but was the bearer of an important dispatch." Eventually he was received in Nagasaki, but no agreement on Sakhalin was reached. The Nipponese were ready to cede the northern part of the island (north of the 50th parallel) to the Russians, but Putyatin insisted that all of Sakhalin should belong to the Tsar. Putyatin left for Shanghai but returned to Japan often in the following years. The Sakhalin issue meanwhile remained unsettled because not only Muraviev but the Tsar himself remained adamant. By a protocol signed on February 7, 1855, Putyatin obtained Japanese permission for Russian vessels to enter certain Japanese ports.

This was the first Russo-Japanese treaty. In regard to Sakhalin, the treaty contained an ambiguous and unusual stipulation: "Sakhalin remains undivided between Russia and Japan, as it has been to this day." [7]

Minimizing Japanese intelligence, Muraviev attempted a crude trick. The Mongolian name for Amur was Sakhalian-Ula. Muraviev argued that since the Amur region belonged to China, the island of Sakhalin was also a Chinese possession; with the cession of the Amur region to Russia, he contended, Russia had also acquired the neighboring island. But Japan did not see it that way, and Muraviev failed to bring about an agreement.

In 1862 a Japanese mission visited St. Petersburg; it proposed the 50th parallel as the border line between Russia and Japan on Sakhalin Island; Russia, in turn, demanded the 48th parallel, which would have given her control of four fifths of the island. Three years later Russia for the first time offered to exchange the Kurile Islands for Southern Sakhalin.

The almost unpopulated Kurile Islands had been claimed by the Japanese since the eighteenth century. Only on the southernmost of the Kuriles, on Iturup, were there any Japanese settlers. A few Russians came to the same island in 1806; since 1830 the Russian-American Company had been in control of all the Kuriles except Iturup. The first Russo-Japanese treaty of 1855 recognized it as Japanese, and all the other islands of the Kuriles as Russian possessions.

Now the Russian plan was to cede the entire chain of islands to the Japanese in exchange for exclusive control of all of Sakhalin. The plan was frowned upon by Tokyo; indeed, Sakhalin was far richer and more promising than the barren and volcanic island chain.

Finally on March 18, 1867, an agreement between the two countries was reached which established a condominium over Sakhalin. The island remained under joint occupation, and the subjects of Russia and Japan were alike free to move and reside in all the unsettled areas. In order to gain possession of as much land

7. James Murdoch, *History of Japan* (London, 1926), III, 593, 612.

as possible the Russian authorities began to transfer to the island convicts sentenced to hard labor or exile.

An exchange of Sakhalin for the Kuriles was formally agreed upon on April 25, 1875. In gaining control of Sakhalin Russia had obviously made the better bargain. However, the Japanese kept their right to fish in Sakhalin waters.

Thus the Russian goal of possession of all Sakhalin was fulfilled long after its initiator, Nikolai Muraviev, and its sponsor, Tsar Nicholas I, had passed from the scene. Sakhalin remained in Russian hands for a period of 30 years, during which it developed into an immense prison. Up to the end of the century its population consisted mainly of prisoners and their families, and the economy of the island—coal mining, lumbering, and road building—was serviced mainly by Russian prison labor. Under these conditions economic progress was slow. At the turn of the century the population of Sakhalin did not exceed 30,000, of whom about 8,000 were women.

THE AWAKENING OF KOREA

As long as Russia stayed far away, Korea's fate depended on her two neighbors, China and Japan. For centuries—until the last quarter of the nineteenth century—China's influence had been by far the strongest in Korea. Chinese was the official spoken language as well as the language of Korean literature. Chinese Confucianism was the Korean religion. Each year Korean delegates went to China to obtain from the Chinese the calendar for the next year—an outward symbol of Korea's dependence on the Middle Kingdom. Independent in her internal affairs, Korea was loosely tied to China as far as international affairs were concerned. An alliance of Korea with a third power inimical to China was out of the question.

Japan tried more than once in the course of centuries to conquer Korea, and wars for its possession were waged among the Japanese, Manchus, and Chinese. Except for short periods, however, Japan was never strong enough to withstand on the continent the overwhelming forces of China, and Korea remained under Chinese sovereignty.

Two events altered Korea's position from the 1860's on: Russia's penetration into the vicinity of Korea, and the rise of Japan after the restoration of the Meiji.

In 1868 Japan embarked on an endeavor to penetrate into Korea, which to all intents and purposes had hitherto been as isolated from the rest of the world as Japan had been only a few years earlier. After a few futile attempts, Japan managed in 1876 to conclude her first treaty with the Korean Government, which provided for the opening of ports to Japanese merchant vessels and the establishment of diplomatic relations between Japan and Korea. The necessary consent of China was obtained; Korea nonetheless remained dependent on China. While the Western world followed in the footsteps of Japan in establishing contact with Korea, a movement started within the "hermit kingdom" against foreign influence, and against Japan in particular. The movement was quelled by Chinese and Japanese troops. In 1884 there was another popular movement, which had Japanese support, in favor of internal reforms, and antagonism between China and Japan over Korea soon became acute.

In April, 1885, China and Japan reached an agreement; both sides were to remove their troops and both pledged themselves not to send any military advisers to Korea. As far as the Korean Army was concerned, the agreement provided: "The two powers agree to invite the King of Korea to hire an officer, or officers, of a third power." This third power was obviously Russia, hitherto absent from Korean affairs.

The Korean Government turned to Russia for military advisers who, under the prevailing conditions, were bound to wield considerable influence in the Korean Army and in Korean domestic affairs in general. In a secret agreement, Russia declared her readiness to grant Korea a form of protection and provide military instructors, in return for a lease of Port Lazareff (near Genzan), on the southeastern littoral of Korea.[8]

Immediately Russo-British antagonism became evident. As soon as London learned of the prospective Russian occupation of Port Lazareff, the British Navy was directed to occupy Port Hamilton, an island off Southern Korea, in order to prevent "probable occupation by another power." The base was seized on April 15, 1885. Now the Russian Government protested in Peking and asked

8. Shuhsi Hsü, *China and Her Political Entity*, pp. 126 ff.

for the evacuation of the British. Chinese pressure was applied in Korea in favor of an annulment of the Korean-Russian agreement. The treaty was not ratified by Seoul, and the British forces withdrew from Port Hamilton in December, 1886, while Russia obligated herself not to occupy Korean soil and pledged herself to "abstain from any encroachments on Korean independence."

In this first encounter Korea's independence was saved by intense Russo-British rivalry, but Russia's interest had once and for all been aroused.

At the moment Russian military activity in Korea was out of the question. In 1888, in a secret memorandum, the Russian Ministry of Foreign Affairs outlined its conception of the Korean situation: since the country was under Chinese influence, it was essential—and it seemed possible—for Russia to oppose China in Korea and to work toward Korea's independence from Peking. In this respect Russian policy coincided with that of Japan. England was opposed, as was China, to Russian advances in the Far East, and was considered another inimical power. The line-up of powers in Korea appeared to be: Russia and Japan against Britain and China.

"The Japanese view on Korea corresponds to ours . . . If need be, we will have to take advantage of her support." [9]

It was, however, a fundamental error to expect Russia and Japan to collaborate in Korean affairs. The error was due to a considerable extent to the appalling lack of information and misunderstanding of Far Eastern matters on the part of St. Petersburg. True, both Japan and Russia were opposed to Chinese primacy in Korea; both Tokyo and St. Petersburg desired Korean independence. For the Russians, however, the program had an anti-Chinese edge; the purpose of Russian penetration of the small kingdom was to effect its independence from Peking. For the Japanese, on the other hand, Korean independence was to be a step against Russia. It was precisely the possibility of Russian predominance in Korea that Japan considered a major menace which had to be avoided by diplomatic and military means. No collaboration between Tokyo and St. Petersburg was possible over Korea, and indeed, within a very few years, it became apparent that there was a parting of the ways. From the middle of the nineties on Korea was a turbulent issue.

9. *Krasnyi Arkhiv*, LII, 54 ff.

INTO SINKIANG

At about the same time that Russia acquired the Chinese territories in the east, she began to penetrate into China from the west, through Russian central Asia into Chinese Turkestan. This drive, too, was part of the Russo-British competition for Eurasia.

The new era in Sinkiang's history begins with the Russian penetration of central Asia less than a century ago. Previously, what is today Sinkiang had bordered on Russia only in the north, in Siberia; to Russia of those days even Siberia was still a distant, unexplored, and sparsely populated dominion. Eventually Russian armies began to push systematically toward the southeast; Tashkent was taken in 1864, Kokand in 1876. At the end of the sixties, Bukhara and Khiva, two independent principalities of central Asia, were made vassal states of Imperial Russia. Military operations continued through the eighties, bringing Russia to the Pamir and what was to become the border of Afghanistan.

Russia had reached the western fringes of the Chinese Empire and rattled the doors of Sinkiang. Russian tradesmen were already crossing the border; Chinese and native merchants tried to establish business ties with Russia. The negotiations between the Russian and Chinese authorities reflected Russia's strength and China's weakness. Russia obtained worth-while privileges for her subjects all over China, and for her merchants in particular. The first of these agreements, signed at Kuldja in 1851, provided for Russian trade facilities at two points along the Russo-Sinkiang frontier. The treaty of 1858 established the right of extraterritoriality for Russia, and provided that Russian citizens were not subject to trial by Chinese courts for criminal offenses; civil cases were to be settled in the presence of the Russian consul. Two years later, Russia obtained from China an agreement to the opening of a Russian consulate at Kashgar (in southwest Sinkiang). Four years later the border line between western China and Russia was defined for the first time. In 1869 the Peking convention opened a 30-mile border to custom-free trade. This clause, which gave Russian merchants a privileged position, was confirmed in the comprehensive treaty of 1881, which provided that "the subjects of Russia shall enjoy the faculty of engaging in commerce under franchise and rights in the towns and other localities of the Provinces of Ili, Tarbagatai,

Kashgar, Urumchi, and others located on the northern and southern slopes of the Tian-shan range up to the Great Wall."

The military and economic penetration of China by Russia aroused serious concern in Britain; in fact, Anglo-Russian antagonism, which was at its height during these years, was in part the product of the Russian expansion into central Asia, which, London feared, would eventually endanger India. Approaching from the south, England penetrated into Tibet and beyond, displaying considerable interest in southwestern Sinkiang, in which were located the principal cities of Kashgar and Khotan. Now both the Russian and British spheres came into contact within Sinkiang—the north obviously falling to Russia, the south to the English.

In 1864 a great uprising took place in Sinkiang under a successful adventurer, Yakub Beg, who expelled the Chinese and for 13 years remained in full control of his "Emirate of Djety-shaar." The British Government, fearing a Russian advance, and being in perpetual conflict with the Chinese, decided to recognize Yakub's state; Russia, on the other hand, refrained from recognizing him. This was the first of a number of instances in which Russia joined hands with China in Sinkiang in opposition to native political movements. On the ground that it was concerned with the maintenance of law and order there, the Russian Government dispatched an army to occupy the Ili district in Sinkiang; it promised to evacuate the area as soon as order was restored. After eight years of occupation, a new Russo-Chinese agreement was reached at the Tsar's Crimean residence at Livadia in 1879, by which China agreed to cede about 30 per cent of the territory of Ili, along with the passes to Kashgar and Yarkand, and to grant Russians important trading privileges.

The Chinese Government refused to ratify the treaty. Chung How, the envoy who had negotiated it, was sentenced to be decapitated. Both sides began to prepare for war. Russia moved 90,000 troops into the Ili region. After further negotiations, however, Chung How was pardoned and another Russo-Chinese treaty was signed in February, 1881. Under this agreement Russia was to evacuate almost the whole of the Ili district—only a small area was to remain under Russian control; in turn, China promised to pay Russia nine million rubles' indemnity. Russian trade privileges for the most part remained in force, and Russian goods were admitted free of duty into the adjacent Chinese territory within a range of 30 miles from the border.[10]

Sinkiang remained a sphere of outstanding Russian interest despite the withdrawal of Russian military forces from the area.

10. *Chinese Social and Political Science Review* (1936), pp. 375–392.

II

The Second Drive to the Pacific

After three decades of relative quiet in Russian Far Eastern relations, the nineties were marked by a second Russian drive toward and onto the Pacific. The great push was related to the construction of the Trans-Siberian Railway, and the great empire builder of this era was Sergei Witte.

After the Suez Canal was opened, Britain and France were able to approach the Far East from the south, thus saving thousands of miles and weeks of travel. At the end of the eighties, St. Petersburg, too, was seeking a direct road to the Far East. In March, 1891, after preliminary studies, Tsar Alexander III signed a decree ordering the construction of the 3,500-mile-long Siberian railway; the importance of the project was indicated by the fact that the future Tsar, Nicholas II, was appointed to head it.

Minister Witte, who is generally known as the father of the first Russian Constitution, was a loyal and ardent partisan of Russia's imperial system from his youth and throughout his official career. According to unconfirmed and possibly inaccurate stories, he had been a member of a secret monarchist group whose purpose was to fight "nihilism"; he had allegedly been sent to Paris in connection with a plan of the Russian police to kill the famed revolutionist, Hartmann, after the French Government had refused to extradite him. Slowly Witte climbed the bureaucratic ladder. When finally he became a minister of the Tsar he soon overshadowed his colleagues by his ambitious and far-reaching plans, his outstanding abilities, and the success of his political and economic measures. The Far East was his special domain, and it was on this area that Witte's main attention was focused in the nineties.

The Trans-Siberian was begun in 1891 and was substantially completed early in the 1900's. It was a one-track railroad from the Volga to Vladivostok. Since large deficits over a long period of operation were anticipated, no private capital was available for the undertaking. The railway was therefore built by the government, mainly with state funds and the proceeds of foreign loans.

The political purpose of the great enterprise was frankly acknowledged by Witte as well as by the Tsars themselves. Crown Prince Nicholas, returning from a visit to China and Japan, attended the celebrations in Vladivostok when work was begun at the eastern end of the line. He later reiterated his conviction that "Russia is in absolute need of an ice-free, open port all year round. This port must be on the mainland [to the southeast of Korea] and connected with our possessions by a strip of land." As for the railroad itself, Witte stated, in one of his reports to the sovereign, that the construction of the Siberian railroad "would be one of those world events which usher in a new era in the history of nations . . . The railway will secure for the Russian Navy all the necessary prerequisites and will give it a firm base in our eastern ports . . . The Navy can be strengthened considerably . . . It will control all international shipping in Pacific waters."[1]

In another report Witte rejected the narrow view that in building the railway Russia was striving only to acquire influence in Manchuria. "Manchuria isn't worth going to all the trouble . . . We shall proceed southward along the road of history," and added:

. . . the more inert countries in Asia will fall prey to the powerful invaders and will be divided up between them . . . the problem of each country concerned is to obtain as large a share as possible of the inheritance of the outlived oriental states, especially of the Chinese Colossus. Russia, both geographically and historically, has the undisputed right to the lion's share of the expected prey . . . the absorption by Russia of a considerable portion of the Chinese Empire is only a question of time . . .[2]

Soon fantastic projects began to arise around the railway. A Mongolian, Dr. Badmayev, a rather dubious character, presented to Witte, and through him to Alexander III, an elaborate plan for the construction of an additional railway from Irkutsk in Siberia, to Lanchow in North China, with Russia in the meantime clandestinely encouraging uprisings in adjoining Mongolia, Tibet, and certain other parts of China. Witte commented with approval: "From the shores of the Pacific and the heights of the Himalayas, Russia

1. B. Romanov, *Rossiya v Manchzhurii* (Leningrad, 1928), pp. 57–60, 71.
2. S. Witte, *Memoirs* (Garden City, 1921), p. 122.

will prevail not only in Asia but also in European affairs." The Tsar liked the idea but found it a little too fantastic to carry out.[3]

The placing in contrast of the contemptible commercial imperialism of Britain with the idealistic motivation of Russia's expansion was inherent in Witte's thinking, just as it had been in that of his predecessor, Muraviev, and as it was to be in that of his successors in the 1940's. "The peoples of Western European civilization [remarked Witte] have assumed the view that this area [east Asia] is exclusively a field for economic exploitation and profit-making." Russia, on the other hand, "has assumed a civilizing, educational mission." [4]

The first political repercussions of the great Russian railroad venture were felt most immediately in Japan and Korea. To Japan, the Russian outpost at Vladivostok and the inevitable drive into adjacent Korea represented a considerable danger; the Tsar's personal intentions with respect to this area were well known.

RUSSIA AND THE SINO-JAPANESE WAR

It was this "Russian menace" that prompted Japan to go to war with China over Korea in 1894. By that time the Trans-Siberian was under construction, and within a few years a direct railroad, capable of carrying not only goods but regiments of troops and heavy artillery, would connect St. Petersburg and Moscow with Vladivostok. In order to secure at least a buffer between herself and Russia and, if possible, bring Korea under her control, Japan was prepared to wage war on China. In the words of Witte, "the war which Japan conducted [in 1894–95] is the consequence of the construction of the Siberian Railway." [5] The British envoy in Japan likewise summed up the causes of the conflict in a confidential report to London: "Whatever the ostensible reason for going to war with China may have been, there can be little doubt that the main object was to anticipate the completion of the Siberian Railway and to prevent Russia from gaining free access to the Pacific Ocean." [6]

3. Romanov, *op. cit.*, p. 63.
4. *Za Kulisami tsarizma, Arkhiv tibetskovo vracha Badmayeva* (Leningrad, 1925), p. 78.
5. Romanov, *op. cit.*, p. 72.
6. *British Documents on the Origin of the War*, Vol. I. Report dated March 26, 1898.

Proceeding in the traditional fashion of oriental diplomacy, Japan, in June, 1894, proposed to China the establishment of joint supervision over Korean affairs. Deeming herself too weak to refuse, and seeking to avoid war, China countered with a proposal for the creation of a three-power control over Korea by Russia, China, and Japan. Russian diplomats in the Far East were inclined to support this move, as it would provide Russia with an easy wedge for the penetration of Korea.[7] Japan, however, turned down the suggestion. The Russian Government, fearing British intervention, decided to abstain from direct action and left the field to China and Japan. London and St. Petersburg, eyeing each other watchfully, assumed a position of neutrality in the negotiations and the ensuing war. The antagonism between them continued unabated. "England wants to take the whole affair into her hands and play the first role," Tsar Alexander wrote a few weeks before his death in commenting on a report received from London concerning the Far East. "Our principal and most dangerous enemy in Asia is undoubtedly England," wrote the Minister for Foreign Affairs in a report to the new Tsar, Nicholas II, in April, 1895 (Alexander III died in November, 1894); and the young Tsar penciled in: "Surely." At a cabinet session in August, 1894, Witte stated that Britain, although neutral, would intervene after the Sino-Japanese war, and "one must be prepared to repulse her." [8]

Britain suggested that the Chinese and Japanese military forces already in Korea withdraw in opposite directions; this implied the partition of Korea between China and Japan—the first time that a partition of Korea was advocated by a great power. The actual partition, however, was not to materialize for another 50 years.

Japan did not accept the British plan and attacked China. In the short war that ensued, Japan was overwhelmingly victorious. China had a population of over 300 million as compared with Japan's 40 million, but Japan was far superior to China in armed forces and it took her only eight months to inflict a decisive defeat on the Chinese. China's Navy was turned over to Japan and Chinese Admiral Ting strangled himself with a silken cord. Japan transmitted to China peace terms which included: independence for Korea; annexation by Japan of the islands of Formosa and the

7. *Krasnyi Arkhiv,* L, 17.
8. *Krasnyi Arkhiv,* L, 32, and LII, 63, 76.

Pescadores; payment of a war indemnity of 200 million taels by China; and, finally, cession of the tip of Liaotung Peninsula, in Manchuria, with Port Arthur, to Japan.

China had no choice but to accept these terms. Japan emerged as the first non-European Great Power in modern history.

The acquisition by Japan of a strategic area in Manchuria was deemed an obvious menace to Russia, and was so interpreted in St. Petersburg. The Russian Government was divided, however, as to the appropriate Russian reaction, and this division contained in embryonic form all the elements of the intense struggle that went on in the leading circles of St. Petersburg in the following decade. One group, headed by the Tsar, was inclined to profess tacit acquiescence in the Japanese advance, but sought the acquisition of other ports on the Yellow Sea or in Korea as compensation to Russia. "In agreement with France," Tsar Nicholas recommended, ". . . we must obtain the reward we wish in the shape of a free port." Witte, on the other hand, recommended concerted diplomatic pressure upon Japan to force her out of Manchuria. This was the view that prevailed in the end. The underlying issue in these formulations of policy was the shape of Russia's relations with England. The Tsar's advice to seize a Korean port in compensation for Japan's gains was an obvious challenge to Britain. The chief of the General Staff, however, issued a warning "not to make any seizures in order not to give England an excuse to make still bigger seizures."

In February, 1895, the Russian Government decided to negotiate with the powers in order to force Japan to relinquish Liaotung. France, as Russia's ally, promptly agreed to go along; Germany, who had a hidden scheme of her own, also gave her consent; England, however, refused—and here was the beginning of the breach. The British Ambassador to St. Petersburg announced quite frankly that England "will scarcely decide upon any forcible measures whatever or upon actions hostile toward Japan, because of late public opinion in England leans more and more toward Japan." At a moment when strong Russo-Japanese antagonism was becoming evident, an Anglo-Japanese rapprochement was evolving which was later to develop into a full-fledged alliance and remain for two decades a cornerstone of Far Eastern power politics.

The "continental bloc," consisting of Russia, Germany, and

France, presented Japan with a note demanding the restoration of Liaotung to China. The Russian note informed Japan:

The Government of His Majesty the Emperor of All the Russias, in examining the conditions of the peace which Japan has imposed on China, finds that the possession of the Peninsula of Liaotung, claimed by Japan, would be a constant menace to the capital of China, would at the same time render illusory the independence of Korea, and would henceforth be a perpetual obstacle to the peace of the Far East.

Consequently the Government of His Majesty the Emperor would give a new proof of their sincere friendship for the Government of His Majesty the Emperor of Japan by advising him to renounce the definite possession of the Peninsula of Liaotung.

Japan deemed it wise to yield. She abandoned Liaotung. Russo-Japanese relations began to deteriorate, and Russia emerged as the savior and protector of China.

For Russia, the main effect of the Sino-Japanese war was the chance to make use of China's weakening, which the conflict had brought about in the Far East. St. Petersburg was still inclined to minimize the extent of the Japanese victories; the traditional view that little Japan was a negligible power compared with giant Russia continued to prevail there. In the official Russian view, the principal result of the Sino-Japanese conflict was a weakening of China that amounted to an almost complete collapse. The areas of China bordering on Russia now appeared to constitute a power vacuum which Russian men and material had to fill—just as they had been for several decades filling the spaces of central Asia. This Russian drive into Manchuria, Mongolia, and Korea was certain to arouse British enmity; but Britain was far away and the risk was well worth taking so long as China could be counted upon to offer no resistance and so long as Japan seemed too weak to interfere.

Thus Russia embarked on the second phase of her Far Eastern drive. The new campaign came sooner than planned; it lasted eight years and culminated in the Russo-Japanese War. It was conceived on an ambitious scale in terms of the territories it was to cover. Swift, sometimes feverish, it treated the world to one sensation after another. It resorted to diplomatic means as well as military pressure. Its traditional anti-British philosophy was interspersed with the fantastic and extravagant notions of new and unknown schemers who were active around the Court and in the Far East. A series of extraordinary successes was scored by this dynamic policy in the face of a bewildered world unable to arrest its course.

As was natural under such conditions agreements were concluded, only to be broken soon after. Russia entered into an alliance with China—but only in order to acquire Chinese territories and ports. Promises were given and retracted.

A rapprochement between England, Japan, and later the United States against Russia was the outstanding product of the crucial decade 1895–1904 in the Far East. It took shape against a background of what appeared to the world in general as a contest between modern, progressive, and liberal ideas against conservative and reactionary tendencies. Russia—a state which had suppressed the Polish uprisings, doomed to failure the revolutions of 1848, populated Siberia with political prisoners, persecuted liberal ideas, and indulged in anti-Jewish pogroms—appeared to be the mainstay of world reaction. The Russian émigrés active in England, France, Switzerland, and the United States provided proof of the regime's primitive and cruel treatment of political opposition. In the Far East Russia supported the moribund empire of the Manchus, and in the Korean struggle St. Petersburg, along with China, was on the side of ancient tradition, illiteracy, and backwardness.

Japan, on the other hand, at that time seemed to be the bearer of the banner of progress and modernization. Since the end of the sixties Japan had been in the throes of a speedy development and adaptation of European science and technique, culture, and hygiene. Industrialization, railway construction, expansion of educational facilities, and promotion of literacy were changing the face of Japan, which had theretofore been turned toward Asia. Political leaders—especially those from China—who were persecuted by their governments found refuge in Japan. Hundreds of young Chinese studied in Japanese universities. Chinese revolutionaries—among them Sun Yat-sen—looked upon Japan as the most advanced state of the Orient and as the future leader in the fight for the liberation of Asia from the Western yoke. It was argued that England's support of Japan, which was prompted by political interest, signified at the same time a combination of the most liberal and advanced country of Europe with the most civilized of the Asiatic nations. Wherever Russian and British influence clashed within another country—Korea, China, or Persia—the conservative elements constituted a pro-Russian party, while the progressive groups tended to side with Britain (or with Japan). Thus it seemed natural that the United States should join the ideological Anglo-Japanese "bloc" against Russia.

Moreover, this placing in contrast of "progressive" Japan and Britain and "backward" Russia was becoming important in the domestic struggle within Russia. The moderate-liberal opposition there was accustomed to look at the British constitutional monarchy as a model worthy of emulation; that Japan was an "advanced" nation as compared to Russia was acknowledged by all factions of the opposition, including the extreme left. The growing activity in the Far East, the new Russian expansionism, and the multitude of ensuing conflicts appeared to be futile, meaningless, and expensive adventures. The Russian public had no sympathy for the government's anti-Japanese policy, and when the time arrived for Russia to go to war with Japan, there was no patriotic rallying behind St. Petersburg's policy. In the wake of that war came revolution at home.

THE TSAR AND HIS CIRCLE

Before 1906 Russia had virtually no cabinet government in the modern sense. There were ministries and ministers, but government as a constituted body, with a premier at the head and an integrated policy, was unknown in Russia. According to the classical precepts of autocracy, all power was concentrated in the hands of the sovereign, and individual ministers served as his assistants only so far as he was unable himself to cope with all the details of government. The Tsar appointed and dismissed his ministers; he was not obliged to inform them of his decisions, and he could take action without consulting them.

During the period when Far Eastern affairs began to assume ominous importance this unparalleled power lay in the hands of a comparatively young man who had just succeeded his father to the throne. "I do not know anything regarding international affairs," the young Tsar confided to his friends. He did feel, however, that it was his right and duty to fulfill the mission of carrying the Russian flag farther into adjacent areas and to add to the splendor

of divinely ordained autocracy. He was, therefore, more willing
to take chances in foreign affairs than were his ministers. He was
inclined to consent to many a risky adventure, as his ancestors had
often been and as, later, his Bolshevik successors in the highest posts
of Russia were to be.

Since his youth Nicholas II has paid special attention to the Far
East. As heir to the throne he had visited Japan and Vladivostok
and had traveled across Siberia; he was the official head of the
Trans-Siberian Railway committee. At the time of the coronation
festivities in 1896, the Chinese Chancellor appeared in Moscow
to sign a treaty extending Russian influence far into northern China,
while an envoy of the Korean King invited the Russian monarch
to establish a protectorate over Korea.

These political trends were in themselves sufficient to arouse
strong antagonism between Russia and England. Domestic issues
further intensified this anti-British attitude in St. Petersburg—an
attitude which at times bordered on genuine and intense hatred. To
the conservative and strongly monarchist groups in Russia, England was the incarnation of a weak monarchy, in which the king
reigns but does not rule.

"Our sovereign has grandiose plans in his head," War Minister
Kuropatkin wrote in 1903. "He wants to seize Manchuria and
proceed toward the annexation of Korea; he also plans to take
Tibet under his rule. He wants to take Persia and to seize not only
the Bosphorus but also the Dardanelles." "His Majesty was most
unfriendly to the English," Minister Witte recalled. "The English
he [Nicholas II] called Jews. 'An Englishman,' he liked to repeat,
'is a *zhid* (Jew).'" [9]

Prince Heinrich of Germany gave Chancellor von Bülow a fair
picture of the Tsar, after a visit to Nicholas II in 1901:

Politically he does not at all like [the British]. He distrusts their policy
and at the same time scorns the English Army as much as the English
system of constitutional parliamentarism. In this respect the Tsar is a
real Russian. While the Tsar likes his uncle, the King of England, personally, the latter instills little respect in him as a monarch. The Tsar
declared: "That one has nothing to say in his country . . ." The Tsar
appeared to consider a clash with Japan sooner or later as inevitable, but
hoped that it would not take place until at least four years from now, by

9. Kuropatkin, "Memoirs," *Krasnyi Arkhiv*, II and V; and Witte, *Memoirs*, p. 189.

which time Russia would gain maritime supremacy in the Pacific Ocean.

The principal interest of the Tsar is the Trans-Siberian Railroad. He hopes that it will be completed within five to six years. He spoke more painfully about France and the French trip. The German fleet has made a great impression on the Tsar; however, he does not at all fear it and even wishes its further development, as he is convinced that Germany and Russia will always go together.[10]

Evidencing his anti-British orientation, the Tsar sent a Cossack captain, Ulanov, to Tibet "to find out what the English were doing there." Ulanov received an order to "incite the Tibetans against England"; he was ordered, however, not to say a word about these instructions to the Russian Minister of Foreign Affairs. The Tsar was glad to receive the advice of the German Emperor that Russia should begin military demonstrations at the frontiers of Persia and Afghanistan, because the "loss of India would be the hardest blow to England." [11]

At times a contradiction appeared between Russia's international position and the trends of the conservative elements and the circles close to the Tsar. The alliance with France, concluded in 1891, was necessary as a safeguard against the growing force of the two Germanic empires in Europe. But France was republican, and anti-clerical; the French Republic had been born out of the turmoil of revolution and her political system still seemed to be a novel challenge to monarchist traditions. The Tsar's personal views and his domestic worries were drawing him toward the German Emperor, who was likewise imbued with faith in the grandeur of monarchical institutions.

Wilhelm II, a personal friend of the Tsar, a more colorful personality and assisted by an able Cabinet, knew how to use the moods and ideas of the Tsar in the interests of Germany. He often appealed to the Russian's monarchical convictions so as to arouse him against republican France; he strove to divert Russia's attention to the Far East so as to reduce Russian pressure in Europe and thus diminish her role as an ally of France. He exaggerated the "yellow peril" —the fantastic nightmare of China and Japan united in a war on the civilized peoples of the West. Russia, Wilhelm told Nicholas, was

10. *Die grosse Politik der Europäischen Kabinette*, XVIII, 34-35.
11. *Krasnyi Arkhiv*, V, 19.

civilization's outpost against the yellow menace, and he offered his assistance to the Tsar against the oriental hordes.

"There is a danger for our monarchical principle," he wrote in a private letter to the Tsar in October, 1895, "in the Russo-French alliance. . . . The republic seems to be raised on a pedestal. . . . This makes it possible for the republicans to imagine that they are quite honest, excellent people, with whom crowned heads can be on an equal footing . . . But republicans are people who should be either shot or hanged." At Christmas, 1898, Wilhelm sent the Tsar a present of a drawing made by himself, which he described as follows: "The two figures symbolize Russia and Germany on the shores of the Yellow Sea, preaching the Gospel, the Truth, and the Light in the East."

"No one could stop Russia from marching with her army to Peking," Kaiser Wilhelm declared in 1898.[12]

At every Russian move deeper into China and Korea, the German Emperor congratulated his colleague in St. Petersburg and promised to see to Russia's interests in Europe if Russia should be occupied in Asia. He grossly flattered the Tsar: "Now you are, properly speaking, the master of Peking." He outlined a promising and hypocritical program: ". . . following the laws of expansion [Russia] must try to get at the Sea for an iceless outlet for its commerce. By this law it is entitled to a strip of coast where such harbors are situated (Vladivostok, Port Arthur). Their 'Hinterland' must be in your Power . . . Korea must and will be Russian." [13]

The Tsar, responsive to the flatteries of the Kaiser, went far beyond the wishes and counsels of his ministers:

"We have to break England's impudence," he repeated again and again. England, and later the United States remained the principal enemies of the right wing in St. Petersburg.

Under these circumstances, strong personalities were often unable to remain at their posts for long. If the influence of a minister upon political affairs, and upon the Tsar himself, became great, the Tsar became suspicious. It was natural that he should find mediocre personalities easiest to deal with. His first Minister for

12. G. F. Hudson, *The Far East in World Politics*, p. 141.
13. *Perepiska Vil'gel'ma II s Nikolayem II* (Moscow, 1923), p. 52. Wilhelm to Nicholas, January 3, 1904.

Foreign Affairs, Lobanov-Rostovsky, was described by his outstanding ambassador, Roman Rosen, as a man "quite ignorant of
Far Eastern affairs . . . [his] ideas of China and Japan were
mostly connected with pictures of pig-tailed mandarins on boxes
of tea, or red lacquer cups and saucers . . . there was a total absence of any clear conception of what the aims of our Far Eastern
policy should be." [14]

Lobanov's successor, Mikhail Muraviev, who was in charge of
foreign affairs in the decisive years from 1897 to 1900, was described by another envoy (Osten-Saken) as a "fast liver" and an
ignoramus.[15] Muraviev's successor, Count Lamsdorff, who remained at the head of the Foreign Office from 1900 to 1905, was
"afflicted with hysterical shyness . . . a narrow-mind" but "devoted to the Throne." [16]

The outstanding personalities during this Far Eastern Decade
were Sergei Witte, officially Minister of Finance until 1903, and
General Alexei Kuropatkin, who was much liked at the Tsar's
court and who had earned military fame in central Asia; somewhat
later, Ivan Bezobrazov and the Minister of the Interior, Vyacheslav Plehve, emerged as the most extreme proponents of reaction
at home and uncompromising opposition to England and Japan in
foreign affairs.

In Far Eastern matters, the differences among these men centered
around the degree of their expansionist dynamism. All of them
accepted the Russian mission in the Far East as a matter of fact;
all of them strove to extend Russian influence over the whole of
northern Asia, including Korea and at least northern China. Witte,
however, who realized better than the others the extent of Russian weakness in Asia, consistently sought to avoid a crisis in Russo-
English relations and therefore became increasingly moderate.
General Kuropatkin, on the other hand, strongly opposed Witte's
middle-of-the-road policy and advocated strong measures against
China; from 1900 on he was able to reduce Witte's influence with
the Tsar and eventually replaced him. Soon Kuropatkin himself
became too circumspect for the extremists, and the most intran-
sigent group, consisting of Bezobrazov, Admiral Abaza, and Plehve,

14. R. Rosen, *Forty Years of Diplomacy*, I, 134.
15. Witte, *op. cit.*, pp. 111–112.
16. Rosen, *op. cit.*, p. 175.

became the favorite advisers of the sovereign. "Bayonets, not diplomats, have made Russia; by bayonets, and not by diplomatic pens, must the Far Eastern problem be solved," declared Minister Plehve in 1903.

There were voices, however, even among Russian officialdom, determinedly opposed to expansionist trends in the Far East. Some saw no reason to court conflict with China and no necessity to acquire lands at her expense; others wanted Russia's energies marshaled for action in Europe. Some of the latter, like Professor Fiodor Martens and Ambassador Roman Rosen, were prevented from rising to leading positions and, on the whole, their views were frowned upon in official circles. In his memoranda, Professor Martens, the leading expert in Far Eastern affairs in the Foreign Ministry, depicted China as a land exploited and oppressed by Britain and France. He believed that Russia, unlike Britain and other imperialist powers, should seek the creation of an independent, sovereign, and strong China:

The great power [he said] which is more than any other interested in maintaining the integrity of China is Russia. For the western European states, China is a *colony* which must be exploited by all possible means, whereas for Russia, China is a great neighbor, entitled to an independent existence. The integrity of Chinese territory . . . must constitute a law for the states of Europe and the United States.[17]

Ambassador Rosen in 1900 presented a memorandum to his superiors in which he said,

Russia is an immense and overgrown empire. One part of it, in Europe, is still underpopulated, and the other, a far greater part, in Asia, can hardly be called populated at all in proportion to its colossal extent. Could territorial expansion in the Far East be considered a legitimate aim of our policy and could its achievement in any way benefit the State and promote the welfare of the people?

Rosen summed up his view:

The acquisition of any new territory in the Far East at such an enormous distance from the centre of the Empire could only contribute an additional weakening element to a position already precarious enough and maintained less by actual power than by prestige.

17. *Krasnyi Arkhiv*, XX, 184–185.

In accordance with Rosen's request, the Minister of Foreign Affairs presented his memorandum to the Tsar, telling Rosen, however, "You must know . . . that most of your arguments run counter to the favourite concepts of the Emperor." [18]

The opinions of such old-fashioned "pacifists" were drowned, however, in the multitudinous choir of strong voices which advocated an advance into China and Korea and fulfillment of a large-scale Russian program in the Orient.

IN CONTROL OF KOREA

After her defeat in 1895 China was compelled to relinquish all claims to Korea, and Japan remained in actual control of the ostensibly independent kingdom. Modernization and reforms were proclaimed at Japan's behest; opposition to Japanese influence was suppressed. The Queen of Korea, opposed to Japanese rule and reform, was assassinated, and the King, fearing for his life, took refuge in the Russian legation in Seoul.

Events began to take a course which had not been anticipated in Tokyo. Russia sought to push the Japanese out of Korea and establish her own protectorate there. Tokyo had hoped to obtain control of Korea by defeating China before Russia's Trans-Siberian Railway was completed; by her victory, however, Japan had provoked Russian penetration of Korea, where until 1894 she had faced a weak China. Now China was out, but Russia was facing her instead.

The intentions of the Russian Government, and especially of the young Tsar, with regard to Korea were unmistakable; yet the general situation was not propitious for the realization of these plans whereby Korea, like the rest of the north Asiatic continent, was to become a part of the Russian Empire. Minister Lamsdorff recalled this program in a memorandum years later: "The fate of Korea, which was bound to become a component of the Russian Empire because of political and geographical conditions, was determined by us in advance." [19] It was the task of Russian diplomacy to maneuver cautiously for a few years longer until it could make available armed forces for the fulfillment of its Far Eastern designs.

18. Rosen, *op. cit.*, pp. 141–147.
19. Romanov, *op. cit.*, p. 66.

The Governor General of the Maritime Province, Dukhovsky, clearly expressed this formula in a memorandum approved by the Tsar:

Russia would be rendered a great service by a diplomacy which would eliminate the least causes for creating unrest and disorder in the Far East in the next four to six years. I mention this period because only in that many years will our armed forces be placed on a new norm of supply, and be trained adequately, and mainly because our railroad from Siberia will be near completion. After the lapse of this period [four to six years], we shall be able to speak a different language.[20]

This principle of careful steering was at first adhered to. In May, 1896, following the Japanese victory over China, Russia and Japan signed an agreement concerning Korea. For the first time in history, the 38th parallel was suggested—by the Japanese—as a border line dividing Korea into two foreign protectorates. Lobanov-Rostovsky, the Russian Minister for Foreign Affairs, rejected the plan. Then the Japanese proposed a joint proclamation of the "independence of Korea." Lobanov-Rostovsky turned down this offer, too. The agreement concluded was rather narrow in scope; it was supplemented a few months later by a new protocol between Lobanov and the Japanese envoy, Yamagata. Both powers were thereby entitled to keep a limited number of troops in Korea (800 Russians and 1,000 Japanese). St. Petersburg did not live up to the agreement, however, and the following year a considerable number of Russian officers were dispatched to reconstruct and train the Korean Army.

A new Russian envoy, Alexis Speyer, who arrived in Seoul in January, 1896, soon came to wield the strongest influence in Korean affairs. He was later joined by a Russian financial adviser, Kiril Alexeyev. The Korean King, who remained at the Russian legation from February, 1896, to February, 1897, was made a tool of Speyer's policy; he signed laws abolishing all the reforms promulgated at the request of the Japanese. The War Department in St. Petersburg detailed a plan for a Korean Army of 250,000 under officers of the Imperial Russian Army. At the coronation of the new Tsar, in May, 1896, Nicholas II received a humble request from the Korean King—who was still in Russian custody—that Korea be placed under Russian protection; the Tsar granted the

20. *Krasnyi Arkhiv*, LII, 87. Marginal note by Nicholas II: "That is correct."

request, and only through the intervention of his Minister for Foreign Affairs was this weighty and potentially dangerous decision revoked.[21]

In February, 1897, the Korean King returned to his palace, but the informal Russian protectorate remained in effect and Russian influence continued to increase. More than 60 Russian "instructors" worked with the Korean armed forces; industrial "concessions," including important lumber concessions at the Tumen River and in the Yalu Valley, were granted to Russian companies; a mining concession in Hamgyŏng Province was also granted. Upon the advice of the Russian envoy, the Korean King assumed the title of Emperor in order to underscore his complete sovereignty. As if in anticipation of political theories of the 1940's, to the Russian envoy national sovereignty meant independence from all nations but Russia. A "friendly government" was established in September, 1897, and a report to St. Petersburg informed the Tsar's ministers that the Korean Council of Ministers was headed by "a person devoted to Russia."

And yet Russia's strong position in Korea was based on prestige rather than power. There were neither considerable troops nor naval vessels to support the aggressive, sometimes arrogant, steps taken by the Russian envoy. His activities aroused protests; ministers chose to resign rather than accept certain of his more extreme demands. In his overconfidence Speyer, in March, 1898, asked for the elimination of a number of persons in the Korean Government "who oppose Russian interests," and threatened that in case of refusal, Russia would withdraw her military instructors from Korea. He was astounded when the King decided against him. The demands were rejected, and the Russian officers were forced to quit; the Russian-Korean Bank, established a short time before, was closed. In April, 1898, a new agreement between Russia and Japan was signed—the so-called Nishi-Rosen Protocol—whereby both powers reaffirmed Korea's independence and pledged noninterference in her internal affairs. Yet, in 1900, Russia obtained privileges in the Korean port of Mosampo.

Russian influence in Korea diminished, and for a period of several years Korea enjoyed a degree of independence due to the rivalry between Russia and Japan.

21. Rosen, *op. cit.*, I, 125, 140.

Russia's withdrawal from Korea was a direct consequence of her nonobservance of the principle of cautious maneuvering which, at least until the turn of the century, had been found to be obligatory for her. Russian control over Korea collapsed like a house of cards. There were, however, additional reasons why St. Petersburg did not press in Seoul for the maintenance of Russian privileges. The attention of the Russian Government was gradually shifting to southern Manchuria; the acquisition of ports and areas now occupied the minds and labor of men in and around the Tsar's court. As for Korea, there began to develop the ominous plan of conquest of the nation by a Russian Army disguised as lumberjacks working on concessions in that country. At the end of 1897, when Russian influence in Korea was greatest, a Russian merchant, Brinner, proposed to sell to the Imperial Government lumber concessions he had obtained from the Korean authorities. Count Vorontsov and Ivan Bezobrazov presented a memorandum to the Tsar advising the purchase of the lumber concessions. The Tsar was impressed by the contents of the report, which urged that Russia must achieve a "completely free hand" in Korea. To this end an "advance troop of 20,000 men" were to masquerade as lumberjacks and work for a time on the more than 2,000 square miles of the concession. At the propitious time these men would strike out into Korea. In May, 1899, the Russian Government acquired the lumber concessions and another was acquired in 1901. In some high government circles this was considered a rather advantageous substitute for the recalled military advisers.[22]

THE RUSSO-CHINESE ALLIANCE

The Russo-Chinese alliance began to take shape in 1895. Russia, as China's helpful protector, found in French banks a part of the millions China needed to pay her indemnity to Japan. Russia's guarantee of the loan was a prerequisite of its being granted. A Russo-Chinese Bank was established. Soon afterward, Li Hung-chang, statesman and virtual ruler of China, came to St. Petersburg at the invitation of the Russian Government to represent his country at the coronation ceremonies for the new tsar. The purposes be-

22. *Russkoye Proshloye* (1923), I, 97–98.

hind this visit were, however, as far as Russia was concerned, predominantly political. Care was exercised not to let the Chinese ruler visit any other European capital before coming to Russia, and when he arrived, an important treaty was submitted for his signature.

This Russo-Chinese treaty of alliance, signed on June 3, 1896, provided for mutual military assistance against Japan and proscribed the conclusion of a separate peace in case of war. "Any attack by Japan on Russian territory in east Asia as well as on the territory of China or Korea will be considered cause for application of this treaty." Both parties pledged themselves to mutual support in case of such a war, by military means as well as with supplies.

The final paragraph of the accord provided for the construction of a Russian railroad across Chinese territory in Manchuria "in order to permit the Russian forces easier access to endangered places"; this was to become the Chinese Eastern Railway, which greatly reduced the traveling distance from Moscow to the Pacific. The political implications of such a trunk line were obvious. Russian offices had to be set up in Manchuria, and an armed railway guard had to be stationed there. It was clear that the treaty opened the door to the penetration of Manchuria by Russia, even though St. Petersburg professed purely economic and strategic aims which would not jeopardize Chinese sovereignty.

The treaty was soon supplemented by a special agreement concerning the new company of the Chinese Eastern Railway. It provided for the construction of only one line across Manchuria, linking Chita with Vladivostok. It was to remain valid for eighty years after the completion of the railway; after that the Chinese Eastern was to be turned over to China. The agreement between the official Russo-Chinese Bank and the Chinese Government provided that extensive areas needed by the future railroad for such purposes as building construction, guard, sand procurement, and the like, were to be ceded gratuitously to the railway by the Chinese state. Later, the possession of these areas greatly enhanced Russian influence in Manchuria.

In these negotiations with the Russian officials, Li Hung-chang gave the impression that he was not averse to receiving "gifts" if they corresponded in value to his power and influence. Subsequently the Russian Government took ample advantage of this peculiar connection with the Chinese dictator.

Later that year the Chinese Government also consented to allow Russia the use of the small port of Kiaochow on the Yellow Sea. This concession was deemed quite secondary at the time, and nobody foresaw the great complications that were later to arise from it.

Now the situation in the Far East seemed to be more propitious for the realization of the designs of St. Petersburg than it had ever been before. There was no power in the East to oppose the advance of Russia. China was defeated. Victorious Japan had been driven from Manchuria by a Russian-led coalition; she had almost been ejected from Korea under Russian pressure. The head of the Chinese Government was willing to co-operate closely with Russia and make significant concessions to her. Russia's power seemed irresistible and the Russian program capable of realization in the immediate future.

The sphere which Russia had carved out for herself was to be established de facto and de jure in the face of intensive but presumably futile British opposition. The sphere, outlined more than once during the preceding years, was now enlarged to embrace, in addition to Extramural China, also the Province of Chili (Hopeh), south of the Great Wall. The control of Chili, which contained the capital of China, Peking, the great port of Tientsin, and had a population of 20 million, was more to Russia than just another Chinese province: it was an ambitious bid for the whole of North China, endangering British interests in the neighborhood of Shanghai, Nanking, and all over central China. In addition, three other provinces of North China—Shansi, Shensi, and Kansu—were often mentioned as part of the future Russian sphere. Inner and Outer Mongolia would automatically fall under Russian influence if this plan were fulfilled. On New Year's Day of 1898 the British Ambassador could report to his Foreign Secretary, Marquis Salisbury:

Producing from a carefully locked desk a map of China, the Minister [Sergei Witte] proceeded to draw his hand over the Provinces of Chili, Shansi, Shensi, and Kansu, and said that sooner or later Russia would probably absorb all this territory. Then putting his finger on Lanchow, he said that the Siberian Railway would in time run a branch line to this town. . . . He considered the lower part of China . . . would be beyond the reach of Russian expansion . . .[23]

The Russian Government outlined its sphere of influence in an official note addressed to friendly Germany:

On the basis of the principle, which has virtually been recognized by the German Government, that the Northern Provinces of China, comprising all of Manchuria, the Province of Chili, and Chinese Turkestan, constitute our exclusive sphere of action, we cannot admit foreign political influence there.[24]

Prince Esper Ukhtomsky, a writer, poet, and head of the Russo-Chinese Bank, outlined the benefits Russia would bestow on those parts of China that would fall under her rule.

Of all the powers [he wrote] capable of exerting a telling influence on [the Far East] Russia occupies first place. It is enough for her to decide —and tomorrow Kashgaria and Mongolia will fly our colors. We could annex regions which for a long time have sought to join us and have begged to be made our subjects. If we do not do so, it is out of high principles and magnanimity . . . On our own, we shall take care of the richest parts of the vacuum of China-beyond-the-wall that seeks our protection.[25]

"Essentially there are not and there cannot be any frontiers for us in Asia," wrote Ukhtomsky,[26] and this attitude was prevalent in leading Russian circles.

To fulfill this program the Russian Government set up industrial and commercial companies in Manchuria and Mongolia and strongly opposed railway construction by other nations (especially British firms) in her prospective sphere. Russian resources were insufficient, and foreign loans were limited in amount: Russia was incapable of embarking on a large-scale development of North China. It was deemed preferable, however, to retard economic progress in the areas to be acquired rather than open them to penetration by other powers.

Russia found her main support for her Far East policy in Berlin. Germany's aid was, however, by no means unselfish. The ambitions

23. *British Documents on the Origin of the War*, I, 8.
24. *Grosse Politik*, XIV[1], 134.
25. E. Ukhtomsky, *Iz kitaiskikh pisem* (St. Petersburg, 1901), p. 27.
26. E. Ukhtomsky, *K sobytiyam v Kitaye* (1900), p. 84.

of Berlin, and especially of the young Kaiser, were likewise directed toward the forging of a vast Far Eastern empire. In this connection the German Government viewed German-Russian friendship as the best means of gaining a foothold in a part of the world where the British Empire was predominant and where Russian and British interests overlapped. Berlin repeatedly assured St. Petersburg that Russia need not worry about her western frontiers in Europe— Germany pledged herself to assure tranquillity there while Russian energies were absorbed in the Far East. "I shall certainly do all in my power," the Kaiser wrote to Nicholas II, "to keep Europe quiet and also guard the rear of Russia so that nobody shall hamper your action towards the Far East . . . the great task of the future for Russia [is] to cultivate the Asian continent and to defend Europe from inroads of the Great Yellow race . . . [I hope] that you will kindly see that Germany may also be able to acquire a Port somewhere where it does not gêne [hamper] you." [27]

In 1897 Germany proceeded to demand payment for her assistance to Russia. During his visit to St. Petersburg in August of that year Kaiser Wilhelm asked whether Russia would object if Germany were to occupy the unimportant Chinese port of Kiaochow, ceded previously to Russia, since Russia did not really need it. But Germany wanted to acquire more than just a harbor in the Yellow Sea. Kiaochow was the threshold into the rich Province of Shantung. The expansion of German-Chinese trade and the building of railways in this contemplated German sphere of China were obviously part of the Kaiser's plan.

The Tsar's reply was evasive; the Russian Foreign Minister was not even consulted. Yet Berlin tended to consider the deal as closed and inquired in London as to the British attitude in case Germany should acquire a port in North China. Striving to hem Russia in and create difficulties for her in China, London gave its consent to the German bid for a base—"the further north, the better." The German Navy was ordered to Kiaochow. Now the Russian Government protested; the Foreign Minister informed the Germans that he "regrets the German step." "*Unverschämt* [impudent]!" was the Kaiser's marginal comment on the report from St. Petersburg. Yet no Russian action ensued. Russian attention swiftly veered toward a more important naval base—Port Arthur. On

27. *Letters from the Kaiser to the Tsar.* Letter dated April 16, 1895.

March 6, 1898, the Chinese Government signed away Kiaochow as a leasehold to Germany.

PORT ARTHUR

When the plans to take over Port Arthur from China were first formulated in St. Petersburg, Count Witte objected strongly; in the end he lost out and the Tsar approved the new program. It was to be pushed against heavy British opposition, but in accord with Germany. The very plan to seize Port Arthur was explained to China as a step to "bar its use to our common enemy—Britain."

While reversing its stand on German penetration of Shantung, the Russian Government demanded German recognition of her future sphere in North China, comprising not only Sinkiang and Mongolia but also the Province of Chili. For Berlin the latter was, however, "ein fetter Bissen" (a choice morsel), as the Kaiser put it. "If, nonetheless, Russia helps us regarding Kiaochow, [he added] and recognizes our interests in Shantung, including the Yellow River, we could leave Chili to them." [28] The deal was perfected as he had outlined it. Now Russia went ahead with her effort to obtain Port Arthur. In January, 1898, simultaneously with the German démarches in Peking, the Russian Government informed China that "it had no intentions as to territorial acquisitions"; as for Port Arthur and Talienwan, they would be abandoned "as soon as political circumstances and the interests of Russia and China permit doing so." [29]

The British Government objected strongly to the proposed seizure of Port Arthur by Russia. "The occupation of Port Arthur would be considered in the East as a commencement of a partition of China," Lord Salisbury cabled to St. Petersburg. But such protests were of no avail. The leading Russian newspaper, the semi-official *Novoye Vremya*, frankly pointed to the "isolation of Great Britain" and to the impossibility of her obtaining assistance from any other power in the Far East.

A Russian flotilla carrying a considerable number of troops arrived in the Yellow Sea. The troops, however, were not disembarked. The Russian envoy in China started negotiations with the

28. *Grosse Politik*, XIV[I], 134–135.
29. Romanov, *op. cit.*, p. 196.

Chinese Government concerning a lease of the ports to Russia, presenting the Russian action as a move to protect China from the Germans, who had seized Kiaochow. The other powers, although alarmed by the developments, had no means of intervening, and the Chinese were obviously unable to resist. In the end the Russian Minister of Finance promised to pay Li Hung-chang a bribe of 3 million rubles ($1,500,000) in three installments, and his assistant Chang In-huan, 250,000 rubles; a certain sum was apparently also promised to the Chinese envoy in Russia. On March 27, 1898, a few weeks after Kiaochow had been ceded to Germany, China signed a treaty with Russia by which the ports of Talienwan and Port Arthur were ceded for 25 years. China kept "sovereign rights" to the Liaotung (Kwantung) Peninsula, yet Russia obtained "complete and exclusive use" of the leasehold. A significant article of the treaty provided for the construction of a new railroad across South Manchuria to Liaotung by Russia.

The significance of this treaty in the history of Far Eastern policy cannot be exaggerated. The same Liaotung Peninsula, with its ports, had been ceded by China to Japan three years earlier as a result of the war in which China was the loser. Then came Russia, appearing as the protector of weak China, and forced Japan to withdraw. As a result Russia then seemed the strongest advocate of China's territorial integrity. Now, Russia herself followed in Japan's footsteps and took possession of what she had denied Japan. "Our seizure of the Kwantung region," Witte wrote later, "was an act of unprecedented perfidy."

And now events were precipitated. The two Far Eastern allies, Germany and Russia, were firmly entrenched in the Chinese ports on the Yellow Sea; China obviously would be unable to resist the further moves that were expected. The other great powers rushed to counteract the Russo-German advances. They did it in the same way that Russia and Germany had before. England drew nearer to Japan; she claimed and obtained Weihaiwei, another port on the Yellow Sea; France received a port in the south, near Indo-China. Even Italy claimed ports but, receiving no support, had to withdraw. Meanwhile the American war with Spain was nearing its end. The United States, a new Great Power, made an appearance in the Philippines and began to exercise a growing influence in the Far East.

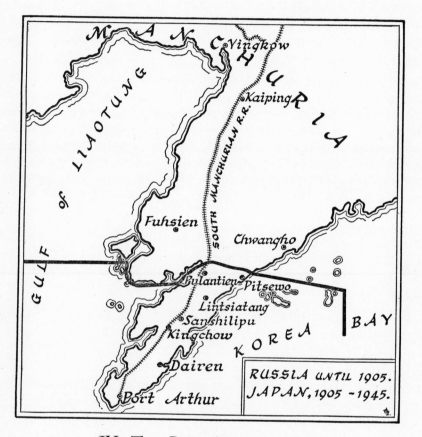

IV. The Port Arthur Area

In England the resentment against Russian policy was mingled with a sense of helplessness. The great British Navy was no bar to Russian advance on the continent of Asia. A British army in the Far East was out of the question. Besides, for many decades British relations with China had been anything but good.

Full of mistrust of Russian policy and full of despair at Britain's impotence to counteract it, the British Ambassador at St. Petersburg, O'Conor, reported to London:

It is evident that the official language and assurances of the Russian Government cover only a small part of their ultimate intentions . . . There is the policy of stopping Russian designs by a combination of Powers; but I confess I do not know the Powers that will take action with us . . . There is the alternative policy of accepting Russian assurances for as much as they are worth . . . This is tantamount at the very least to accepting spheres of influence, for which Her Majesty's Government had shown no proclivity, but it secures a share and a preponderant share in the semi-disintegration of China which has already unfortunately commenced. Russian policy is to obtain from China all they want by so-called friendly negotiation . . . they will take China more or less under their protection . . . and will . . . be able speciously to argue that they acted throughout in agreement with the Chinese Government.[30]

The only peaceful solution for England would be an agreement with Russia, concerning China and at the expense of China. In London it seemed that the situation was favorable for a partition of spheres of influence in China between Russia and England, so long as the Siberian railroad was not yet fully in operation. The British envoy at St. Petersburg advised his government to negotiate a modus vivendi in the Far East. "The Russian Government," he wrote in January, 1898, "and particularly the Emperor, are greatly afraid of complications arising before the Siberian Railway is completed. The moment is opportune for making amicable arrangements."

The British plan was to recognize the whole of northern China as a Russian sphere of influence, while the southern part, especially the commercially important Yangtze Valley, was to constitute the British sphere. The negotiations over the agreement lasted for

30. *British Documents on the Origin of the War*, I, 17. Report dated March 13, 1898.

more than a year. The two spheres at first were planned to be both political and economic. In the course of the negotiations, however, it was thought preferable, because of suspicions on all sides, to consider the spheres in the written agreement merely as economic units. The agreement, which was signed on April 29, 1899, covered mainly the building of railroads in China. Its real implications extended, of course, into the political field also. The British zone was described as "the provinces adjoining the river [Yangtze] and Honan and Chekiang." The sphere obtained by Russia was defined as the territories lying "to the north of the Great Chinese Wall."

The Russian concession to Britain consisted in the abandonment of her claims to the Province of Chili. As far as Manchuria was concerned, the doors remained, however, effectively barred to the other powers as a result of this agreement. It was never violated during the years that it remained in force—down to the war of 1904-5, but it proved to be of no help in the growing political crisis. Russia's advance continued, and Britain was unable to check it—unable so long as she had no ally in the Far East.

By the turn of the century a rapprochement between the United States and England was beginning to take shape, and, with it, the traditional Russo-American friendship of the nineteenth century was coming to an end. Nonetheless the reaction of the United States to the changing situation in North China differed from that of Britain. While the British Government tried to arrive at a compromise with Russia in order to safeguard its extensive political and economic interests in China, the United States was free to oppose continually the process of partitioning China. Washington now espoused the earlier British principle of an "open door" for foreign trade in China and other parts of the British sphere, and Secretary of State John Hay began to labor on the creation of a treaty system guaranteeing the "open door" in China as protection for American political and economic interests.

Formally the "open door" policy was concerned merely with facilities for American trade and investment in those parts of China which, in one way or another, had been placed under control of third powers. The "open door" meant the absence of discrimination against American businessmen, merchants, and investors, through special regulations, railway tariffs, customs duties, and similar means, and the assurance that, in particular, they would enjoy the same commercial and financial rights and privileges that were accorded to nationals of the power predominant in a given province of China. By implication, however, the "open door" was a political weapon that operated also against Russia in Manchuria. To thrust open the doors of Manchuria to foreign trade, and to American and other railway construction—with Russia herself, being short of capital, unable to compete—obviously foreshadowed the gradual undermining of Russian political control of Manchuria by expanding the economic power of the United States, Britain, and other states. Thus the "open door" was an economic countermove against Russia's political advance in the Far East.

On September 6, 1899, John Hay dispatched his first open door note to three of the Great Powers and, somewhat later, to the other three powers "interested" in China. In his note to St. Petersburg, Hay said that one year earlier the Russian Government had promised China "all the rights and privileges formerly guaranteed by China in the area of Port Arthur," and that in August, 1899, the Russian Government had confirmed this pledge when establishing the free port of Dalni (Talienwan). Now the United States wished to arrive at a comprehensive agreement concerning the entire "so-called Russian sphere of interest in China." In substance, John Hay asked, first, that no power "in any way interfere with any treaty port or any vested interests" within its sphere in China; second, that Chinese tariffs and duties apply to all merchandise, no matter to what nationality the ports or spheres belong; and third, that harbor dues and railway charges in any "sphere" not exceed those levied from China's own subjects.

Hay's proposals were accepted by the powers to whom they were addressed. Russia's answer was somewhat ambiguous, and there were obvious signs of hesitancy and reluctance, but generally the reply was in the affirmative: a public rejection of the "open door" principle was impossible. Hay was aware of the limited practical value of the Russian reply, but he wished to assure himself of a legal foundation for future American activity in China and therefore pretended to be fully satisfied that the Russian reply subscribed to the "open door" policy. "We want to take it for granted," he wrote, "that Russia has acceded to our proposals without much qualification." [31]

A few months later Hay had occasion to make use of the pretended international accord concerning the application of the "open door." In his second circular note in July, 1900, he proceeded to project the "open door" principle into the political field. Now he proclaimed it to be a tenet of American policy to preserve "China's territorial entity." This was the moment of the Boxer Rebellion and international intervention against China, which for a time appeared to be the overture to the final partition of the Chinese Empire among the powers. The United States' objective, Hay stated, was a solution of the Chinese problem "which may bring about permanent safety and peace to China, preserve Chinese territorial and administrative entity, protect all rights guaranteed to friendly powers by treaty and international law, and safeguard for the world the principle of equal and impartial trade with all parts of the Chinese Empire." [32]

In February, 1902, Hay again addressed Russia regarding the "open door." In his note he protested against the Russian draft of a treaty with China, which would have created a Russian monopoly "in opening mines, establishing railroads, or in any other way industrially developing Manchuria."

Hay's notes ushered in a policy toward China which was to become a tradition in the State Department. Though inconsistently applied and at times warped by concessions to other powers, it provided the basis for a Sino-American understanding and more than once led to diplomatic controversies between the United States and Russia. Later this policy found its clearest expression in the Nine-Power Treaty concluded at the Washington Conference in 1922. Whereas John Hay had had Russia in mind when he inaugurated the "open door" policy, a quarter of a century later Charles Evans Hughes directed the same policy against Japan, and another 25 years later, James F. Byrnes and George C. Marshall again used the same principles in seeking to contain Russian ex-

31. United States Ambassador Charlemagne Tower reported to Hay from Russia that "the Russian Government did not wish to answer your propositions at all . . . it did so because of the desire upon its part to maintain the relations subsisting between the two countries." Tyler Dennett, *John Hay* (New York, 1933), p. 294.

32. Edward H. Zabriskie, *American-Russian Rivalry in the Far East* (University of Pennsylvania Press, 1946), p. 61.

pansion under novel circumstances—the same principles which John Hay had formulated half a century earlier.

PARTITION OF CHINA?

The great popular uprising known as the Boxer Rebellion, which started at the end of 1899 and lasted through 1900, was a consequence of the defeats and humiliations which China suffered at the hands of the Great Powers. The movement, spontaneous and cruel, was directed against the "foreign devils" who, in the eyes of the fanatical members of the insurrectionist groups, symbolized the outrages and insults suffered by the Chinese people. Many Christian missionaries lost their lives in the rebellion; the lives of foreign diplomats were also endangered, and the German envoy and a Japanese official were killed. The Boxers issued artful proclamations such as the following:

Today the Sky, full of ire against the Street of Jesus for its insults to the Spirits, its destruction of the Sacred Teachings, and its failure to worship Buddhism, has swept away the rain and sent 8 million heavenly fighters for the annihilation of the foreigners. Soon after a short rain a great war shall break out, causing privations to the people . . . If we do not destroy the foreigners, the Sky will not send us a great rain.

When the movement reached serious proportions, the Chinese monarchy decided to side with the Boxers: now the rebellion took on the characteristics of a holy war against all foreign influence on Chinese soil. The Western Governments sent small expeditionary forces into China whose first task was to relieve the diplomatic staffs in Peking. By the time the main forces arrived from Europe, a few weeks later, the uprising had already been suppressed. Had it not been for the political ambitions of the intervening powers, normal conditions could have been re-established in September, 1900.

Each of the Great Powers, however, had its own policy in China, and when the first news of the unexpected events reached the various foreign offices in Europe, the question immediately arose: how do the Boxer Rebellion and the collective action of the powers fit into the existing plans and programs for the Far East, and what use can be made of these latest events to promote a given scheme of policy?

Japan, for example, considered the moment propitious for a new military advance on the continent, from which she had been driven by Russia a few years earlier. Japan was nearer to the Chinese theater than any other nation. She declared herself ready to send into northern China a force of 20,000 men and more, if necessary, to quell the rebellion. Her political aims of course were extensive: to forestall the advance of Russia and to take China under her tutelage against the northern giant.

Germany considered the Boxer movement a boon. Three years earlier she had taken over a port in Shantung Province, but at that time saw no way of expanding deeper into China. Now there was a pretext not only for dispatching an army to the Far East, but even for claiming leadership of all the armies of the Allied Nations: "Our special position," Foreign Minister von Bülow reported to the Kaiser, "is based on the fact that we have a murdered diplomat." Von Bülow made use of the intense rivalry between the British-Japanese and the French-Russian coalitions, and by means of this accomplished his goal: the German General Waldersee was appointed Commander in Chief of all the Allied Armies. The German Government hoped that this success would be only the start of the growth of Germany's importance in Far Eastern affairs, and vehemently protested when the other nations hastened to bring the Boxer affair to a close; she preferred to protract it.

To the Russian Government the Boxer Rebellion appeared to be a signal to fulfill the Russian program in Manchuria and northern China. For two years now Russia had been entrenched in Port Arthur and had certain police forces stationed along the new railroads in construction across Manchuria. No plausible reason existed, however, and no pretext arose, for occupying the rest of the great area. Now the pretext for an advance into Manchuria presented itself. An acute conflict began between War Minister Kuropatkin and the Witte group. While Witte tried to exercise caution and to steer carefully, Kuropatkin saw the moment approaching for the fulfillment of the great design for Manchuria. "On the day when the news of the rebellion reached the capital," Sergei Witte relates in his *Memoirs*,[33] "Minister of War Kuropatkin came to see me at my office in the Ministry of Finance. He was beaming with joy. I called his attention to the fact that the insur-

33. Witte, *op. cit.*, p. 107.

rection was the result of our seizure of the Kwantung Peninsula. 'On my part,' he replied, 'I am very glad! This will give us an excuse for seizing Manchuria.' " Kuropatkin's star shone bright during that period; the brilliant general was becoming one of the most influential persons at court. He sometimes even put Witte in the shade, since the latter was becoming more cautious and advised against precipitating events. "We must make of Manchuria another Bukhara," Kuropatkin said. (Bukhara, now a part of Soviet central Asia, was then a small independent nation which was transformed by military force—General Kuropatkin was one of the military leaders—into a dependency of Russia.) Obviously, Manchuria must expect the same fate.

The struggle between Witte and Kuropatkin was a battle of memoranda to the Tsar as well as a web of intrigues. Witte repeatedly submitted reports to the Tsar telling him that "Kuropatkin is leading into a plight." "If we assault China with fire and sword," he wrote, "we are forever making out of China our sworn enemy," Kuropatkin, on his part, submitted a memorandum advocating plainly that "North China must be occupied."

I and Count Lamsdorff [Witte wrote in a private letter in the summer of 1900] are in all seriousness more afraid of Kuropatkin than of the Chinese. He simply amazes me in his lack of conscientiousness or mental limitations—whichever it is. Besides the dispatch of masses of troops, the huge expenditures, the unnecessary daily orders by telephone and communications, etc., I am also incensed by his accounts, by all his descriptions of supposed battles in which—according to him—we never sustain any casualties or where at worst we lose a dozen men, while the Chinese suffer hundreds of killed, always flee and abandon their weapons and trophies.[34]

The chief difficulty in the path of Russian policy was the fact that the events in China were taking place precisely in the Province of Chili which had been designated as a part of the future Russian sphere. The invasion of Chili by the troops of a number of nations was also a check on the Russian advance from near-by Manchuria. The collective invasion of China, provoked by the Boxer Rebellion, caused Russian policy to become devious. In Manchuria, Russia was the most aggressive force against China, while in Peking she tried to separate herself from the assembly of the "intruders,"

34. *Krasnyi Arkhiv*, XVIII, 33, 37, 40.

protect China from too far-reaching demands, and speed the evacuation of foreign troops from Chinese soil. This Russian "separatism" aroused protests and indignation not only in Japan and England, but even among the friendly German diplomats and generals. "Russia wants to show the Chinese," the German Ambassador reported from St. Petersburg, "that its attitude is milder than that of the other powers and that it is not willing to participate in a further action against China." [35] The real aim of Russian policy was to remove all the foreign expeditionary forces—first of all the Japanese—from China and to prevent the Germans from gaining a foothold in Chili. That policy was pursued with great vigor.

No mistake was being made in St. Petersburg, however: Britain remained the main adversary. Germany's estrangement was considered to be temporary. She could obviously be wooed back. France, Russia was sure, remained her ally. In his instructions to the Ambassador in France, the Russian Foreign Minister wrote at that time: In your conversations with the French Foreign Minister you must support the idea of the desirability of co-ordinated action by France and Germany with the purpose of frustrating the efforts of England, in which endeavor they [France and Germany] can count fully on all possible moral support on the part of Russia.[36]

The general impression in the outside world was that the Boxer Rebellion signified the beginning of the break-up of China and that the hour had struck for the interested powers to execute their territorial programs in the disintegrating oriental empire. Any small event could precipitate developments. The rivals watched one another jealously and awaited the signal for final action.[37]

Since Russia possessed the greatest power and had carved for herself a vast territory, her policy inspired the greatest fear and suspicion. Germany's reaction to her policy was to move away from Russia for a time. Germany unexpectedly concluded a treaty with Britain, the first draft of which frankly stated: "Should another power proceed to obtain territorial acquisitions of this kind

35. *Grosse Politik*, XVI, p. 115.
36. Instructions of August 9, 1900, in *Krasnyi Arkhiv*, XIV, 23–24.
37. When the German envoy in Peking alluded, among his colleagues, to the impending partition of China, Bernhard von Bülow, the Foreign Minister, reprimanded him: "Not every truth is suitable to be uttered" (Nicht jede Wahrheit ist auszusprechen nützlich).

and should [Germany and Great Britain] consequently consider it necessary themselves to proceed to territorial acquisitions, then the two governments will come to a previous understanding on this subject." [38] The treaty was signed on October 16, 1900. In the final draft the wording lost its sharpness, and the phrase "proceed to territorial acquisitions," as relating to Germany and Great Britain, was omitted. However, the tradition of excellent Russo-German relations in the Far East was broken, and to the outside world the Kaiser's visit to London in January, 1901, was significant of the new state of things. Except for the support of France, Russia was isolated.

The possible spheres of the four European powers in China—should China disintegrate—were tentatively indicated. The southern part of China, bordering on French Indo-China, would obviously fall to France. The great central region, the so-called Yangtze Valley, including Nanking and Shanghai, would fall to Britain. Farther to the north, an area up to the Yellow River would obviously be claimed by Germany. Finally the whole north of China from Sinkiang to Chili and Manchuria, including the capital of Peking, would fall to Russia (see Map V). The United States would claim no part of China's territory. Japan would have to be content with Formosa, acquired by her a few years earlier.

But China escaped partition at that time. The fact that she did was due neither to her military power nor to the strength of her national unity. Only the intense competition among the Great Powers, the anti-imperialist trend in American policy, and the unsatisfied ambitions of Japan saved her. Not opposition to imperialism and territorial conquests but, paradoxically, a profusion of imperialism on the largest possible scale achieved the miracle of China's continuance.

The Boxer incident was officially closed in 1901, and the powers, with the exception of Russia, began to evacuate their troops from China. Russia left her armies in Manchuria and obviously did not intend to withdraw them.

The first draft of a treaty concerning Manchuria as well as other northern territories was presented by Russia to China at the end of 1900. It was tantamount to granting Russia extensive privileges

38. *Grosse Politik*, XVI, 223.

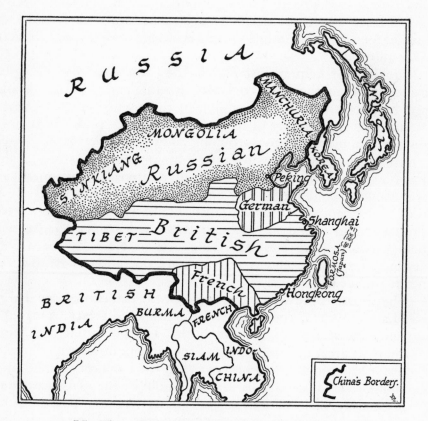

V. THE PLANNED PARTITION OF CHINA

and permitting her to extend her influence over the Tarbagatai area, Kashgar, Yarkand, Khotan (all in western China), Mongolia, and Manchuria. This version of the treaty did not permit China to maintain armies in these areas—Russia was to take care of law and order—and prohibited the import of arms. The size of the police force was to be decided by consultation with Russia. No concessions (railroad, mines) or leases of land to other nations were to be allowed.

Looking for help against Russia, the Chinese envoys divulged the contents of the draft to Japan and England. Minister Witte also revealed to the foreign diplomats the essence of the outlined treaty. The temperature of Russo-British and Russo-Japanese relations rose immediately to the boiling point. Even Germany advised China to reject the Russian draft. The imminence of war in the Far East became the main topic of international discussion. Japan was growing bold and openly opposed Russia ("China's ally") in the Chinese capital. Moreover, Japan acted as China's self-appointed protector and friend in opposing Russian demands. "Japan will help China achieve clearing Manchuria of Russian troops . . . Japan would not hesitate to start military operations if Russia does not renounce her treaty." [39]

The situation grew so menacing that St. Petersburg decided to yield and in April, 1901, recalled the proposed treaty. Its troops, nonetheless, stayed on in Manchuria. The government did not abandon its great design. In July of the same year—1901—Foreign Minister Lamsdorff asked his envoys in the Far East to state their opinion—"just theoretically—what would be the consequence of an official Russian statement concerning its intention to annex Manchuria." Commenting upon this request, the Foreign Minister explained: "From a political point of view, the annexation to the Russian possessions of an extensive Chinese area, rich in resources, could only serve to enhance Russia's prestige among the peoples of Asia . . . but one should avoid international complications."

It was in order to avoid such "international complications" that Witte and Lamsdorff tried to promote economic expansion in Manchuria without dangerously encroaching on Chinese sovereignty. They tried to keep out of Manchuria all foreign industrial and especially railway investments; they contemplated the build-

39. Romanov, *op. cit.*, pp. 306–307.

ing of a Russian railroad as far south as Peking; they sought to obtain from China as much land as possible around the Chinese Eastern Railway; they insisted on keeping Russian "armed guards" and administration in all the settlements along the railway; and they wished, if possible, to draw out the occupation of Manchuria until the completion of the Chinese Eastern.

While this program aimed at the economic control of Manchuria Witte and Lamsdorff were inclined to practice appeasement of Japan and refrained from new advances against Korea. Their influence, however, was gradually waning.

III

Isolation and Defeat

TWO GOVERNMENTS IN RUSSIA

After 1900 new personalities, quite unknown to the public, began to gather around the Russian throne and acquire influence. Among the rival factions in Russia's leading circles, one circle represented the most extreme trend, both in foreign and internal affairs. To this circle belonged: the uncle of the Tsar, Grand Duke Nikolai Alexandrovich; Adm. Alexei Abaza; Prince Vonlarlarski; later, Gen. Eugene Alexeyev (said to be an illegitimate son of Tsar Alexander II) joined the group, as did the shrewd and reckless Minister of the Interior Vyacheslav Plehve. The spiritual head of the group, and the least selfish among them, was Ivan Bezobrazov, with the title of Privy Counselor.

Minister Witte, who was becoming hesitant, was, in their eyes, a traitor. Even Kuropatkin, the audacious War Minister, was far too moderate for them. As a precaution, in the event their correspondence fell into the hands of their rivals in the official government, the group at first used cover names for their hated enemies. Witte was called "Nostril," Minister Lamsdorff, "Tadpole," General Kuropatkin, "Black Grouse." The Tsar was called "the Boss." Witte, Lamsdorff, and Kuropatkin, most resented by the group, constituted the "lousy triumvirate."

This was a unique situation. "Witte, Lamsdorff, and myself," General Kuropatkin sadly relates in his *Memoirs*, "are concerned about the personal correspondence between the Tsar and this visionary and adventurer [Bezobrazov]."

In one of his reports to the Tsar, Bezobrazov outlined his program: "The Far East is still in a period when a stubborn struggle is necessary in order to assure the consolidation of our realm; domination by us is the ultimate aim of this struggle; without such domination we are not able either to rule the yellow race or control the inimical influence of our European rivals." [1]

1. Kuropatkin, *Memoirs*. Bezobrazov's report of July 23, 1903.

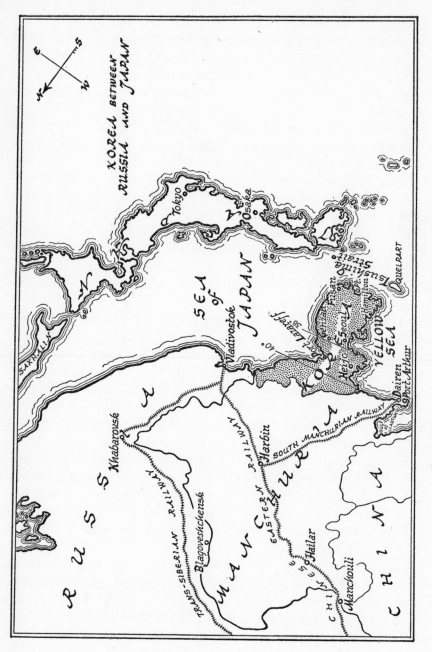

VI. Korea between Russia and Japan

Manchuria, a controversial issue for the members of the Russian Government, was no problem for the Bezobrazov group. The latter took it for granted that northern China would be annexed to the empire. The significance of Korea in the expansionist program of this party of extremists was outstanding. Korea would have rounded out the possessions of the Russian Empire in northern Asia; possession by Russia would have closed Korea to penetration by any other power—Britain or Japan. The inclusion of Korea in any Russian program could not appear otherwise than as a challenge to her eastern neighbor since Japan had openly stated that she would go to war over that area. Bezobrazov's group was fully aware of the danger and, while exaggerating Russia's might in the Far East, prepared for a war against Japan.

What the Japanese Government tried to achieve was recognition by Russia of Japan's complete dominance over Korea. More than once it proposed a deal: Manchuria to become a Russian and Korea a Japanese sphere. Although some members of the Russian Government (among them Foreign Minister Lamsdorff and Sergei Witte) were inclined to accept partition with Japan of the Far Eastern areas, an agreement was never reached. On the contrary, the determination to dominate Korea grew stronger among high circles surrounding the court, especially since Bezobrazov's group was gaining the upper hand. At the same time, the fantastic plan described above was evolved: to make use of the forest concessions on the Yalu River (in Korea) as a screen for a Russian military advance. A swarm of officials was dispatched to Manchuria and Korea. Admiral Abaza was placed at the head of this peculiar venture. "We must take Korea by the spider's method," Bezobrazov declared. He was extremely confident, since his group had the support of the Tsar. The Russian envoy to Korea bluntly announced that "Korea must be Russian."

Somewhat naïvely, the Tsar was convinced that the forest concession at Yalu would also become a genuine industrial enterprise that would yield profits. When he ordered an appropriation of two million rubles for Bezobrazov, he simultaneously prepared an estimate of future dividends and even a schedule of their disbursement.[2]

2. Kuropatkin, *op. cit.*, entry for October 31, 1903. On the eve of the war against Japan, Witte "took the documents from his secret panel and showed me two of them," Kuropatkin recalled. "On the reverse side the Tsar had filled almost the whole page with pencil writing. These were the anticipated profits from the forest concession."

Russian Government circles did not realize how rapidly the international situation was changing in 1901. China stubbornly refused to sign the treaty with Russia in spite of all the pressure applied by St. Petersburg and in spite of changes in her favor accepted in the course of negotiations. China went so far as to prohibit the granting of new concessions in Manchuria to Russian companies. Li Hung-chang, Russia's white hope in China, died late in 1901. In their resistance to Russia the Chinese were encouraged by Japan, and Japan in turn was backed by Britain. The rapprochement between London and Tokyo was making rapid headway, and from July, 1901 on, a formal alliance between London and Tokyo was being discussed at London's suggestion. Thus Britain found an ally in the Far East to oppose Russia and resist her moves on the Asiatic mainland. Before the Anglo-Japanese treaty was signed on January 30, 1902, Marquis Ito went to Russia with a last offer of compromise, suggesting that Russia claim Manchuria in compensation for abandonment of Korea. This plan, which had been repeatedly discussed in earlier years, was firmly rejected by St. Petersburg. The Tsar wrote on the report concerning the Japanese proposal: "Russia cannot renounce her right to maintain as many troops in Korea as do the Japanese."

The most significant part of the Anglo-Japanese treaty was its preamble, in which both signatories affirmed their "special interest" in the maintenance of "the independence and territorial integrity of the Empire of China and the Empire of Korea." Only six years earlier Russia had concluded her alliance with China and pledged her support against encroachments against the latter by Japan. In the short intervening years the situation had changed to such an extent as to make Russia, and not Japan, appear to be the main menace to China, and Japan, not Russia, the protector of her integrity.

By the treaty of alliance each power obligated itself to remain neutral in case the other party became involved in war; if, however, any third power joined in the war against Britain or Japan, the other signatory was pledged to enter the conflict. In practice this meant that Britain would remain neutral in a war between Russia and Japan, but that she would join as Japan's ally if either Germany or France entered the conflict on Russia's side.

Now Russia confronted a powerful coalition in the Far East.

The two new allies were supported, albeit informally, by China and the United States; the latter was gradually assuming an attitude of hostility toward Russia. The knot of this international combination was of course in London, and the traditional Russo-British rivalry now assumed a more overt and bellicose tone. Ambassador Isvolsky, the future Foreign Minister, correctly estimated the situation in a report home from Tokyo in May, 1902: "Henceforth the knot of Russian-Japanese relations lies no longer here [in Tokyo] but in London, and it will scarcely be possible to work out any agreement between us and Japan without the full knowledge and approval and perhaps even without the more or less direct participation of the Court of St. James's." [3]

The first fruit of the new alliance was the Russo-Chinese agreement of April 8, 1902, concerning Manchuria. The demands which Russia had made on China during the preceding year were dropped, and the evacuation of Manchuria by Russian troops—after a stay of more than two years—was agreed upon. The evacuation, however, was not to begin until six months later, in October, 1902, and was to be accomplished in three stages, the last one due to take place in October, 1903. By means of a bribe of 30,000 lan out of the so-called Li Hung-chang funds, the Russian negotiators managed to condition this withdrawal upon the "mode of action of other powers." [4]

For a time it seemed as if the danger of war had been averted. Influential groups in Russia, however, considered the agreement with China as merely a timesaving maneuver that put off the conflict with Japan. Indeed, only the first stage of the evacuation was carried out; the pledge concerning the withdrawals scheduled for April and October, 1903, was broken. In fact, new Russian troops arrived in Manchuria. The Russo-Chinese accord continued to be violated.

Russia tried to counter the Anglo-Japanese alliance by a new rapprochement with Germany. The friction of 1900 was forgotten, and when the Tsar met the Kaiser in the Baltic in the fall of 1901, their relations were most cordial.

3. Romanov, *op. cit.*, p. 356. Report of May 17, 1902.
4. *Ibid.*, p. 348.

Tsar Nicholas termed the English policy as most egotistic . . . He spoke vehemently against anarchists [i.e., socialists and revolutionaries] who find asylum in England. He said that he was an enemy of the revolutionaries—even in this respect he is in complete accord with His Majesty [the Kaiser]. He said he would never grant a constitution . . . [Leo] Tolstoy is doing great damage by his works.[5]

This rapprochement with Germany was to some extent dictated by Russian domestic considerations. In the Far East, Germany's assistance, which was at best only halfhearted, did not mean very much in practical terms. In case of military conflict between Russia and Japan, Germany could not be counted upon to act so long as France remained neutral.

The policy of moderation and prudence which had been foisted upon Russia by the new power alignment in the Far East did not last. By the end of 1902 the extreme expansionist trends were again winning out, and Russian policy now took a sharp turn against Britain and Japan. The decisive day proved to be February 7, 1903. On that day a special conference was summoned by the Tsar to decide whether the evacuation of Manchuria was to be continued. Here Witte, supported by a number of other ministers, demanded agreement with Japan. He, as well as Foreign Minister Lamsdorff, advocated a compromise solution calling for the withdrawal of all Russian claims to Korea and South Manchuria. Even General Kuropatkin advised limitation of Russian interests to North Manchuria. The final decision lay with the Tsar. He decided against them, and the second deadline for the evacuation of Russian troops from Manchuria passed unobserved.

In order to reduce the influence of the more cautious among his ministers, the Tsar proceeded to adopt a quite unusual reform. On July 30, 1903, he created the post of Viceroy of the Russian Far East, the viceroy to be empowered to conduct diplomatic negotiations with China, Japan, and Korea. General Alexeyev was appointed to this new post. From that time on, the influence of the Russian Minister of Foreign Affairs on the Far East was almost nil. A Special Committee for the Affairs of the Far East, actually

5. Von Bülow's notes in *Grosse Politik*, XVIII[1]. When the Tsar again met the Kaiser in 1902, he reiterated, "Tolstoy is Russia's evil genius."

headed by Bezobrazov and Abaza, was created in St. Petersburg. It was as if a second government had been established, and the most important problems of Russian foreign policy were taken out of the hands of the official cabinet. The military forces in the Far East were virtually subordinated to this second government and took orders from the Committee on the Far East rather than from the War Minister. "What I cannot understand," Count Vorontsov wrote in a private letter in May, 1903, "is the duality of our policy in the East: the Tsar's official and the Tsar's unofficial policy, each of which has its agents, quarreling with each other."

Acting logically, Sergei Witte resigned. Besides being personally offended he was disinclined to accept the responsibility for the war against Japan and Britain which appeared increasingly imminent. Kuropatkin soon followed his example. In his *Memoirs* he recalls a conversation with the Tsar when he told the sovereign of his desire to resign. "Your Majesty's confidence in me will grow when I cease to be a minister," Kuropatkin said. "His Majesty stopped me and said, 'You know, however strange that may seem, it might be psychologically true.'"

The last six months before the outbreak of war with Japan were full of crises and struggles behind the scenes; the Tsar himself wavered and frequently changed his mind. The true, almost unbelievable, events of this period did not become known until two years later, when a collection of documents was published under the title *Crimson Book*. Unlike the usual White Books and Blue Books and the like, this one was published without the knowledge of the government; printed in only 400 copies, it was intended for distribution among a select group of persons. In its 39 documents, the prologue to the war is painted with devastating evidence: the official Russian Government remained out of the picture; the obscure Admiral Abaza loomed as the real master; orders and counter-orders of the Tsar followed each other in chaotic sequence. The government ordered all the copies of the *Crimson Book* immediately seized and withdrawn.

From these documents, and from all other sources, Russian policy on the eve of the Russo-Japanese war appears as a series of zigzags, oscillations, and reversals, a model of confusion and indecision. In June, 1903, the Tsar was inclined to cede Korea to

Japan. General Alexeyev, from the Far East, was also counseling moderation. In September the Tsar signed a telegram submitted to him by Foreign Minister Lamsdorff, ordering "that there be no war!" In his report to the Tsar, Kuropatkin declared, in October, "We should keep only North Manchuria. The new frontier will not touch Korea and will provoke no complications with Japan. A conflict with China is possible—but not war." General Subotich, Kuropatkin's adviser, submitted a report questioning the very basis of Russian policy; according to Subotich Russia did not need "warm ports" in the Far East; she could not obtain military superiority there. He came to the same conclusion that Kuropatkin and others had reached before him: only North Manchuria must be kept under Russian control.

The "clandestine government," however, subscribing to the thesis of Russian superiority and a Russian mission in Asia, and to a program of defiance of both Japan and Britain, wielded greater influence than did the cautious experts. Since July, 1903, Japan had been making offers to Russia but had received no answer. In November, 1903, the King of England tried to mediate between Russia and Japan, but his efforts were frustrated in St. Petersburg. While both sides were preparing for war, the Japanese envoy, in January, 1904, told the Russian ministers that there would be war if no answer to the Japanese proposals were forthcoming. But the Ministry of Foreign Affairs was paralyzed. "I can do nothing," Lamsdorff said, "I take no part in the negotiations." [6]

Reversing his previous orders, the Tsar, on February 8, 1904, wired General Alexeyev in the Far East:

It is desirable that the Japanese, and not we, be the ones to start military operations . . . But if their navy should cross the 38th parallel on the western coast of Korea, with or without a landing, you are hereby given discretion to attack them without waiting for the first shot from their side. I rely upon you. God help you.[7]

Two days later, on February 10th, the Japanese Navy, without a declaration of war, shelled Russian warships at Port Arthur.

6. Witte, *op. cit.*, p. 126.
7. Russia, Special Committee on Far Eastern Affairs, *Crimson Book*, Document 39.

THE RUSSO-JAPANESE WAR

The war against Japan was from the first a series of unprecedented defeats for the Russian Army and Navy. The military debacle brought catastrophe to the whole internal political system as well, and by the end of the war the centuries-old Russian monarchy was shaken to its roots. The peace of Portsmouth, which brought to an end the eighteen months' war, reduced Russia's position in the Far East as well as her prestige in Europe.

In the first three months of the war (February to April, 1904) Japan's armies landed unopposed in Korea. In April they crossed the Yalu River, and on April 18 inflicted a heavy defeat on the Russian Army, commanded by General Zasulich. A month later the Japanese occupied Talienwan. At the end of July the Russian Pacific Navy was destroyed near Port Arthur. The next important event of the war, the battle at Liao-yang, which lasted from August 16 to 22, ended in a disaster for Russia. Japan's might appeared to be overwhelming and it seemed that her victories might extend too far. President Theodore Roosevelt's first steps to achieve a compromise and end the war were taken following Liao-yang; they proved futile at this time.

On January 1, 1905, the fortress of Port Arthur capitulated after a long siege. In February a huge Russian army was beaten near Mukden, the defeat amounting to a rout. The Russian Government put its hopes in its European navy, which reached the Far East in May, 1905. The navy was annihilated at the battle of Tsushima. This was practically the end; further Russian resistance might have led to the occupation by Japan of eastern Siberia. Japan, however, was also exhausted. President Roosevelt and Kaiser Wilhelm succeeded in convincing both countries to agree to a peace conference and, eventually, to sign the peace treaty.

Japan's star rose high during the war. There were few who had believed that this small nation, almost unknown to the world, would be able to beat the Russian colossus. Japan had displayed a high degree of military preparedness, efficiency, and technical skill, and her admirals and generals proved to be not inferior to the military leaders of Europe. The Japanese intelligence service was amazingly efficient, and Japanese espionage work in Russia during the war was most thorough. Japan spent 120 million yen (about 10 per cent of her war budget) for intelligence work in Russia.[8]

Russia, on the contrary, surprised the world by her lack of military efficiency. She had no definite strategical plan; her generals and officers displayed insufficient interest in the operations. The one-track Siberian railroad was jammed, and the chaotic situation impeded the transport of troops and supplies from Europe. A series of commercial scandals occurred in connection with war supplies. The quality of military matériel was inferior, due to the network of bribery surrounding the War Department.

As far as the Russian population was concerned, the war with Japan was one of the most unpopular in Russian history. In the very first weeks of the war the government attempted to organize patriotic demonstrations in the cities. These, however, were no more than processions of small groups, guarded by police, with a few government officials, carrying a large picture of the Tsar, at the head. The Tsar himself traveled over the country to greet the regiments departing for the Far East; his presence, however, did not evoke any great enthusiasm, particularly when the news of the defeats became known.

These defeats strengthened the revolutionary movement in Russia, which had been growing in the years preceding the war. Events bore out those who had pointed at the intrinsic decay of the obsolete political system. It was precisely to disprove this viewpoint and to achieve a new prestige for the political system that influential members of the government considered the war necessary. Vyacheslav Plehve, the Minister of the Interior, who considered a defeat impossible, stated frankly, *"We need a small victorious war to stem the tide of revolution."* [9]

The series of defeats produced the opposite effect: the revolutionary tide spread far beyond the small groups of the underground Socialist parties. The whole population was astir. Plehve himself was killed by a bomb thrown by the student Sazonov, a member of the terrorist group of the Social-Revolutionary party. On January 22, 1905, a large procession of workers, headed by the priest Georgi Gapon, marched toward the Winter Palace to present a

8. Cf. Alexander Votinov, *Yaponski shpionazh v russko-yaponskuyu voinu 1904–1905 gg.* (Moscow, 1939).
9. Witte, *op. cit.*, p. 250.

petition to the Tsar. Before it reached the palace it was met by a barrage of bullets and dispersed. Hundreds of dead and wounded were left lying in the streets. A wave of political strikes followed in the cities, and so-called "agrarian disorders" among the peasants spread over the country. The mounting opposition to the regime included even the most moderate elements of Russian society. The Imperial Government, isolated and confused, began to make concessions. The first Russian constitution and the establishment of the Duma were immediate consequences of the Russo-Japanese war.

No other war had engendered among the Russian people so strong a defeatist attitude as did that against Japan. The extreme left, comprising all the Socialist parties, was openly defeatist. At the International Socialist Congress in Amsterdam in 1904, during the Russo-Japanese war, the veteran Russian Socialist, Georgi Plekhanov, publicly shook hands with Sen Katayama, the leader of the Japanese Socialists; Plekhanov acted for all the factions of Russian Socialism—Mensheviks, Bolsheviks, and Social-Revolutionaries. Lenin, whose influence was rising in step with the tempo of revolutionary events, deemed the military reverses a boon for Russia. In his eyes Japan was an advanced country, Russia a backward one, and "the war of an advanced country against a backward one [Lenin wrote at the time] has again, as it has more than once in history, played a great revolutionary role." [10] He did not desire a quick conclusion of the war, since each new defeat increased popular discontent. When the Menshevik faction proclaimed its slogan of "peace at *any* price," Lenin protested. "The cause of Russia's freedom depends greatly upon the military defeats of the autocracy . . . The Russian people have gained by the defeats." [11]

The differences between the foreign policies advocated by the Bolsheviks and those advocated by the other Socialist parties—the differences that became so important in 1917–18—can be seen in these polemics of 1904–5. Lenin's defeatism contained the seeds of his later theories concerning the benefits of a war which develops into a civil war. A war is of course a calamity, Lenin said, but it is wrong to base a policy on "this trivial reasoning."

Agents of Japan tried to strengthen the revolutionary move-

10. Lenin, *Collected Works* (Russian ed.), IV, 165.
11. *Vperiod* (January 14, 1905), No. 2.

ment in Russia and offered through interim financial assistance as well as weapons to the revolutionaries. Konni Zilliacus, a leader of a Finnish "active resistance party," approached Russian Socialist leaders with an offer of aid, but the proposal was turned down. The only exceptions were Pilsudski's faction of the Polish Socialists and a group of Georgian separatists, who did accept the assistance offered by Zilliacus.[12]

The negative attitude toward the war and outright defeatism were also widespread among the moderate non-Socialist opposition groups. Peter Struve, one of the leaders of the future Constitutional-Democratic party, for instance, wrote upon the outbreak of the war: "The occupation of Manchuria and the outlet to the sea were economically nonsensical for Russia . . . The loss of Manchuria and the Kwantung Peninsula will be no loss at all but will be to our advantage, for, in the pursuit of our own interests, we should long ago have abandoned this awkward adventure. And our enemies will ask no more than that from us." [13]

Finally criticism of the government policy which was presumed to have precipitated the war and defeatism were rather common even in government and monarchist circles. Esper Ukhtomsky, formerly a staunch supporter of the drive to the east, declared in an interview with the *Frankfurter Zeitung:*

Why is the public apathetic? Because there can be no war less popular than the present one . . . We have been involved in the East Asiatic venture against the will of the people—using that term in its broadest meaning.

. . . Port Arthur was in no way essential to us; as a port it is no better and no worse than Vladivostok; at any rate, it is no less subject to freezing . . .

. . . Nobody wants this war, and it will do nobody the least bit of good.

For a short time after the outbreak of the war it seemed that it might develop into a great world war. It was considered possible that Germany would join Russia in the Far Eastern venture. Japan sought to induce China to participate in the conflict on her side. The situation was so alarming that England's joining the war seemed probable, in accordance with the Anglo-Japanese treaty

12. L. Martov, *Istoriya russkoi Sotsial-demokratii* (Moscow, 1923), p. 92.
13. *Osvobozhdeniye* (1904), Nos. 17–18, pp. 299, 311.

of alliance (Britain would be obliged to come to the aid of Japan as soon as any other nation joined Russia). Within a few months, however, these apprehensions were dispelled and the war continued to be confined to the Far East.

Nevertheless England remained more than a loyal ally of Japan until the very end. She threw her whole diplomatic weight into the Japanese scale. British relations with Russia during the entire course of the war were poor, and during the last phase the ties between Britain and Japan were even strengthened. Japan demanded from Britain recognition of Tokyo's future protectorate ("special interests") over Korea. England, on the other hand, wanted to obtain Japanese assistance in case of possible British conflicts with Russia in the Far East and even in India. After a few months of negotiations a new treaty of alliance was concluded in August, 1905, which covered both items: Japanese dominance over Korea and the "maintenance of peace in India." The alliance was modified in such a fashion in 1905 that England and Japan would support each other if either were attacked by one state. This treaty remained in force during the decade following.

Of paramount importance in the situation was the fact that the United States actually was a member of the anti-Russian coalition. American public opinion had been against Russia since the end of the 1890's; the Russian advance into Manchuria had increased the bad feeling in America. The internal situation in Russia—the anti-Jewish pogroms, the persecution of the opposition parties—strengthened the anti-Russian sentiments. President Roosevelt, in using the strong language that he did, spoke for the great majority of Americans. He described the Tsar, for example, as a "preposterous little creature." "Those responsible for managing [Russia's] foreign policy," he wrote, "betrayed a brutality and ignorance, an arrogance and short-sightedness which are not often combined." [14]

Before attacking Russia Japan had obtained the pledge of the United States that the latter would observe "a *very benevolent* neutrality"; it was only after she received this reassurance that Japan sent her great army to Korea. Roosevelt proceeded to act as though he were a member of the Japanese coalition. "As soon as this war broke out," he wrote later in a letter, "I notified Germany and France . . . that in the event of a combination against

14. Tyler Dennett, *Roosevelt and the Russo-Japanese War* (New York, 1925), p. 47.

Japan . . . I should promptly side with Japan and proceed to whatever length was necessary on her behalf." [15] When George Kennan, the American expert in Russian affairs, suggested to President Roosevelt in May, 1905, that the United States enter the Anglo-Japanese alliance, Roosevelt replied: "I personally agree entirely with you," but "have you followed some of my experiences in endeavoring to get treaties through the Senate? I might just as well strive for the moon."

American public opinion was pro-Japanese. Each Japanese victory was hailed with delight, and the American press vividly described corruption and atrocities attributed to the Russians. "When the report of the Japanese victory [at Tsushima] reached America, Admiral Dewey and other officers of our Navy listened with breathless interest, and the comments reported were 'wonderful, wonderful.' " [16]

After the autumn of 1904, however, President Roosevelt began to become aware of the growing force of Japan. His idea had been a balance of power in the Far East, with Japan and Russia on opposite sides of the scales. In Japan's ultimate aims, of course, America had no confidence. As President Roosevelt wrote to Senator Henry Cabot Lodge: ". . . while Russia's triumph would have been a blow to civilization, her destruction as an eastern Asiatic Power would also in my opinion be unfortunate. It is best that she should be left face to face with Japan so that each may have a moderative action on the other." [17]

Years after he left the White House, Roosevelt gave his basic concept of American foreign policy. He spoke of Europe, but his formula was equally applicable to the Far East:

As long as England succeeds in keeping up the balance of power in Europe, well and good. Should she, however, for some reason or other fail in doing so, the United States would be obliged to step in at least temporarily to reestablish the balance of power in Europe; never mind against which country or group of countries our efforts may have to be directed. In fact, we ourselves are becoming, owing to our strength and geographic situation, more and more the balance of power of the whole globe.

15. Dennett, *op. cit.*, p. 2. Later investigations, however, were not able to find these Roosevelt statements in the archives.
16. Tupper McReynolds, *Japan in American Public Opinion* (New York, 1937), p. 8
17. Dennett, *op. cit.*, p. 165.

In the face of Japanese victories, Roosevelt started, wherever possible, to sound out feeling concerning the peace terms and to press for an early conclusion of the Russo-Japanese war. In view of his unsatisfactory relations with the Russian Government, Roosevelt acted through Berlin (this helped produce a certain rapprochement between the American and German Governments in these years). Roosevelt's efforts, however, were not successful so long as Russia could hope to score at least a partial success. Not until June, 1905, when the battle of Tsushima was lost, did both parties agree to the proposal of Roosevelt and Wilhelm II to convene a peace conference.

Germany's policy during the Russo-Japanese war was a series of complicated moves and intrigues which often puzzled other governments. Before the war started Germany had encouraged Russia to oppose Japan; it appeared that Germany intended to join Russia in case of a military conflict. Actually the German idea behind these moves was to divert Russia's attention (and her armies) from Europe and to isolate France. A protraction of the war was therefore advantageous to Berlin. A weakening of Russia and loss of Russian prestige strengthened Germany's position in relation to France, the "hereditary enemy."

Documents published a few decades after the war reveal the existence of a conflict between the Kaiser and his Chancellor developing out of this war. Wilhelm II feared the growing revolutionary movement in Russia and wanted to see the Tsar emerge victorious from the Far Eastern war; besides, his personal theory concerning the "yellow peril" was still alive. His government, on the other hand, and especially the shrewd von Bülow, regarded Russia's internal affairs with more equanimity than did the Kaiser and were more concerned with Germany's *grosse Politik*. Heated discussions took place between Wilhelm and von Bülow. The Chancellor rejected the "yellow peril" theory and disapproved the Kaiser's exaggerated interest in the personality and autocratic methods of the Russian Tsar. No, Wilhelm replied to his Chancellor, I cannot follow your road. I am myself an Emperor, and have the duty to assist the Emperor of Russia. The dualism in Germany's policy during the war was manifest.

The two monarchs corresponded with one another, the Kaiser advising the Tsar to resist Japan and even to send his best regiments to the Far East. The Tsar was grateful for the Kaiser's sympathy. On August 28, 1904, he authorized Prince Heinrich to deliver this message to the Kaiser: "Willy need not be at all anxious; he may sleep well at night, for I vouch that everything will come perfectly right." [18] Two months later the Tsar sent another message to the German Emperor: "Russia will fight this war to the end until the last Japanese is driven out of Manchuria."

At the end of 1904 negotiations were begun between Berlin and St. Petersburg for the conclusion of an alliance between Germany and Russia (aimed, of course, at England). The German Government, which did not want to provoke England unnecessarily, was not too anxious to conclude such a treaty, yet the discussions between the two capitals, which had appeared to be leading nowhere, suddenly ended with the signing of the agreement at a meeting between the Kaiser and the Tsar at Björkö in May, 1905. It was one of those tragi-comic incidents wherein the German Kaiser took advantage of the naïveté of the Tsar and the absence of his ministers. When Lamsdorff, the Russian Foreign Minister, learned about the treaty signed by the two emperors, he was desperate. When he made attempts to extricate Russia from this spider's web, the Kaiser replied: "What is signed is signed!" Neither was Berlin enthusiastic about the agreement, and Bülow was greatly relieved when Lamsdorff finally fell back on the stipulation of the treaty which provided that France's adherence to it was necessary—and buried it.

In the beginning of June, 1905, even the German Emperor began to advise Tsar Nicholas to enter into peace negotiations. On June 9 both Russia and Japan consented to avail themselves of the services of President Roosevelt, and the peace conference opened on August 5, 1905, in the United States. Russia's chief delegate was Sergei Witte who, two years earlier, had been ousted from the government because of his cautious policy in regard to Japan.

The original Japanese conditions contained a few clauses which were not acceptable to Russia. Japan demanded limitation by treaty of the future Russian Navy in the Pacific and the payment of a war indemnity; also the cession of the whole of the island of Sakhalin. In spite of the intervention of President Roosevelt and the German Kaiser in Tokyo and St. Petersburg, the peace talks

18. *Grosse Politik*, XIX[1], 216.

approached an impasse. But Japan, financially exhausted and prodded by the Anglo-Saxons, finally had to give in on certain points. Russian naval activity in the Far East was not curtailed by the treaty, no indemnity was required, and only the southern half of Sakhalin was ceded to Japan.

The Treaty of Portsmouth was signed on September 5, 1905. Russia undertook to evacuate Manchuria and to place it again under the sovereignty of China. The much disputed Liaotung Peninsula, containing the two ports of Talienwan and Port Arthur, was turned over as a "leased territory" to Japan, contingent on Chinese consent—which China, of course, could not refuse. Railroads in the southern part of Manchuria, constructed by Russia, were ceded to Japan without payment. Japan obtained fishing rights in the seas adjacent to Russia.

As to Korea, which had been the main bone of contention between Russia and Japan on the eve of the war, Japan scored a total victory. Even before the war had ended, Tokyo had secured Britain's acknowledgment of Japan's "paramount political, military, and economic interests in Korea." By the treaty of August 12, 1905, Britain recognized "the right of Japan to take such measures of guidance, control, and protection of Korea as she may deem proper and necessary." Similarly the United States concluded an unpublicized agreement ("a recorded conversation" between Secretary William Taft and Premier Count Katsura) by which Japan pledged "not to harbor any aggressive designs against the Philippines," while the United States agreed to Japanese suzerainty over Korea. Later President Theodore Roosevelt assured Tokyo that "the reorganization of Korea by the Japanese would meet no opposition from the United States."

Now in the peace treaty of Portsmouth, Russia was compelled to recognize the "paramount political, military, and economic interests" of Japan in Korea; Russia agreed "not to interfere or place obstacles in the way of any measure of direction or protection and supervision that the Imperial Government of Japan may deem necessary to adopt in Korea."

As a result of the war Russian power was reduced and Japan emerged as the strongest power of the Far East. Japan owed her successes in good part to the support of Britain and America. Yet her ambitions went far beyond her wartime accomplishments.

IV

The Last Decade of the Empire

Following the Russo-Japanese war, Far Eastern international relations took a quite unexpected, almost sensational, course.

After the Treaty of Portsmouth, the world expected that Russia would withdraw from Chinese territory and that Manchuria would be restored to China. Japan was expected to limit her activities on the continent essentially to Korea and the Liaotung Peninsula. On the whole the integrity of China appeared secure so far as possible action on the part of Russia and Japan was concerned.

The Treaty of Portsmouth provided, in Paragraph 3, that

Japan and Russia mutually engage to evacuate complete and simultaneously Manchuria [(except Liaotung), and to] restore entirely and completely to the exclusive administration of China all portions of Manchuria now in the occupation or under the control of the Japanese or Russian troops. The Imperial Government of Russia declares that it has not in Manchuria any territorial advantages or preferential or exclusive concessions in impairment of Chinese sovereignty or inconsistent with the principle of equal opportunity.

In spirit as well as in letter, this paragraph coincided with the wishes of the other powers, especially with those of the United States.

What really emerged from the peace treaty was a Russo-Japanese alliance directed primarily against China and secondarily against every power which supported China's opposition to Russia and Japan. This alliance was the outstanding feature of the Far Eastern situation for an entire decade, down to the Russian Revolution of 1917. Premier Katsura told the Russian envoy in Tokyo succinctly: "If the friendship between our peoples continues to develop further in the same direction, we shall not only have predominance in influence in the Far East but all over the world, especially from the moment on when the Pacific Ocean becomes the center of rivalries among various powers." [1]

Russia's defeat in the war with Japan did not spell national catastrophe; it did not compare with the defeat of Germany in 1918, or the defeats of Germany and Japan in 1945. The Russian army was still a formidable force; Russian resources were not diminished; France continued to provide assistance to her eastern ally; Russian economy had not sustained any lasting losses from the war to any significant degree; in the realm of politics, the revolutionary movement of 1905–6 was soon crushed and suppressed. The Russian Government was again master of the situation. Nor did Russia's importance in international affairs deteriorate, since the rising German danger increasingly forced Britain and France toward collaboration with the St. Petersburg government.

Before both Japan and Russia lay the great, tired, defenseless body of China. The old dream of unilateral Russian predominance in China had vanished and now the only means of expansion was through collaboration with Japan. The spoils were enormous; why not divide them? As far as Russia's policy was concerned this meant a repudiation of the programs of the Bezobrazov clique and a reversal to the ideas of Witte and Lamsdorff. Indeed, the leading personalities of the decade 1906–17—Stolypin, Kokovtsev, Isvolsky and Sazonov—traveled the roads charted by their unhappy predecessors.

What Russia and Japan possessed in China after the war were Manchurian railroads. The world wanted to view these railroads as purely economic enterprises. Not so the two interested powers; to them the railroads were bases of a future political structure, the initial lines of an expanding influence which would eventually lead to a partition of Manchuria between them. Starting thus in Manchuria, the Russo-Japanese alliance widened in scope from year to year, from treaty to treaty, and soon embraced the whole of China's northern peripheries.

The milestones of this alliance were the four Russo-Japanese treaties of 1907, 1910, 1912, and 1916. Each signified a further step into China. To each was attached a secret agreement in which the

1. *International Relations in the Epoch of Imperialism* (*Mezhdunarodnyya otnosheniya v epokhu imperializma*), Series 2, XVIII[1], 205; hereafter cited as *International Relations*. Report from Tokyo dated July 10, 1911.

more important points were covered.[2] In a world full of diplomatic espionage, the parties did not succeed in keeping the treaties secret. The respective allies of the two parties were informed—Britain by Japan and France by Russia. The help of Britain and France was often needed to mediate the numerous difficult questions arising between Russia and Japan. The other powers, too, in some way or another managed to learn the substance of the agreements.

THE RUSSO-JAPANESE CONVENTION OF 1907

The first Russo-Japanese postwar convention, signed on July 30, 1907, delimited the Russian and Japanese spheres of influence in Manchuria and bound the two powers to defend the new state of affairs. The line of demarcation (see Map VII) gave northern Manchuria to Russia and southern Manchuria to Japan.

In a report summarizing Russo-Japanese relations, Russian Foreign Minister Sazonov clearly and frankly stated the reasons for the rapprochement between his government and Japan after the Russian defeat:

According to the peace of Portsmouth, Manchuria was to be evacuated and returned to Chinese administration. The Chinese Government as well as the Great Powers were inclined to . . . deny Russia any preferential position in China in territories adjacent to the Manchurian railroads. Evidently neither we nor the Japanese were able to agree that Russia should be deprived to such a complete extent of the fruits of her labors. The agreement on Russian and Japanese spheres of activity, concluded less than two years after the Treaty of Portsmouth, was an expression of the sense of solidarity in Manchurian affairs.[3]

It was as if the two allies were saying to the world, "You are wrong. Not the Manchurian railroads, but Manchuria herself, will be our *exclusive* sphere. China's sovereignty over Manchuria will be recognized by us de jure but not de facto; Chinese administration and Chinese law will not be altogether abolished, but we have our own designs and ideas about Manchuria, and at the right moment we will annex the respective areas."

Japan proceeded gradually to convert Korea into a colony and wanted Russia again to confirm her "exclusive rights" there; as

2. The treaty of 1912 was entirely secret.
3. *International Relations*, Series 3, VII[I], 469–472.

compensation, Russia demanded Japanese recognition of Mongolia as a part of the sphere of Russian influence. Japan hesitated—the southeastern corner of Mongolia, bordering on southern Manchuria, was becoming important to Japanese expansion. Negotiations over this point covered a period of several months in 1907; finally, France, experienced in the creation of "spheres of influence," came to the aid of the parties and a compromise was arrived at: "Outer Mongolia" was carved out and the area recognized by Japan as a Russian sphere. The rest of Mongolia (Inner Mongolia) was unaffected by this first treaty. Drawing a line of demarcation between North and South Manchuria, the convention divided the country in accordance with the "gravitation of political and economic activity" toward either country.

It became obvious that the emerging collaboration of Japan and Russia was an alliance for expansion and conquest, although the formula "safeguarding the status quo" was often used in the published treaties. The two governments were associates in a risky, large-scale enterprise. They were aware of each other's feelings, and each watched with strained attention lest his ally make too great strides. For each step forward on the part of one there had to be a reciprocal advance by the other. There was no doubt on the part of either ally that one day the game of dividing Chinese spoils would come to an end, and that when that day came they would have to fight each other. It was because of this peculiar alliance, based on the premise of eventual conflict between the signatories, that the Russian Government proceeded to build a new railway in the Far East, running on Russian soil from Chita to Vladivostok around the northern borders of Manchuria: this was the so-called Amur Railroad. Its only purpose was to provide a safe alternate route to the Far East in case of war in Manchuria when the Chinese Eastern would be lost or put out of operation. The construction of this line was begun, at a considerable cost, in 1908, and completed in 1916.

Almost openly, while they planned joint action, the two governments were also preparing for war between themselves. Diplomatic dispatches and memoirs dealing with this period reveal startling details about the actual attitude of the allies toward each other. In July, 1910, for instance, Count Jutaro Komura, the Japanese Foreign Minister, informed the British envoy in Tokyo of the contents of the new treaty with Russia, adding, "with a laugh," that the line of demarcation between the Russian and the Japanese spheres in Manchuria would become more important "when Russia is stronger and ready to go to war again." "Conventions or no conventions," the envoy added in his report to London, "the two powers will keep a pretty sharp lookout one upon the other." [4] In 1911, when Russia was preparing for a military expedition into China, the friction with Japan assumed serious dimensions. At the end of 1913 Russia once again became nervous and the government decided to erect new fortifications in Manchuria "in case of military complications with Japan." The Russian envoy in Tokyo, when requested to report on the situation, informed his chief that "the military party insists upon an increase of armaments because of the alleged aggressiveness of our actions in Manchuria and Mongolia." [5]

Incidents of this kind occurred repeatedly. This was natural, since the influence and the strength of Russia and Japan were not growing correspondingly. To maintain a balance was impossible. In the period immediately following the war Japan was naturally the stronger of the two. Russia, however, gradually recovered, and after 1910 was prepared even for a more audacious policy than Japan. But since early in 1914, when Russia became occupied in Europe, it was Japan that took first place.

THE UNITED STATES AND GERMANY AGAINST RUSSIA

The grouping of the Great Powers in the last decade before the Russian Revolution is now only of historic interest. Some of the nations that were most active at that time have since disappeared from the Far East; others have changed their policies. What is surprising, however, is the number of elements that have remained constant in the policies of those powers which are still active in the Orient today. Many of the problems are much the same as they were three decades ago. Many political moves of our time are reminiscent of the days when Theodore Roosevelt, Taft, and Wilson were the spokesmen for America, and Sazonov and Isvolsky for Russia.

4. *British Documents on the Origin of the War*, VI, 485.
5. *International Relations*, Series 3, I, 156, 158 (January 26 and 29, 1914).

RUSSIAN EMPIRE, 1905
JAPANESE EMPIRE, before 1905
New JAPANESE acquisitions
  1. Southern Sakhalin (Karafuto)
  2. Liaotung Peninsula
New JAPANESE sphere of interest:
  3. Korea

VII. RUSSIA AND JAPAN,

RUSSIA

SAKHALIN

TUVA

MANCHURIA

OUTER MONGOLIA

SINKIANG

INNER MONGOLIA   Peking

SEA of JAPAN

JAPAN

CHINESE REPUBLIC

TIBET   Shanghai

INDIA   Canton

BURMA   Hongkong

FORMOSA

▨ RUSSIAN EMPIRE, 1915
▨ JAPANESE EMPIRE, 1915
▨ New RUSSIAN sphere of influence:
    Outer Mongolia, Tannu Tuva, northern Manchuria
▨ New Japanese sphere of influence:
    Southern Manchuria and eastern Mongolia

1905 AND 1915

During this decade humanity was moving toward the great war and was soon plunged into it. New coalitions were forming in Europe. France was firmly bound to Russia. Britain first settled her differences with France and then with Russia and later joined them in the war. Eventually the United States, too, entered the wartime coalition. In the Far East, however, quite different groupings of powers were at work, groupings which might at first glance appear paradoxical.

The Russo-Japanese alliance was cemented not so much because of the resistance of China but because of the opposition of the four big powers (the United States, Germany, Britain, and France) to Russian and Japanese policy in China. In the more intimate language of Russian diplomacy these powers were contemptuously referred to as "the trading powers"—implying that the four nations were in Asia for money—trade and investments—whereas Russia was fulfilling a great political mission in the Orient. (Japan was considered to be in the same position as Russia.) The fact was that Russia and Japan were not rich enough to grant large loans to China, build railroads out of purely economic interest, and develop an important trade. "The open door" to the rest of China did not seem so important to Russia and Japan as did their territorial and political interests and the great dreams of future empires.

Fundamentally the four "trading powers" were opposed to Russian and Japanese expansion on the continent. They presented anything but a united front, however, and Russia and Japan were successful in keeping them from forming a coalition.

Among the four powers, the United States occupied the extreme position in the antagonism to Japan and Russia. The United States possessed no ports or spheres in China and was opposed to territorial acquisitions in China by the other five powers. Consequently, expansion of spheres and privileges aroused more opposition in America than elsewhere. Japan, cognizant of American attitudes, was cautious and moved slowly, at least until 1915. It was Russia that provoked most of the American indignation. In addition, the United States was not bound to any of the "political powers" by ties of alliance and, unlike Britain and France, appeared to be in no need of assistance from these powers in any possible future war.

The United States acted freely, although not persistently. She was not prepared to go to war over Far Eastern issues, and the world was aware of this. Therefore, American protests and declarations in favor of China's integrity were not taken very seriously; they were not considered as of any real danger to the concepts of Russia and Japan.

The American policy strove to solve Asiatic problems by economic means—to achieve the "open door" and territorial integrity of China by vast investments and by industrialization of China. The American aim was the salvation of China through internationalization of foreign economic intervention: construction of railroads by an international syndicate rather than by particular national groups; purchase by the syndicate of the existing railroads, including those in Manchuria; establishment of facilities for foreign commerce everywhere in China ("open door"); provision of sizable loans to the Chinese Government, to enable it to build up an effective administration and to equip a national army for resistance to encroachments. This policy was in contrast to that of Russia and Japan, which were not interested in strengthening China and were unable to offer China 10 per cent of what America was ready to deliver.

The history of the Far East during that decade presents a unique picture—and how instructive for our times!—of an international struggle in which certain powers make use of force, others of economic tools. It is a struggle between military-political and economic means; between centralized will power and mailed fist on the one hand, and financial and commercial pressure on the other; between millions of soldiers and millions of dollars. The outcome of the struggle gave an unequivocal reply to the fateful question, which was the stronger of the two?

The German attitude toward Russia and Japan in the Far East was in many respects analogous to that of the United States. In this policy of antagonism to Russia and Japan, Germany was prompted partly by economic motives, as her trade with China was growing rapidly. Mainly, however, it was dictated by the state of affairs in Europe, where the antagonism against Germany-Austria was becoming acute. Far from entertaining anti-imperialistic ideas and far from adhering to any principles concerning the integrity of China (Germany was herself entrenched in Shantung), she was yet ready to support the American policy.

After 1905 Germany opposed the Russian as well as the Japanese advance in China, and persistently refused to recognize Russian or Japanese "special rights" in Chinese territories—in particular, Russian claims to a privileged position in Mongolia and in Chinese Turkestan. A revealing discussion took place when the Kaiser and the Tsar, in the company of their respective ministers, met again in the Baltic in July, 1912. In his usual somewhat arrogant manner Wilhelm II explained to the Russian ministers what the correct Russian attitude to China should be. "Russia must see the desirability," he said, "of co-operating in the strengthening of China in order to free her from Japanese influence and to make of her a barrier against any unfriendly Japanese plans."

"I pointed out to His Majesty," Sazonov, the Russian Foreign Minister, reported, "the danger that a regenerated and strong China might as well turn against Russia, in concert with Japan." He then proceeded to explain frankly to the German Emperor the divergence between the German and Russian policy in China:

"Germany is interested in China's buying power and she fears China's disintegration . . . Russia, on the contrary, as a nation bordering on China, and with a long unfortified frontier, cannot wish for a strengthening of her neighbor; *she could therefore quietly witness the downfall . . . of modern China.*" [6]

Since 1905 the idea of a continuing collaboration with the United States in the Far East had been a favorite idea of the German Government.

In 1906 the Kaiser proposed to the Chinese envoy an alliance between the United States, Germany, and China. In the fall of 1907, the State Council of China decided to sound out Berlin and Washington on this subject. Von Bülow, the Reichskanzler, instructed his envoy in Washington to talk to President Roosevelt about an alliance of the three nations. Roosevelt replied on November 8, 1907: "Communicate to His Majesty that I am prepared to go hand in hand with Germany in the great questions of eastern Asia . . . I foresee the probability of common actions of the navies of Germany and the United States against Japan." [7]

The negotiations looking toward an outright convention between the United States, Germany, and China did not materialize.

6. *International Relations*, Series 2, XXᴵ, 271 (July 8, 1912). Italics mine.
7. *Grosse Politik*, XXV, 78–79.

China herself became hesitant. Indeed, what could be the consequences of a declaration of political war on the part of these three nations against Japan and Russia? The United States was obviously not prepared to fight. Germany had her European troubles. China would still be alone, and her new alliances would only serve to provoke a stronger policy on the part of Japan and Russia.

The collaboration between the United States and Germany in the Far East continued until the very outbreak of the World War. It had no important results, however, and was limited essentially to declarations and protests.

BRITAIN AND FRANCE BETWEEN TWO FIRES

Britain and France occupied the middle position between the two extreme groups, that is, Russia-Japan on the one side, and United States–Germany on the other. Britain, however, inclined more toward Japan, while France was bound to Russia.

The traditional, anti-Russian bias in British policy was mollified after Russia's defeat in 1905, and a degree of readjustment in their rival interests became possible. In 1907 the two nations concluded a treaty to end the old disputes in the Middle East and central Asia. The treaty delimited the respective rights, interests, and spheres of each in vast regions of Asia. As far as China was concerned, Tibet was the only item covered by the agreement.

While Japan, Britain's bellicose ally, was entering an era of collaboration with Russia, Britain herself looked for a rapprochement with the government of St. Petersburg. In a political sense the British-Russian treaty of August 31, 1907, and the Russo-Japanese treaty of July 30, 1907, were an entity.

In China, Britain belonged to the "trading powers." British trade with China was important, British investments there were large, and the expansionist policy of Russia was still a thorn in Britain's flesh. She tried, therefore, to maintain a mediating position between the vigorous offensive of the Russian Government and the opposition presented by the United States and Germany. Britain was, of course, not anti-imperialist in the sense that America was. She possessed ports in China and enjoyed privileges and "unequal treaties." Time and again Russia pressed London to recognize the projected Russian "sphere" in northern China. Britain was uncertain whether to reject the demand or to negotiate a deal at the expense of China.

France's policy was similar to the British in the one respect that it was equally uncertain and inconsistent. France also belonged to the "trading powers" and was essentially opposed to the creation of a large Russian sphere in China. However, she was forced by circumstances to yield in a great degree to the Russian demands in northern China.

During that period a close alliance with Russia was becoming an issue of life and death for France. All Far Eastern problems appeared unimportant to France when compared to the German danger. The need of Russian assistance in the event of a European war was a decisive factor in French policy; the Russian Government realized this and exploited the situation. The Franco-Russian alliance was confined only to Europe, and the French Government showed reluctance in supporting Russian demands in the Far East. At such times Russia reminded France of Russia's significance in Europe. Should France dare to oppose Russia in Peking and lend assistance to China, "this would compel us," the Russian Premier told his Foreign Minister in March, 1912, "to strengthen our military position on the Chinese frontiers, and this, in turn, would necessarily lead to a weakening of our forces on the western front and *might deprive us of the means necessary to give France the assistance* which is provided for by our military convention." [8] Such threats usually accomplished the desired results.

RUSSO-JAPANESE RIVALRY AND COLLABORATION

After the treaty of 1907, Russia and Japan proceeded to build their spheres in Manchuria into potential protectorates or future possessions. Foreign activity in these spheres was barred and investments by third powers were discouraged.

Until 1910, however, there was a constant disproportion between the progress made by Russia and that made by Japan. Tokyo was able to make ample use of the privileges gained by the Russo-Japanese convention of 1907, while Russia was still recovering from the war. A new tension arose between St. Petersburg and Tokyo in 1908–9, at times threatening to produce serious conflicts.

8. *International Relations*, Series 2, XIX^II, 311 (March 21, 1912). Italics mine.

Looking for support against Japan, Russia set out to improve relations with the United States in order to checkmate Japan in Manchuria.

These developments coincided with the plans of American railway builders, of whom Edward Harriman was the most prominent, to acquire the Manchurian railways or to construct new lines there. Intended as a strictly economic affair, the American venture nonetheless was full of political implications: it would have deprived both Russia and Japan of the basic vehicle of their expansionist policy in this part of Asia. The Russian Government, however, pressed as it was by Japan and fearful of a new military encounter, tended to accept a deal with the American companies. Japan vehemently rejected the Harriman offers. The controversy reached its peak when the Americans developed a plan to build a railway running parallel to the Japanese South Manchurian. Now a certain divergence of views inside the Russian Government became apparent, especially between Finance Minister Kokovtsev and "pro-Japanese" Foreign Minister Isvolsky. At the same time the menace of an American-Russian alliance, or even of a larger multipartite economic intervention in Manchuria, prompted Japan to ease the tension with St. Petersburg and try to negotiate a new Russo-Japanese agreement. Japan proposed a "formal alliance" to Russia; "not only China but also other powers will bow," Baron Motono, the Japanese envoy, told the Russian Minister of Foreign Affairs. Isvolsky was in favor of such a "common Russian-Japanese guardianship over Manchuria" to the exclusion of all the other powers. Nicholas II approved of this "very close agreement with Japan." Russia thus turned away from the United States and began to negotiate with Tokyo, eventually to conclude the treaty of 1910.

Since the attempt of private American interests to gain a foothold in Manchuria had been frustrated by Japanese opposition the United States Government decided to broaden the private venture into an ambitious political program. Despite the unfavorable turn which the Russo-American negotiations had taken and despite the new Russo-Japanese rapprochement, Secretary of State Knox proposed in December, 1909, that the existing railroads in Manchuria be taken over by an international syndicate backed by the Great Powers and that an industrial and railroad construction program be launched in Manchuria as an international economic enterprise—which would in effect have restored Manchuria to China.

The Knox proposal met with rejection in St. Petersburg.[9] Relations between Russia and the United States became strained. Isvolsky termed the American proposal "naïve." Indeed, the idea of stopping the Russian political and military advance by means of financial combinations appeared naïve not only in St. Petersburg but in most of the other capitals. What Knox did not anticipate, however, was rejection of his proposal by England and France. Only Germany evinced some enthusiasm. The Kaiser expected great things from the American scheme: "The collaboration of the German-Anglo-Saxon nations," he wrote, "will be demonstrated to the world for the first time!"

Wilhelm II was glad to receive from his ambassador in Washington reports on the numerous friendly talks with the Secretary of State. "The Secretary of State has a high opinion of his plan," the German envoy wrote to Berlin. "It means the creation of a sort of a buffer state between Russia and Japan. Knox says, either Japan is honest in her assertion that she wants the open door in Manchuria [here the Kaiser made his marginal remark, 'she is certainly not'] in which case Japan must be happy, or she is not. . . . Knox used the expression, 'we have to smoke out Japan.'" (The Kaiser's remark: "With British smoke? That would be a comedy!")

Another report from the envoy stated, "Knox is very angry with Russia and Japan and also with England, which is being taken in tow by Japan . . . China is too weak. She must be strengthened, and this can be done only by the two unselfish powers."[10]

Knox's plan of defeating Russia and Japan by means of financial operations proved a failure. The failure did not prevent him, however, from repeating the attempt a year later. The results of the second attempt were likewise negative. An unexpected outcome

9. *Grosse Politik*, XXXII, 73, 78. When the Russian Foreign Minister gave his negative reply to the American envoy, William Rockhill, the latter told him that the United States could proceed to build parallel railroads to rival the Russian ones. Rockhill got such a sharp reply from Sazonov that he declared he would be compelled to avoid personal contact with the minister and limit himself to writing notes.

10. *Ibid.*, XXXII, 68, 71, 92. The German envoy in Tokyo, however, did not share the overoptimism of his sovereign. "In my opinion," he wrote to Berlin, "the American proposition reveals a sort of naïve impudence which is peculiar to the little-experienced State Department in Washington."

of Knox's policy was a pronounced tightening of Russo-Japanese relations. In the face of the "American menace" the tie between them really became an alliance. This alliance found expression in the second Russo-Japanese convention, concluded in 1910, which was a countermove against the United States.

RUSSIA AND JAPAN vs. THE UNITED STATES

The reaction to Knox's policies in St. Petersburg as well as in Tokyo was a decision to make a strong gesture against interference of other powers in those regions of continental Asia which consituted the sphere of "special interests" of the two powers. "The solidarity of the two powers is to be given expression not only for China's sake but also for that of the other powers. No doubts can then be harbored as to the ability of Russia and Japan independently to solve the Manchurian question by mutual assistance." In these words the outstanding Japanese diplomat, Viscount Goto, expressed the main idea of the new treaty. The Japanese envoy in St. Petersburg, Motono, frankly commented: "The American proposal is a clear proof of the necessity of bringing about an understanding between Russia and Japan on the Manchurian question." [11]

The new convention was signed on July 4, 1910, and consisted again of a public and a secret accord. The public protocol reaffirmed the integrity of China yet omitted the formula used in the treaty of 1907 concerning the "independence and territorial integrity of the Empire of China and the principle of equal opportunity." (The latter formula was the equivalent of the American-sponsored "open door" principle.) The essence of the agreement was the sentence contained in the secret treaty that in the event the "special interests" of Russia and Japan "should come to be threatened," the two nations "will agree upon the measures to be taken with a view to common action . . ." This was the first time Russia and Japan envisaged "common action."

The State Department in Washington was aware that the new treaty was aimed primarily at the United States and suspected that a secret agreement had been concluded also. The American press was bitter. Germany reacted with even more resentment. On the margins of the message from St. Petersburg, the Kaiser gave

11. Siebert, *Entente Diplomacy*, pp. 9, 11.

way to his feelings: "Gangsters!" "Division of booty!" "Brazen-ness!" "Nonsense!" "Wait and see!" And a few days later, he reiterated: "On this question we are in the same boat as America." [12]

In defiance of Germany and the United States, Japan and Russia, as soon as the new convention was signed, started to display a new activity in the Far East. Plans matured rapidly. A few days after the signing of the treaty, Japan formally annexed Korea. Russia intended to compensate herself for this by annexing the western part of her sphere—Outer Mongolia or Sinkiang.

The possibilities appeared great, and the martial spirit grew. A conflict with China would present no danger since the neutrality of Japan was assured. "There is no reason," the Russian envoy in Peking reported to his minister immediately after the signing of the new convention, "to depart from the basis of the policy we have followed hitherto of territorial acquisitions . . . Perhaps the Ili territory [in Sinkiang] . . ." And in order to hold China in check, he advised a realistic measure: "The only peaceful means of exercising pressure on China at present is to lay down a double track on the Siberian Railway. Only this measure is feared by China." [13]

A few months later, the Russian envoy in China advised his government to give more attention to Outer Mongolia. (Although theoretically included in the Russian sphere by the Russo-Japanese secret treaty of 1907, Outer Mongolia actually remained under Chinese administration.) The Russian envoy recommended direct negotiations with London. England (he suggested) could obtain compensation in Tibet while agreeing to a new Russian move into Mongolia.[14]

China reacted to the growing new menace with two moves. First, a special envoy, Liang Tun-yen, was again dispatched to Germany and the United States. In Berlin he proposed the creation of a new Chinese armed division of 20,000 men under German command.[15] In both capitals he again proposed an alliance of the three nations. The negotiations lasted from September, 1910, to June, 1911, but resulted in no action. Obviously, the idea of an outright assumption of an obligation to go to war in defense of China was not accept-

12. *Grosse Politik*, XXXII, 121.
13. Siebert, *op. cit.*, p. 19.
14. *Graf Benckendorff's Diplomatischer Briefwechsel*, ed. Siebert, I, 378–383.
15. *Grosse Politik*, XXXII, 153.

able to the two powers. Russia was prepared to cut the Gordian knot.

WAR WITH CHINA?

Russian activity in the Far East was most intense in the two years following the Russo-Japanese treaty of 1910. It was hampered, however, by the condition of European affairs which demanded concentration of Russian forces and attention in the west. Then, in 1914, as the European war approached, Russian activity in the Far East rapidly diminished.

By 1910 Russia had recovered from the defeat in the war and from domestic crises: now the old designs could be revived. Once again, just as ten years earlier, the creation of a vast Russian sphere in Asia and the control of new areas became a program for action —with the significant difference, however, that this time no encroachment on Japan's sphere was intended. The resumed advance could be directed on northern and western China. The semi-official *Torgovo-Promyshlennaya gazeta* in 1910, gave a picture of the desired new boundaries in Asia:

Our frontier with China is incorrect, winding, difficult to defend, and does not correspond at all to physical-geographic conditions. The natural frontier between Russia and China must be the Gobi desert. These sandy dead seas may be compared to oceans which divide men and states. Two different and incompatible races, the yellow and the European, must be separated by an effective barrier against mass invasion.

An acute controversy developed, however, on the question whether the time was more opportune for a new advance in Asia or whether Russia's energy ought to be focused on European issues, as German policy threatened to unleash a new war. Just as during the preceding decades the most conservative and extreme rightist political groups advocated a dynamic policy of expansion in Asia, whereas the liberal opposition—essentially anti-German, pro-British, and pro-French—demanded moderation in Asia and closer co-operation with the Western Powers.

Foreign Minister Sazonov was made the target of attacks by the rightist press for his efforts to avoid all risky adventures. Sazonov himself told a Russian official in December, 1911: "I am against annexations [in Asia], especially since Russia can not even digest its present Siberian areas. All that [a policy of expansion in Asia] would do would be to give our policy an adventurous character, create hostility between us and China, entail enormous expenditures, and, finally, weaken our position in Europe." The annexation of Tannu Tuva, for instance, which was demanded by the Russian military, in Sazonov's opinion would have been "a mistake and would divert us from our direct tasks." [16]

While the War Minister and rightist spokesmen were urging "action" to take advantage of the disintegration of China, Sazonov appeared before the Duma in April, 1912, and rejected the call for an immediate campaign in Asia:

Our state emerged and thrived not on the shores of the Black Irtish but on the banks of the Dnieper and Moskva Rivers. The aggrandizement of Russian possessions in Asia must not constitute the aim of our policy; it would lead to a weakening of our position in Europe and in the Near East . . . We should not annex territories bordering on our lands just because that can be done without taking great risks.

But *Novoye Vremya*, the leading newspaper, editorially disagreed with the Foreign Minister's views:

Not in Europe, but in the Far East are those considerable changes possible, yea indeed imperative, upon which depends the future of our empire . . . Chinese anarchy, on the one hand, and Russian imperial problems, on the other: this situation leads us to the inescapable conclusion that it would be criminal folly to let slip by so favorable an opportunity and to fail to profit by the weakness of our [Chinese] neighbor in order to achieve our imperial ideals.

In a series of eloquent articles *Novoye Vremya* outlined the whole theory behind Russian aggrandizement, the role of its emperors, and the immediate tasks ahead:

Our time-honored policy, from the days of the Varangians down to the reign of Emperor Alexander III, was founded on the axiom that Russia must expand territorially at the expense of her neighbors. In spite of her thousand years of existence, Russia is still on the road toward her national and political frontiers. The present as well as future generations will still have to expend much effort, strength, and talent before this task is completed . . .

16. I. Korostovets, *Von Cinggis Khan zur Sowjetrepublik* (Berlin, 1926), pp. 127–128.

Which of the European powers can look with favor on the unification, reformation, reorganization, and fortification of the immense masses [of China]? These developments would manifestly be a handicap to those powers which are compelled to have territorial clashes with the new China: Russia, England, and France.[17]

This program of the most aggressive elements in and around the government was rejected, at least formally, and Sazonov won out: no outright annexation of Chinese territories was to be sought. This was 1912, and Balkan affairs absorbed the attention of the European governments; armed forces had to be kept in readiness at Russia's western borders. Actually, however, the proponents of forceful action were winning out. Their program called for the separation from China of territories bordering on Russia and for their establishment as autonomous provinces without formally being annexed to the Russian Empire.

The Russo-Japanese treaties were correctly interpreted in Washington as overt challenges to Knox's program for economic and political penetration into North China. Nevertheless, the United States Government proceeded to continue its old policy. Soon after the signing of the Russo-Japanese agreement of 1910, China applied to the United States for a loan of 50 million dollars. The American banks, with the approval of the State Department, consented. They proposed, however, that the banks of the other three "trading nations" participate. This proposal was the origin of the famous "Consortium." Outwardly a purely businesslike combination of financial groups, the Consortium soon began to make diplomatic moves and countermoves, and its members, essentially bankers, began to act as agents of governments, spokesmen of "power politics." The connection between *Hochpolitik* and economy was obvious. In practice the "open door" would mean the dislodging of Russia and Japan from China.

Even loans to the Chinese Government might serve the same purpose. Because China was not considered a solvent and solid debtor, loans to her were usually "guaranteed" by specific state revenues—customs duties, salt revenues, etc. The agencies of the creditor nations were entitled, under the conditions of the loans, to supervise and control certain items of state income and collect

17. March 31, April 12, April 17, and April 30, 1912.

the receipts. China felt humiliated by this infringement of her sovereignty and the popular movements which resulted played a great role in the revolutionary movement during those years—1910–11. Only under such conditions, however, was it possible for China to secure loans abroad.

The United States and the other three nations were ready to lend money to China, under certain conditions, to establish order in her finances, and to develop certain of her industries.

Russia and Japan were, from the very beginnings of the consortium, extremely hostile to it. Since state revenues were to be a "guarantee" of the loans, the income of northern China, including Manchuria, would be applied to payments of interest and repayments of the loans. Foreign nations would send their agents; local customs offices and branches of the treasury would be controlled by foreigners—in a territory which, as the Russians and Japanese saw it, was their prospective possession.

The Russian Ministry repeatedly explained to its envoys that the Chinese Government wanted a loan to be used

"for political aims which are opposed to our influence in Manchuria and Extramural China . . . There has lately become manifest a Chinese tendency to create in Manchuria international interests which would serve to counteract the Russian interests. It is to be feared that [the Chinese Government] will take the same attitude in Mongolia and in Chinese Turkestan." [18]

The simplest way to put an end to the "American threat" would be outrightly to annex Manchuria. At first many of the leading personalities in St. Petersburg were prepared to answer the Consortium by taking over northern Manchuria. It was clear that such a step would mean war—a small war if China remained isolated, and a large war if any of the Great Powers were to give her aid. The world did not know at that time (the winter of 1910–11) how near it was to a war in the Far East. Such a war, had it occurred, would hardly have been limited to Asia. The first World War might easily have started in 1911. That it did not, was largely due to the fact that there was profound divergence of opinion in leading circles in Russia.

At a meeting of the Russian Cabinet on December 2, 1910, the

18. *International Relations* Series 2, XVIII^{II}, 79 (October 5, 1911).

Minister of War, Sukhomlinov, demanded military operations and outright annexation of northern Manchuria on the pretext that China had begun to reorganize her military forces. Cautious Foreign Minister Sazonov told his colleagues that he was "convinced that the annexation of northern Manchuria was for us an imperative necessity"; he considered the moment unfavorable, however, since the situation in Europe called for attention and military reserves. The Premier offered cautious support to his Foreign Minister. "Future events," he said, "may move us to annex northern Manchuria when a favorable situation presents itself," but not immediately. The decision of the government was a compromise between the two tendencies: "The Council of Ministers considers annexation dangerous at this moment; later developments may force us to such a step. All departments must work on the assumption that our treaty rights in northern Manchuria must be upheld, in order that we may be able to proceed to annexation at a later date." [19]

Activity was heightened despite the cautious compromise. An ultimatum was presented to China on February 18, 1911. In accordance with the governmental decision it was limited to economic and trade demands; northern Manchuria was not mentioned. "In view of the position taken by the powers in regard to our present demands," Minister Sazonov commented in a letter to his envoy, "we have considered it advisable to eliminate from the ultimatum the points which do not constitute a direct conclusion from the existing treaties." The fact, however, that these demands were presented as an ultimatum and that the ultimatum was subsequently repeated created great nervousness in St. Petersburg as well as in Peking. Russian troops were concentrated at Dzharkent, at the border of western China, and were increased around Tsitsihar in northern Manchuria. Daily conferences took place in the Tsar's palace in which the Minister of War, Chief of General Staff, and various members of the government participated. The ultimatum to China had no fixed date for a reply. When a few weeks later no reply was forthcoming, Russia repeated the ultimatum. Military operations appeared imminent. The Chinese Minister of War wrote that he "is prepared to accept a war with Russia and is aware of the consequences, but an honorable death is preferable to disgrace."

19. *Diplomatische Aktenstücke*, ed. Siebert, pp. 272 ff.

Russia informed Japan that "the time has come to demand . . . the fulfillment of the promises made us on the occasion of the annexation of Korea." Japan was obliged, of course, to tolerate a Russian diplomatic and possibly a military offensive against China; but such a strengthening of the Russian position was undesirable. Japan, under coercion of the United States, and probably also of England, was unable to follow Russia in the great adventure. She therefore tried to induce the Russian Government to take a calmer view. Advising China to accept the Russian demands Japan at the same time pointed out in St. Petersburg that there was no plausible reason for a war, and that the Chinese troops, which allegedly menaced the Russian-owned North Manchurian Railway, were actually no menace at all. "The only danger he [the Japanese envoy] can foresee, would come from America, whose fleet in the Pacific, after the completion of the Panama Canal, will be so powerful." [20]

China accepted the main provisions of the Russian demands, and the war threat was dispelled for the time being. But the danger continued to hang over the Far East for several years, and Russian policy remained persistently offensive. Soon attention shifted to another province of China—Mongolia. The separation of Outer Mongolia from China became the major goal of Russian policy in the Far East between 1911 and 1913. By the time the World War broke out, the creation of a Russian protectorate over Mongolia was substantially completed. [21]

At this time Japan was less insistent. China, always siding with the less aggressive of the two powers at any given moment, was prepared to align herself with Japan against Russia. The Japanese envoy in Peking publicly advocated "protection by Japan of China's integrity," and this was correctly translated by the Russian press as advice to China to reject any new Russian demands. The Foreign Ministry in St. Petersburg was disappointed about the "*arrière-pensée* which is directing Japanese policy in this case; undoubtedly Japan has the aim of establishing relations of confidence with China." [22] And the Russian envoy in China, in his reports to the minister, drew these conclusions: "Japan has made it her pri-

20. *Grosse Politik*, XXXII, 31.
21. Cf. Chapter V below.
22. *International Relations*, Series 2, XVIII¹, 23 (May 23, 1911).

mary task to establish with China relations of friendship and confidence ('a fatherly patronage over China,' as they express it) and will not undertake any common steps with us . . . This circumstance must impel us to take care of our military preparedness in the Far East." [23]

In order to counteract the Japanese-Chinese rapprochement, the Russian Government launched the idea of a Russian-Japanese-Chinese alliance. The policy was conceived not only to oppose the "trading powers," with their "integrity-for-China" slogans, but also to prevent Japan from conducting a separate policy. Japan rejected the new scheme. She preferred to try a unilateral "pro-China" policy. Russia was isolated. The government faced a decision as to whether to go further in the dangerous course or to retreat. The clever Benckendorff, Russian Ambassador in London, advised the shrewdest caution: let Japan take the first steps, he urged—Japanese aggressiveness will provoke American opposition, and the policy of the United States will be directed primarily against Tokyo, not St. Petersburg.

RUSSIA AND THE REVOLUTION IN CHINA

At the end of 1911 revolutionary developments came to a climax, and early in 1912 the ancient monarchy crumbled amidst an atmosphere of universal discontent, excitement, and humiliation. Soon the southern provinces were at war with the north; the new government proclaimed as its goal the establishment of a strong central regime, financial recovery, an alleviation of the tax burden, efficient administration, and the creation of a strong army. However, the international issues which had contributed so decisively to the upheaval, continued to be uppermost among the problems plaguing the new China.

Most people in and out of China were inclined to assume that revolution was the road to the rejuvenation of stagnant China; that national forces which had been suppressed by the old bureaucracy would now succeed in bringing about a general transformation of Chinese internal and external policies; that the Chinese people had taken their affairs into their own hands and would now demonstrate their ability and strength. The world was wondering whether

23. *Ibid.*, Series 2, XVIII[1], 93 (June 6, 1911).

China, after her revolution, would follow the Japanese road to national resurrection.

At this point a profound abyss divided "the trading powers" from the two "political powers"—Russia and Japan. The trading nations were inclined to expect the emergence of a great new market in China with investments safeguarded under the new civilized political system. Russia and Japan, on the other hand, asked themselves whether they were interested in a national resurrection of China at all, whether a strong China would not be a detrimental factor in their far-reaching schemes, and whether the upheaval was not the appropriate moment for them jointly to fulfill their plans.

The Russian Government considered the moment appropriate for the launching of a campaign for the realization of its long-planned sphere—Manchuria-Mongolia-Sinkiang. With all of China already in the throes of the revolutionary movement, the Russian Foreign Ministry reported to the Tsar: "From the point of view of our interests, the dissolution of the present Chinese Empire would be desirable in more than one respect. Even in the event that various parts of China will not become entirely independent, there will develop between them a rivalry which will weaken them."

"Yes," the sovereign noted on the margin of the report, and the following communication went out to the Russian envoy in China: "Dismemberment of China into more or less independent states would, in our view, be in accord with our broad interests." [24]

In a subsequent report (January, 1912), the Foreign Minister stated: "Russia and Japan must . . . use this exceptionally favorable moment to make their position in China secure . . . This moment, when a new government emerging in China is in need of our recognition and support, presents opportunities that should not be missed . . . Point One on the program is Manchuria: Chinese resistance must be eliminated there . . . Actions must be taken in concert with Japan." "Agreed," was the Tsar's remark on the report. The very next day negotiations with Japan were begun concerning the partition of new spheres. [25]

To counteract the Russian policy, the new Chinese Government

24. *Ibid.*, Series 2, XIX¹, 56 (November 22, 1911).
25. *Ibid.*, Series 2, XIX¹¹, 33–34 (January 23, 1912).

strove to consolidate the young republic and to establish its unity. A decree dated April 21, 1912, said that "Mongolia, Tibet, and [eastern] Turkestan must belong to the territory of the Chinese Republic"; the administration and status of China's different parts must therefore be reconstructed upon homogeneous bases. The Chinese decree aroused indignation in St. Petersburg. It was taken as proof "that China does not want to take into account our program of an autonomous Mongolia and is planning further active steps in the Mongolian question."

"We must see to it," the daring and persistent envoy Krupensky reported from China in July, 1912, "that China remains in her present state of helplessness as long as possible." China "should not be permitted to extricate herself from her various financial difficulties for a long time." As far as the negotiations concerning an international loan to China were concerned, Krupensky saw the advantages to Russia in torpedoing them: "Either the loan must not materialize at all, or it must be tied up with such foreign control and supervision that it will arouse indignation in the people; the acceptance of such conditions by a central government will lead to disorders in the provinces and perhaps even to an uprising in the south of China."

At that time the new Chinese Government was seeking recognition by the Great Powers. The United States was inclined to grant recognition. Krupensky, however, advised rejection of the request. "A strengthening of the Chinese Government," he said, "is to the interest of the United States and of the other trading powers. As far as we are concerned, consolidation of the Chinese Government is not to our interest." Krupensky's advice that the new Chinese Government not be recognized was approved by the Tsar: "Why hurry?" The negative reply to the request for recognition was given on July 17, 1912.

Krupensky demanded outright military operations against China. In his correspondence with his government he argued against his chiefs; he rejected their cautiousness: "We must prepare to put real pressure upon China." As far as the other powers are concerned, he contended, "we need not fear resistance in case we should deem it necessary to apply such measures in northern Manchuria, in Mongolia, and in western China." Nor did he expect any serious resistance on the part of China herself. "I am aware that we cannot act openly against the wishes of friendly France and England . . . I never speak out frankly before my colleagues . . . in order not to divulge the task that I have set myself, which is to hinder the creation of a China reorganized after European or Japanese models."

Krupensky's advice was not fully accepted by the Russian Government. The situation in Europe was impeding Russian action in China. "Essentially I am of your opinion," Krupensky's chief answered him from St. Petersburg, "but in world politics we are acting in common with England and France. These two powers, especially the former, consider it desirable not to permit a disintegration of China . . . If we should proceed openly against France and England, it would mean loss of their support of our privileged position in Extramural China." [26]

THE UNITED STATES AND THE CONSORTIUM AGAINST RUSSIA

Despite the fact that the annexation of northern Manchuria was not on the agenda for the immediate future, the international Consortium again loomed as the great problem and danger to Russian expansion in China. In Russian eyes, the United States was rising to the stature of Enemy Number One.

The first Russian counterplan was simple: "We are working for the destruction of this Syndicate." [27] Nothing less than its total destruction seemed to answer the need. In international discussion it was proposed that in order to appease Russia, the Consortium indicate its willingness to exclude northern China from the scope of its operations. This step alone was considered by Russia to be insufficient, however, as loans advanced to the Chinese Government would make possible a reorganization of the Chinese Army and a strengthening of the Chinese state, and this was precisely what the Russian Government feared most. Only a complete abolition of the "American plan" would do; or, at least, the exclusion of the United States from the Consortium.

But how could this be accomplished? "It will be rather difficult," the Russian Ambassador wrote from Paris, "to exclude America

26. *Ibid.*, Series 2, XX^{II}, 86 ff. (August 24, 1912).
27. Stieve, *Isvolsky and the World War* (London, 1926), p. 29.

from the future Consortium since, under the present situation in China, the financial groups count primarily on the support of the Americans." [28] But, Minister Sazonov said, "I doubt whether we and the Americans will be able to collaborate in China in one financial combination."

The interesting idea then arose in Russia of detaching France from the American combination and creating a new Consortium— Russia-Japan-France—against England–United States–Germany. France was considered to be in such need of Russia's assistance in Europe that she would be obliged to follow the lead, and it was expected that her great financial resources would help to develop the northern areas of China. A special governmental conference, on June 7, 1911, under the chairmanship of Premier Stolypin, decided to propose a delimitation of Chinese territory as between the consortiums, the northern part of China (Extramural China) to constitute the field of activity of a new Russian-French-Japanese combination and the rest of China to be left entirely to the American-British-German group. Partition of China was again in the cards.

Despite strong Russian pressure, France declined. Separation from Britain was impossible for her; besides, French banks would not risk the dangers involved, even if the government gave its approval to the idea. France instead proposed to Russia another plan: to include Russia and Japan in the great Consortium and to make of the Consortium a universal combination of the Big Six, that is, all the great powers of the Far East. Technically, participation in such a Consortium would have amounted to a reversal of Russian policy, since the program of the Consortium called for unification and strengthening of China, while Russia's avowed goal was dismemberment of China. Actually, however, Russian membership could be converted to the achievement of the latter aim. It would be easy for Russia to prevent, from within, any action by the Consortium which was opposed to Russian interests; it might even be possible to prevent any activity of the Consortium in general. The idea was a forerunner of the "veto" of our days. Besides, joining the Consortium provided an occasion for Russia to advance, as a precondition of her joining, a demand for international recognition of a large exclusive Russian sphere in northern China. These

28. *International Relations,* Series 2, XVIII², 248 (July 20, 1911).

arguments seemed so compelling that the government began negotiations which resulted in Russia consenting to enter the Consortium, together with Japan.

The political crisis through which China was passing at the time
did not put an end to the negotiations about an international consortium. China's financial needs increased, and her dependence on
foreign assistance became acute. While Russia and Japan under-
scored their political goals, the United States, as the main spokesman of the Consortium concept, increased its counteractivity in
favor of Chinese "integrity" by economic means. In the course of
the ensuing negotiations, no government was as hostile to Russia
as that of the United States. St. Petersburg made it clear that Russia
would "participate in the Consortium only on condition of a reconstruction of it which would guarantee our predominant influence in enterprises north of the Great Wall." The United States was
strictly opposed to such a reconstruction of the Consortium and
therefore to Russia's inclusion. When pressed by England and
France to compromise, Secretary Knox gave way. At the same
time, however, he addressed a note to the powers (February 12,
1912), obviously directed against future separate actions of Russia and Japan, advocating "concerted action in China." To emphasize this American policy, Knox allowed the press to publish
his note and told the Russian Ambassador that his aim was "to make
an end to all talk about a division of China." [29]

Irritation with Washington mounted. This was a moment in
history when Russia appeared finally to be in condition to fulfill
her mission in the Far East; such a situation might not occur again.
And here America barred the road! Count Benckendorff, the influential Russian envoy in London, wrote privately and in a sar-
castic tone, to his minister, ". . . America decided to play politics
[through the loan to China] . . . and that has spoiled the whole
business . . . Then came Yuan Shi-kai who threatened to make
China a real Great Power . . ."

The struggle for a Russian "sphere" entered an acute stage. Russia demanded unequivocal recognition of such a sphere by the
powers.

In a note to France, Russia had already formulated her conditions in the following somewhat clumsy terms: France would be

29. *Ibid.*, Series 2, XIX^{II}, 112 (February 9, 1912).

obliged "not to lend assistance to efforts of the Chinese Government to weaken the political situation in Manchuria, Mongolia, and Chinese Turkestan by introducing changes in the existing administrative and military situation of these regions and by creating international interests there contrary to the special interests of Russia."

The British Government was also informed that the intentions of the four-nation Consortium "constitute a menace to Russian interests in regions [of China], the development of which was made possible by Russian genius and Russian capital and in which Russian interests have played a predominant role." [30]

In March, 1912, Britain and France declared to their associates, the United States and Germany, that they would not proceed without their allies, Russia and Japan. France went a step further in meeting the Russian demands by proposing the exclusion of Manchuria, Mongolia, and Chinese Turkestan from the scope of "guarantees" for the loans. Only the use of the loans for improvement of China's Army remained a controversial point between Russia and the other powers. Even in this respect France tried to acquiesce in the demands of the Russian Government: "It is out of the question," Poincaré wrote on April 4, 1912, "that we [France] should assist in the creation of an army which would menace our interests and yours." Japan was inclined to view the military reorganization of China with equanimity. She communicated to Russia her inclination to enter the Consortium since "China will not be able to reorganize her army by means of the loan and no danger therefore threatens the interests of Japan or Russia."

A dispute then arose between Russia and Britain concerning the extent and meaning of Russia's "special interests" in Extramural China, and London tried to limit the Russian privileged rights by using the phrase: "as far as they are based on agreements with China." But this limitation was just what Russia wished to avoid, since the creation of the sphere she desired would have to proceed along lines contrary to these agreements. The Foreign Minister, in his reply to Britain, presented his formula of a Russian sphere in China: "The natural geographic and economic gravitation of northern Manchuria, Mongolia, and western China to the Russian possessions in Asia is creating a special position for Russia in these

30. Note to Britain, September 27, 1911, and to France, October 5, 1911.

regions; that special position is not necessarily expressed in treaties."

Britain did not accept this concept; the "open door" would become a shut door if Russia's sphere were recognized. This British resistance was the main cause of Russia's failure to fully realize her plan in northern China.[31]

Russia finally decided to participate in the Consortium. In the process, she had occasion more than once to reiterate the formula, so disquieting to Washington and so disagreeable to London, too, that the conditions of the Chinese loans "shall contain nothing that could be harmful to special Russian *rights and interests* in northern Manchuria, Mongolia, and western China."

"If we do not get satisfaction," Premier Kokovtsev wrote, "we shall have to quit the Consortium."

These "preliminary discussions" continued for months even after Russia and Japan joined the Consortium in June, 1912.

Meanwhile China in her great need established contact with certain foreign banks which had remained outside the Consortium. In September, 1912, it became known that a German bank had arranged for a small loan to China. A London group agreed to grant China a loan of nearly 50 million dollars. This was a heavy blow to the Consortium; what was the use of the endless political discussion, its members asked, if no practical results were achieved? They pressed now for an easing of the conditions. But Russia was firm and uncompromising. Might the Consortium possibly dissolve? Such a development, which would mean a defeat for the United States, was not at all disturbing to Russia. "If the Consortium falls apart," the Russian Ministry told its ambassadors, "this will serve our interests."

This, in fact, was the end of the Consortium. Technically it remained in existence for a few months more, but actually it was moribund. England and France retreated before the strong policy of Russia; the threatening situation in Europe caused them even to move closer to Russia. A new combination emerged in the Consortium—the triumvirate of Russia, England, and France. With a feeling of deep disappointment, the American Ambassador reported, in February, 1913: "Everything indicates a readjustment of relations of England, France and Russia on lines of a triple

31. *International Relations*, Series 2, XIX[II], 456, 502–503 (April 25, and May 6, 1912).

entente; otherwise complete volte face of British cannot be explained." [32]

For the United States this combination created an intolerable situation. Its only companion in Chinese affairs remained Germany. Even Chinese public opinion, aware of the difficult conditions of the proposed loans and of the imminent introduction of foreign control over China's finances and economy, was indignant. The American financial plan, meant to save China, now aroused Chinese protestations.

President Wilson took office in March, 1913, and soon the United States withdrew from the Consortium. For all practical purposes it ceased to operate, and thus ended for the United States a curious experiment. In a sense the Consortium was a predecessor of the League of Nations with its faith in peaceful collective action against aggression, and with its exaggerated trust in the efficacy of economic pressure as opposed to military-political conquest. The fate that befell the Consortium—it was actually a great fiasco—later overtook the institution erected at Geneva.

RUSSO-JAPANESE CONVENTION OF 1912

The negotiations between Russia and Japan which were prompted by the Chinese developments progressed during the year 1912. Both governments considered the moment favorable for an extension of their spheres from Manchuria into Mongolia; Russia demanded, in addition, recognition by Japan of "special Russian rights and interests" in Chinese Turkestan. In the course of the negotiations Tokyo alluded to the fact that Japan would have to demand the Chinese Province of Fukien (opposite Japanese Formosa) if Russia insisted upon Turkestan; such a demand, however, would greatly complicate matters, since the "trading powers" would never agree to it. The question of Turkestan was dropped from the new agreement.

The main object of the new treaty was partition of Inner Mongolia into a Russian and Japanese sphere. "During recent years," a Japanese note (April 20, 1912) said, "Japan has acquired special rights and interests in the eastern part of Inner Mongolia . . . In-

32. United States Department of State, *Papers Relating to Foreign Relations* (1913), pp. 163-164.

ner Mongolia must be divided." After a short period of bargaining, the border line between the Japanese and the Russian sphere was drawn in accordance with Russia's proposal; that is, it ran along the meridian of Peking (see Map V). The new agreement was signed on July 8, 1912. This treaty, too, although a secret one, was communicated to the allies—France and Britain. Rumors immediately appeared in the Japanese press which the Tokyo government officially denied.

To Russia the treaty represented new proof of the value of collaboration with Japan. Important possibilities in the future were implied. This treaty, with the treaties of 1907 and 1910, was a base of Russian policy in the Far East until the Revolution.

In 1913–14 Russo-Japanese relations again began to deteriorate. The policies of Japan and of Russia seemed no longer to be synchronized.

Japan's sole preoccupation was China. All her forces and resources were devoted to the goal of penetrating the continent. She built new railways in Manchuria which, besides having great economic significance, threatened the master of the other half of Manchuria—Russia. She developed her trade in central China by investing capital in Chinese industry. She had informers in all important cities and was better acquainted with Chinese affairs than any other nation. Her ambitions grew from year to year.

Russia, on the other hand, watched with great envy the display of Japanese energies with which she was unable to cope. The Balkans were already aflame. Russian armies, resources, and the energies of her leaders were almost entirely absorbed by the growing conflicts with the western neighbors. For Russia new operations in Asia would be dangerous adventures. For the time being she had to prefer stable conditions.

Japan now found Russia to be a weight, hampering her moves. Any act taken without Russian consent would arouse indignation and possibly armed resistance. Japan hinted that now Inner Mongolia, too, could be detached from China, united with Outer Mongolia (which was already in the Russian sphere) and the whole of Mongolia made into a joint Russo-Japanese protectorate.

The Russian Government did not openly respond to this hint but became increasingly—often almost ridiculously—suspicious of

Japan.[33] In July, 1914, a week before the outbreak of the Great War, the Japanese Minister of Trade, Oura, nonetheless declared in a public address: "Many Japanese believe that a war between Russia and Japan will not occur sooner than in 30 to 50 years. There are, however, reasons to suppose that the second war will begin in a few years." [34]

It was the Japanese thought that if Russia should be unable to continue the advance into China in common with Japan, Japan could proceed alone. But if Russia should become an obstacle on the road, if the great Japanese ambition to rule China could not be realized because of Russian rivalry and jealousy, then the opposition of Russia must be broken. Japanese ambitions had gone far indeed by that time. As the World War developed, Japan felt that she was the only real heir to eastern Asia.

RUSSIA AND JAPAN IN THE WORLD WAR

The war speeded up the realization of these plans. Japan sided with the Allies, declared war on Germany, and in a matter of weeks occupied not only the German archipelagoes in the Pacific but also the German-held port of Kiaochow in China. This was, however, only the beginning. The next step—the famous "twenty-one demands"—was aimed at China. The demands were a comprehensive program for the acquisition of a dominant place in Chinese affairs: a program directed primarily against Chinese sovereignty but simultaneously against the position of other powers in east Asia, and particularly against Russia and the United States. In a secret letter written on April 3, 1915, to the Japanese military attaché in China, the Japanese General Staff explained the great significance it attached to the demands: "The demands connected with the Fukien Province . . . are the most vital points against America [and have as their object] the lessening of the value of the Philippine Islands." Other demands were "directed against Russia as they would reduce the value of the Siberian Railway as a military weapon." The important document (which fell into Russian hands in China) concluded on the following note: "The Army

33. *International Relations*, Series 3, II, 168; X, 618 (March 31, 1914, and April 12, 1916). The Russian envoy in Mongolia, for instance, reported home that "one Japanese watchmaker arrived with his family."

34. *Ibid.*, Series 3, V, 24 (July 23, 1914).

has spent over ten years in formulating these plans . . . We, the Japanese General Staff, have always urged those in government to push ahead this forward policy . . . China is the first country to bear the brunt of our expansion policy." [35]

The deep secrecy which at first, on the insistence of Japan, surrounded the negotiations between Japan and China did not last for long. When the Great Powers learned of these negotiations, they were unable to take any decisive step to counteract them. The superiority of Japan's political strategy became evident. The powers were involved in a hard war in Europe and could not risk a new conflict in China.

Only the United States was neutral, but its reaction, although energetic, was not impressive. Secretary of State Bryan officially recommended to the Japanese that they act with "moderation"; he asked the governments of Russia, France, and Britain to support the démarche. All three governments, however, declined. Bryan then let it be known that the United States would not recognize an agreement between Japan and China contrary to American interests or to the "principle of equal opportunities." This threat made no impression on Tokyo. The Japanese Foreign Minister, Baron Kato, told the Russian envoy that the American declaration was "impudent." Kato spoke "not without irony about American diplomacy," the envoy reported, "and made the observation that after the departure of [Dr. John Bassett] Moore, there was no one left in the State Department who is informed in matters of diplomacy and diplomatic technique." [36]

The situation in China was unprecedented. Mighty Russia was uneasy, making no moves, while Japan advanced at high speed. The Chinese press and political circles looked at Russia with interest and hope. Krupensky, the aggressive diplomat, expressed Russian feelings of sympathy to the President of the young Chinese Republic. Amazed at the change in the atmosphere, he wrote, in May, 1915: "At this moment we have better relations with China than at any time since the Russo-Japanese war . . . Lately, the Chinese have been looking to us for help. Yuan Shi-kai [the President] wants to return to the times of Li Hung-chang" (i.e., to the time of the Russo-Chinese alliance against Japanese aggression). [37]

35. *Ibid.*, Series 3, VII^{II}, 364–366 (English text in original).
36. *Ibid.*, Series 3, VII^{II}, 479 (May 18, 1915).
37. *Ibid.*, Series 3, VII^{II}, 427; VIII^{II}, 52–53 (May 12 and August 11, 1915).

Actually the pursuit of an anti-Japanese policy was out of the question for Russia. While Japan was ready to fight, Russia was preoccupied in Europe. Moreover, Russia was badly in need of armaments; the supplies from Britain and the United States were insufficient, but Japan was able to deliver a considerable number of rifles and other arms. Russia was forced by circumstances not only to remain passive in the face of a powerful Japanese expansion in China but even to agree to many a demand which ran counter to her interests.

China had no choice. She signed the humiliating agreements with Japan after a few changes in her favor were made in them. On the whole, Japan now regarded China as a nation deprived of sovereignty and not equal in status to the independent nations of the world. Japan was anxious to emphasize her dominant position and to exclude China from international conferences and negotiations on an equal footing; in the Japanese scheme of things, China was to sink to the level of an India. Japan opposed China's entry into the war against Germany in order to prevent her participation in the peace conference. Japan also opposed the elevation of Yuan to emperor. Japan even aided the revolutionary movements in China's southern provinces in order to weaken the Central Government. In a secret message the Foreign Minister, Viscount Ishii, wired his envoy in Russia setting forth his program as follows:

1. To create for Japan a privileged position in China and to impress on the Chinese people the sense of Japan's might.

2. Yuan Shi-kai must be removed from authority . . .

4. The government is aware that the powers in Europe and America will under no conditions agree to this intervention in Chinese internal affairs.[38]

Japan's first objective on the road to "Greater East Asia" was complete elimination of Germany and of German trade from China. No sooner had China accepted Japan's demands than negotiations were begun with Russia concerning a new treaty. Russia needed Japan's weapons as well as a guarantee that this dominant power of the East would not make use of the war situation to penetrate into the Russian spheres in China. For Japan's arms Russia was prepared to pay a high price. She offered Japan a section

38. *Ibid.*, Series 3, X, 345–346 (March 7, 1916). The telegram was intercepted by Russian intelligence and decoded.

of Russian railroad in southern Manchuria. She even alluded to the possible cession of Northern Sakhalin to Japan.[39] Japan, on the other hand, wanted a guarantee against Russia's making a separate peace with Germany, as well as assurance that no Russo-German collaboration would emerge in China after the war.

Dissension arose mainly in regard to China's participation in the new agreement. It was logical that China's signature should be required to a treaty whose purpose it was to close China to Germany (and Austria-Hungary) after the war. The Russian Government, in its new role of protector of China's independence, wanted such a treaty with both Japan and China. But Japan emphatically rejected the idea: China was no longer considered to be a nation on an equal footing with Japan or Russia.

After a year of negotiations, the new treaty was completed; it was signed on July 3, 1916. In its public as well as its secret part it was a treaty of alliance against a "third power hostile to Russia and Japan"; the secret treaty described the conditions under which assistance was to be given respectively by Japan and Russia in the event a war arose between one of them and the "third power."

The "third power" was not named in the treaties, although there was no obvious reason why Germany could not be singled out. Later the opinion was expressed that the United States had been one of the targets of the treaty.[40] Russian archive documents, published in the late 1930's, make reference to Germany and Austria only. Nonetheless, the strange wording of the treaties indicates the possibility that both governments had mental reservations concerning the potential application of the alliance against the United States.

The treaty was valuable to Russia because the three previous agreements (1907, 1910, and 1912), which had guaranteed Russian privileges in North Manchuria and Outer Mongolia, were declared to remain in force. In addition, Russia now secured a quantity of rifles from Japan.

After the signing of the Russo-Japanese alliance in July, 1916, the co-operation of the two powers seemed closer than ever. A few months later, however, the Revolution in Russia put in question all her treaties, privileges, and obligations.

39. *Ibid.*, Series 3, VIII^II, 236; X, 222 (September 6, 1915, and February 18, 1916).
40. Cf. E. B. Price, *The Russo-Japanese Treaties.*

V

The Russian Sphere in China

THE ACQUISITION OF MONGOLIA

The Mongolian area that came under Russian domination during the decade 1906–16 was small in population, of little economic value, and of little cultural significance. In extent, however, and also in its significance for international relations, it was large. The area in question was the northern part of the Chinese Province of Mongolia.

Among the Asiatic nations, the Mongols, a people numbering only a few million, are a very small group, and their "heroic epoch" lies in the distant past. Nomads for the most part, their level of civilization is far below that of their two great neighbors, the Russians and the Chinese. But it was precisely this circumstance—the small backward nation lying between two powerful rivals—that gave such significance to the Mongolian problem.

It would be only slight exaggeration to say that Mongolia's significance lies in her territory rather than in her population. Outer Mongolia is almost as large in area as China proper.[1] Mongolia is seven times the size of France and ten times that of Japan. To complicate the problem further, there are about half a million Mongols living in Russia, around the Baikal, in the areas adjoining Mongolia. The latter constituted a sort of political bridge to the Chinese province, and their importance has increased during recent decades as Russo-Chinese relations have from time to time involved the Mongolian question.

For about two centuries the Mongols actually enjoyed a great deal of autonomy within the framework of the Chinese Empire. Removed from Chinese centers, poor and non-bellicose, they were of little use and presented no danger. Their officials were mainly Mongols; no Chinese army was stationed in their land; and there

1. Outer Mongolia has 1,380,000 square miles; China proper, 1,550,000.

was practically no Chinese immigration into Mongolia. Some economic ties, however, had bound them to China. The small trade of the country has been carried on by Chinese merchants. Early in the present century, a Chinese bank opened credits to politically influential Mongol leaders.

Since the end of the nineteenth century, as Russia has exerted increased efforts in Siberia and the Far East, Mongolia has assumed greater importance in China's policy. This borderland, which was clearly a doorway to further Russian expansion into central Asia, now commanded more attention. The Peking government began to tighten Chinese ties with Mongolia and to curtail Mongolian autonomy. It strove gradually to extend the general system of Chinese administration to the Mongols, it encouraged immigration of Chinese peasants into Mongolia, and it was prepared to break, by force if necessary, the opposition which must naturally and inevitably develop there.

An anti-Chinese movement headed by lay and religious Mongol leaders sprang up, and Russia soon tried to make use of it to foster the separation of Outer Mongolia from China. Before the autonomy movement had gained momentum, however, the Russo-Japanese convention recognized Outer Mongolia as part of the Russian sphere. Russian agents stimulated the movement and directed it into pro-Russian channels. Indeed, Russian assistance was necessary if the Mongol cause was to achieve any success; without Russian aid the movement could easily be crushed by Chinese forces. But Mongols, with their childish notions of international relations, believed that pure sympathy and benevolence guided policies and that Russia would aid in creating a new independent and sovereign Mongolian state embracing all of the various Mongolian lands.

In 1910–11 the situation in Mongolia became aggravated. Chinese activity was increasing: Chinese Army units were arriving; a whole Chinese division was expected at Urga, the capital, and barracks had already been built. The Chinese *amban* (head of the local government) in Urga began to persecute Mongolians who were sympathetic to Russia. Colonization of Mongolian lands by the Chinese was meanwhile being pushed forward.

In July, 1911, the Khutukhtu (the "living Buddha") and the princes met in the capital and decided to appeal to the Russian Tsar for help against Chinese aggression. A delegation was sent to the

Tsar. It carried a long and interesting letter signed by the Khutu-khtu himself and four high princes.

The omnipotent White Tsar of the great Russian people, being power-ful, strong and charitable, protects the yellow peoples and is himself the incarnation of virtue; if we assist one another, we will not lose our former position. The yellow peoples will flourish and eternal peace will reign.

According to the experience of many nations, any small people can become strong if it is supported by a great and powerful people. There is a saying that a great and strong state aids the small state.

Mighty Tsar, consider our condition with pity and magnanimity. Humbly imploring aid and protection as do those who long for rain in times of great drought, speaking but the truth, we present you this worthless gift.[2]

This development was not unwelcome to the Russian Govern-ment. It was obvious, however, that a Russian move would pro-voke not only China's protests, but also a Japanese and British reaction. The Tsar did not receive the Mongolian delegation, but acting Foreign Minister Neratov reported to him that "the move-ment that has emerged among the Mongols can be made use of in our relations with China."

On August 4, 1911, the Russian Cabinet dealt with the delicate situation. The protocol of this session of the cabinet stated quite frankly that "some of our agents in Mongolia have assisted in a large measure in the creation among the Mongols of the conviction that they can count on Russian support in case they attempt to break with China." However, "at present the Imperial Govern-ment is obliged to participate actively in the solution of various acute questions in the Near and the Far East . . . it would be un-desirable, at this political conjuncture, to take any active step in connection with Mongolia."

It was decided to promise the Mongols certain assistance "in the preservation of their racial integrity"; to augment the small Russian military force stationed in the Mongolian capital (as "the guard of the consulate") and, also, to point out to the Government of China that its measures in Mongolia would be regarded as inimical to Russia. On the whole, however, the Russian Govern-ment preferred to act cautiously. In his report to the Tsar, the

2. *Novyi vostok*, XIII, 352–354.

Minister of Foreign Affairs expressed his conviction that Russia must "watch quietly the events in Mongolia." The Tsar, remembering no doubt the days of his own *Drang nach Osten* when Mongolia was viewed as one of the next objects of expansion, made the following note on this report: "Quietly watch, yes—but not miss the opportunity!"

Outright Russian annexation of Mongolia was impossible because of the international situation. The Japanese Ambassador was beginning to make inquiries of the Russian minister as to Russian plans concerning Mongolia. To British and American ears, too, annexation of Chinese provinces by Russia would have sounded inauspicious. At the very least, new agreements with Japan and Britain would be necessary in advance of any definite moves in Mongolia. Early in October, 1911, the Chinese Revolution began and in February, 1912, the monarchy was abolished. Drawing their own conclusions from this event, the Mongols declared their complete separation from China and their constitution as a sovereign state. On December 16, 1911, the Khutukhtu was proclaimed the head of Mongolia.

Mongolia therefore accomplished as a result of the Chinese Revolution what it had expected Russian aid to accomplish for her. The weakness of the young republican government of China made it impossible to apply force in its relations with Mongolia; rather, it tried to persuade the new Mongol ruler, by means of letters and telegrams, that Mongolia must submit to Chinese authority. These Chinese letters were another piece of seemingly naïve yet shrewd oriental diplomacy.

"Honorable Lama!" wrote Yuan Shi-kai, the new President, in a telegram to the Mongol leader. "Our army commanders . . . are aching for a fight with the Honorable Lama. It is only I, the President, who holds them back, out of compassion, in the hope that a peaceful solution may be reached . . . You, Honorable Lama, have started military operations . . . arrested princes and dukes and inflicted suffering on the population . . . You have outdone the brigands by your looting and unruliness." Since the Mongols had insisted that their allegiance to the Chinese Empire had ceased with the downfall of the monarchy, Yuan emphasized his rights: "The Empire of the Tsings did not recognize the independence of Mongolia, consequently I am unable to do so. Urga is an area subject to China."

The Chinese Government followed this up with a statement in which it promised the Khutukhtu, if he would submit, a reward "which will be different from usual rewards. May the sky and the earth be witness that this promise will be kept! However, if you continue to menace and if you will not be peaceful, then the five nationalities which constitute the Republic will make you feel the brunt of their rage, and you shall be punished by fire and sword!"

The Mongols suddenly displayed an amazing knowledge of history. "Is it not known to you," the Khutukhtu replied, "that England and America once stood under the rule of one monarch and that later America, having become independent, concluded with England a treaty which up to the present has not been renounced?" The Khutukhtu declined to yield, and accused the President of cruelties. He concluded his message on a highly diplomatic note: "Take care lest you be cut up in pieces like a melon!" [3]

Russia proceeded slowly. Her first effort was to prevent China from taking any measures in or affecting Mongolia without consulting Russia, thus taking upon herself the role of mediator between China and Mongolia, although this obviously meant intervention in the internal affairs of China. On January 11, 1912, the Russian Government finally published a statement on Mongolian affairs. It mentioned "great Russian interests in Mongolia," offered its services to both sides, and explained why it must recognize the new regime in Mongolia, while at the same time it was delivering arms to the Mongol leaders. The Russian consul was right when he stated in his report that "the willingness of our government to supply arms to the Mongols, and the advice of Korostovets [the Russian envoy] . . . have strengthened the Mongols in their determination to separate [themselves from China]." [4]

China was naturally resentful. Russia's demand that no Chinese military units be kept in Mongolia, coupled with the arrival of new Russian detachments, was particularly difficult for the Chinese to accept, and they resisted as long as they could. Likewise the Russian demand for priority rights in railroad construction in Mongolia

3. Korostovets, *op. cit.*, pp. 226–228.
4. *International Relations*, Series 2, XIX^I, 178 (December 11, 1911).

met with protest. The Chinese asserted that they alone were able to "maintain order" in Mongolia. But Russia stood firm: the Mongols, they declared in Peking, do not believe Chinese promises unless endorsed by Russia.

In the meantime Russo-Japanese negotiations concerning the division of Inner Mongolia into spheres of interest of the two nations were progressing. Russia was prepared to recognize the eastern part of Inner Mongolia, adjoining the Japanese-protected southern Manchuria, as a Japanese sphere; Japan, satisfied with this acquisition, was prepared to agree to a Russian policy in Outer Mongolia directed at an actual though not a formal separation of that area from China. The Russo-Japanese treaties were signed on July 8, 1912.

As a result Russia's tone in her dealings with China on the Mongolian problem became more and more insistent. The new Chinese president, on the other hand, was striving to unite and strengthen China and to display to the outer world as well as to his own people a large degree of independence and force. In August, 1912, a Chinese unit composed of guards, infantry, and cavalry and armed with machine guns was to go to Mongolia. Russia made a strongly worded declaration and threatened to dispatch an army. Later, China proposed to annul all Mongolian debts to China if the Mongolians would return to their former status; weapons, too, were offered on that condition.[5] The Russian Government likewise proposed granting arms to the Mongols, on condition, however, that these would not be used in territories other than Outer Mongolia, since Inner Mongolia was becoming taboo as far as Russian expansionist activities were concerned.

Chinese protests, however strong, remained ineffective. Japan had stepped aside, Britain was interested in other fields, and China alone was not able to withstand the strong Russian pressure. On November 3, 1912, Russia, in defiance of China, concluded her decisive treaty with Outer Mongolia, which brought about the separation of that province from China and the emergence of a new Russian protectorate in central Asia. The first point of the treaty read as follows: "The Imperial Russian Government will lend Mongolia its assistance in order to preserve her present autonomy and also her right to keep her national army, forbidding entry to Chinese

5. *Ibid.*, Series 2, XXII, 245 (September 23, 1912).

armies and colonization of her lands by the Chinese." Most of the other paragraphs dealt with personal and commercial rights and privileges of Russian citizens in Mongolia.

The negotiations between Russia and Mongolia concerning this treaty and its final wording were a great disappointment to the Mongols; for a time it even appeared likely that the talks would break down and that no agreement would be reached.

First of all, the Mongols intended to create a really sovereign state independent of both China and Russia. Their first draft of a treaty referred to an independent Mongolian state. Russia's hands, however, were tied by numerous declarations and treaties obliging her to respect the "integrity of China." Therefore on paper, at least, the sovereignty of China over Mongolia was to remain. But to the Mongols the "autonomy" referred to in the treaty and the continuation of Chinese sovereignty were a disappointment.

Secondly, the Mongols intended immediately to enter into diplomatic relations with a number of states. They were disappointed to find that no nation except China and Russia was ready to negotiate with them officially. Later, they naïvely took certain steps looking to the establishment of diplomatic relations with Japan, France, and others. It was on the advice of Russia that their letters were returned to them unopened.

The third disappointment was the hardest, and it concerned the most important phase of the situation: Mongolia was to be divided, and only Outer Mongolia was to acquire autonomy. The status of Inner Mongolia was to be unchanged; it was to remain a Chinese province (with Japanese privileges in its eastern part). The negotiating Mongolian princes were unable to understand the reasons for the division and they questioned it again and again, although the Russians plainly stated Japan's position and rights and pointed to the Russian treaty obligations. The Mongols remained dissatisfied. If this was to be the situation, they argued, would it not be wiser to return to China and remain united with the Mongols of Inner Mongolia? A Mongol delegation was already on its way to Peking.

Finally, the Russian draft of the treaty was signed, not, however, without threats on the part of Russia. But a big question remained

—whether and when a reunion of the Mongol people would be possible.

No sooner had the treaty been signed than feeling in Mongolia toward the Russians began to cool. The disappointment and disillusionment of the Mongolian leaders were great. The achievements were not what they had dreamed of. For them the treaty with Russia was a hard lesson in international politics. In his memoirs the chief Russian negotiator and envoy in Mongolia, Ivan Korostovets, is frank about the feelings of the Mongols toward Russia.[6] Everyone seemed to have turned suddenly against the Russian policy; the Mongols became suspicious and considered Russia untrustworthy.

A Mongol leader, DaLama, tried to go to Japan in the hope of getting international recognition of Mongolia's sovereignty; on Russian advice a Japanese visa was refused him. "Russia wants to isolate the Mongols and to bring them under her rule." Such was the impression. With a few exceptions arms for the Mongols were also refused. Strange events transpired. The Russian envoy complained about the anti-Russian activities of a Mongol leader, Bingtu Wang; soon after, the latter was found poisoned.

Russia's negotiations with China concerning a new order in Mongolia progressed slowly because of the reluctance of both the Chinese and the Mongols. The Chinese government, unable successfully to oppose the Russian policy, strove to prolong the negotiations in the hope that some unexpected event might bring about a reversal in the situation.

The Russian envoy in China reported, on October 10, 1912, that "the Chinese seem to base their policy on rumors about a revolutionary movement in Russia; they figure on complications in Europe because of Balkan affairs." While the Russian government was prepared to give China only a paper sovereignty over Mongolia, China wanted to observe the letter of the provision and claimed actual influence. A "Chinese party" emerged in Outer Mongolia and made rapid headway.

Finally, a Russo-Chinese agreement was concluded on November 5, 1913. In the first paragraph Russia recognized that Outer Mongolia "remains under Chinese suzerainty," but in the second and third paragraphs China recognized Outer Mongolia's auton-

6. *Op. cit.*, pp. 255-290.

omy, and China's actual rights were held to a minimum (essentially, to the protection of Chinese citizens in that area). Russia promised not to colonize Mongolia and to limit her own military force to a protecting detachment. But most important of all the provisions was the stipulation that questions concerning Outer Mongolia and the latter's relations with China could not be resolved without Russia. Practically, a Russian protectorate over Outer Mongolia was now recognized by the two governments, Japan and China.

The next Russian step was to conclude a railroad agreement with Outer Mongolia (November 10, 1914), and to enlarge Mongolia's territory by including in it the Province of Barga. Final settlement, however, of all outstanding questions called for an agreement of all three—Russia, China, and Outer Mongolia—and the Russian Government, as soon as the agreement with China was reached, invited the other two governments to a conference to discuss such an agreement. But here, again, almost insurmountable difficulties arose.

The Mongols were indignant that behind their backs Russia and China had agreed between them to maintain Chinese "suzerainty" and to cut Mongolia in two. On November 4, 1913, the Mongolian Government officially had informed Peking and St. Petersburg that it could not accept the proposed solution. A long series of conferences took place in Urga between the Mongols and the Russian envoy. The latter reported: "Despite all my verbal assurances that Outer Mongolia cannot expect to evolve immediately from a Chinese province into an efficient, independent state . . . the Mongolian ministers obstinately hope to achieve complete separation from China and a juncture with Inner Mongolia. They obstinately repeat the same arguments." [7]

In Inner Mongolia, therefore, military operations on the part of the Mongols, on a small scale but accompanied by atrocities, took place against the Chinese; the Government of Outer Mongolia and its princes assisted in the struggle. This created a difficult situation for Russia because of the pledges to Japan. "We could not give aid to this Mongolian imperialism," wrote the Russian Foreign Minister, explaining why arms were not delivered to the Mongols. But the fight continued for a long time. Again and again

7. *Krasnyi Arkhiv*, XXXVII, 30–31.

the Mongolian Government sent notes and declarations to Russia asking for her assistance against China; it demanded withdrawal of Chinese troops from Inner Mongolia. These efforts were fruitless.

Since Russia, bound by the treaty with Japan, was not prepared to help, the Mongols began to look to Japan herself. This was exactly what Russia feared. The Mongol idea was, with Japan's assistance, to separate Inner Mongolia from China and then to unite the two parts of their land into one state—if necessary, under a joint protectorate of Japan and Russia. The next step would be Japanese penetration into all of Mongolia—a development eagerly sought in Tokyo, but feared in St. Petersburg.

The Mongols began their negotiations with a Japanese official named Kodama. Receiving encouragement from him, the Khutukhtu wrote a letter to the Japanese Emperor, in January, 1914, in which he asked that the Emperor send a Japanese envoy to Mongolia and help unite the nation. The Mongols naïvely sent their letter through the only existing channel—the Russian. When it was presented in Tokyo by the Russian envoy, it embarrassed the Japanese Foreign Office, since, according to the existing treaties, Outer Mongolia was a Russian sphere and, in international diplomacy, the Khutukhtu was not recognized as the head of a state. An overt act against Russia was out of the question. The letter was returned to the Mongols "unopened." But Japanese intrigue, of which the Russians were well aware, continued.[8]

Finally the "tripartite conference" of Russia, China, and Outer Mongolia opened in Kiakhta in September, 1914. Russia was already preoccupied with the war in Europe, and China was inclined to procrastinate. Nor did the Mongols expect to achieve their objectives at that conference. The conference lasted nine months, and the accord was not signed until June 7, 1915. The new agreement was essentially a combination of the two earlier treaties, the Russo-Chinese and the Russo-Mongolian. Chinese suzerainty over Outer Mongolia was to be maintained and—for the first time since 1911—was recognized by the Mongols. No international treaties of a political nature could be concluded by Mongolia. A small military guard was allowed both the Chinese

8. *International Relations*, Series 3, X, 618–619 (April 12, 1916).

and the Russian envoys. The dominant position, of course, was held by the Russians.

Before long, however, the Russian position began to deteriorate. The Russian defeats in Europe had repercussions throughout Asia. Russia's prestige was sinking, and to the degree that it went down the prestige of China was enhanced.

A Russian bank, with government backing, opened a branch in Mongolia, but no loans were made to Mongols. The head of the Russian military force stationed in Mongolia gave expression to his sense of racial superiority and made himself hated by the people. The Russian officers of the Mongol troops considered their assignment in Mongolia a temporary one; they did not bother to learn the Mongol language, the military instruction they gave was inadequate, and the Mongol soldiers kept running away.

"The sad disappointment of the Mongols in the Russians and in Russian policy," a Russian traveler and explorer sums up the experience, "was reflected in every one of their words, in all their relations and dealings with the Russians. The solemn chord that had been audible in their spirit [earlier in the century] had completely vanished; at all encounters, at all conversations there were notes of bitter disillusionment, of a reality that satisfied no one." [9]

When the Revolution broke out in Russia, Mongolian affairs were in bad shape. It was obvious that Outer Mongolia benefited but little from her ties with the Russian Empire; the economic advantages accruing to Russia were minimal too. Soon the revolutionary events found their reflection in the far-off colony. In 1918 Russo-Chinese relations in Mongolia reached a new crisis.

NORTHERN MANCHURIA

Much smaller in size than Outer Mongolia, northern Manchuria was of far greater political and economic importance to Russia than any other of her territorial acquisitions during the century following the Napoleonic Wars.

For Manchuria as a whole the first decades of the present century were a boom time. From a backward, empty country with a population of 8 to 10 million (1890), she advanced within this

9. A. Baranov, *Khalka* (Harbin, 1919), p. 4.

short period to the rank of one of the most important agricultural and industrial regions of the Far East. Her population was 23 million in 1920, and about 40 million in 1940. The chief stimulus to this development came from the two railroads built in Manchuria by Russia between 1896 and 1903. One of them, in the southern part of Manchuria, had to be turned over to Japan in 1905, and has since then served as the initial base of a great development of southern Manchuria as a Japanese protectorate.

Northern Manchuria, on the other hand, constituted the Russian zone and its development was based on the Russian-owned Chinese Eastern Railway. Though lagging behind the Japanese zone in progress, northern Manchuria also showed signs of a speedy evolution. It was larger in area (310,000 square miles) than the Japanese zone (80,000 square miles); the Japanese zone, however, was densely populated. More than half of Manchuria's inhabitants lived (as they also do today) in the southern zone. Before the construction of the railroads, in the nineties, northern Manchuria had a population of about 2 million. This figure rose to 5,700,000 in 1908, 8,000,000 in 1914, and 14,000,000 in 1928.[10] The rapid growth was due to Chinese immigration, which amounted to several hundred thousand a year. In both the Russian and the Japanese zones the Chinese were about 95 per cent of the population, and today, too, the Chinese represent a similarly large percentage.

From a legal point of view Manchuria was a province of China. Neither the Chinese Government nor the government of any other nation ever recognized the colonial or semicolonial status of the country. Russia's rights were based on the treaty of 1896 concerning the Manchurian railroads by which China had agreed to cede to Russia, for the duration of the Russian ownership of the railroads (80 years), "lands which are necessary for the building, maintenance, and guarding of the railroad"; these lands to be "free from estate taxes, the railroad company to possess the exclusive right to administer its lands." China was generous at the beginning, and agreed to lease to Russia a large belt of land alongside the railroad tracks, particularly at points where stations were to be built. This leased territory was so extensive that large cities soon emerged in the Russian-owned territories. The total area of the leased lands was 232,000 acres; 29,000 acres of this land later be-

10. *Vestnik Manchzhurii* (1928), No. 7.

came the city of Harbin, the capital of North Manchuria. The situation was a paradoxical one: all the cities in this part of China stood on Russian soil and there were no cities which did not adjoin the Russian railroad tracks.

To protect the railroad property against brigandage, a police force was necessary, and China agreed to allow a Russian guard to be stationed in Manchuria. In accordance with the Portsmouth Treaty, 15 armed men per kilometer of railroad were admitted. In this way a Russian armed force of 30,000 men—a large force by Chinese standards—was stationed in northern Manchuria.

The main offices of the Russian railroad were located in Harbin. Before long these offices developed into a sort of Russian government of northern Manchuria. New, unexpected departments of the railway manager's office were opened, for instance, a school department, health department, church department, and others, including a sort of foreign office. Russian high schools were soon established; three Russian newspapers were published daily. There was even a "People's University"—a type of educational institution which was becoming popular in Russia at that time—established in Harbin. Russian courts were set up to judge civil suits arising between Russians.

The lessening of Chinese control over northern Manchuria and the strengthening of Russia's influence proceeded gradually during this decade. One Russian demand followed another; pressure was exerted to have the Chinese Government agree to them. Since 1896 Chinese import duties for Russian goods brought into Manchuria had been reduced by one third. Now other privileges were granted in connection with coal mining in the railroad zone; all coal mines at both sides of the tracks, for a distance of 19 kilometers, were restricted, so that no foreigner (meaning a non-Russian) was entitled to engage in mining operations without the consent of the Russian administration. Similar agreements relating to timbering were also concluded.

In 1910 an agreement was reached between Russia and China regarding shipping on the Sungari, Manchuria's main river. The agreement created almost a monopoly for the Russians. Other nations, even the Japanese, were excluded.

A hard struggle went on between China and Russia concerning the local administration of the cities of northern Manchuria, and

other governments, including the United States, soon became involved in this dispute. In 1907, without the consent of China and
in disregard of Chinese laws, Russia introduced the Russian system of local administration. In January of 1908 the Government
of China formally protested, and a diplomatic dispute ensued. In
the meantime the Russian city administrations had begun to collect
taxes, but some of the foreigners residing in northern Manchuria
refused to pay these taxes. (The United States Consulate supported
the claims of Americans.) Despite the support given, China finally
had to accept the Russian demands, and in May, 1909, an agreement
was signed by which the administrative bodies of northern Manchurian cities were subordinated to both the Chinese authorities
and the manager of the Russian railroad. Actually this meant recognition on the part of China of Russian control.

The Russian population in northern Manchuria, which increased
from year to year, reached about 100,000 in 1914–16. It was a
small minority compared with the millions of the Chinese population. Russian control of economy and policy, however, was firmly
established. By agreeing to preferential customs for Russian im-
ports to Manchuria China actually consented to a privileged position for Russian foreign trade. Russia sent textiles to northern
Manchuria and received from Manchuria the rapidly growing exports of soya beans, wheat, and tobacco, the exports coming
through the Russian port of Vladivostok. Almost all northern Manchurian flour mills belonged to Russians. Branches of Moscow
firms selling Russian kerosene, sugar, and textiles were opened in
Harbin.

The political struggles which developed in Russia's internal
affairs were reflected in northern Manchuria. Russia's revolutionary
parties had their groups among Russian workers and intellectuals
of northern Manchuria, and the political strikes, street demonstrations, and arrests which occurred there were on the Russian pattern.
Trade-unions emerged also about 1906–7. As far as political life
was concerned, northern Manchuria was part of Russia, since the
Russian minority constituted the wealthier and politically maturer
part of the population, the Chinese majority being passive.

From the start of the twentieth century, the international economic situation was extremely favorable for Manchuria, and the

progress of her Russian zone was only a part of the general growth of the country. It has often been argued that if other, richer nations had been admitted to Manchuria, and if the door had been opened wide to economic activity, Manchuria would have benefited from it and developed to a far greater degree. This may be true. The Russian capital and Russian commerce that fertilized Manchuria were of necessity on a small scale; even Japan was able to do more in her zone to foster industry and commerce than was Russia.

The fact is, however, that the Russians placed their imprint on the evolution of northern Manchuria during the first two decades of the latter's sudden rise and growth. Russian influence remained constant during the succeeding decades, even after Russia retreated from Manchuria and even after she ceded her railroad to Japan. Geographically situated between Chita and Vladivostok, constituting a sort of a bulge into Russian territory, northern Manchuria obviously presented a problem for the future. The efforts to solve the problem, which have not as yet succeeded, proceeded most dramatically during the decades following the first World War.

TUVA

An area at the northwestern corner of Mongolia constituted a separate problem in Sino-Russian relations. This was the Uryankhai region, later renamed Tannu Tuva, or Tuva.[11] A country almost the size of Great Britain, it had a population of about 60,000 at the turn of the century. So long as Mongolia was part of China, Tuva was a part of the Province of Mongolia. With the separation of Outer Mongolia, Tuva became inaccessible to the Chinese Army and to Chinese officials. It could now remain with Mongolia, be annexed by Russia, or else be made into a separate state.

The people of Tuva regarded Mongolia as a great nation with an advanced culture, economy, and politics, just as the Mongols in their turn looked up to the Chinese. Nomads and hunters, the Tuvinians did not even have a written language until Soviet linguists invented an alphabet for them in the early 1930's.

Tuva was difficult to reach from Russia. Russian merchants began to get there in the 1860's; they were the first to do business there. Foreign trade reached more important proportions in the

11. This region will be referred to throughout as Tuva.

1890's, when Chinese merchants began to penetrate from the east through Mongolia. The word "trade" had, however, a specific meaning for the Tuvinians: it was a sort of barter activity, similar to that existing in colonial areas during the early period after their discovery. Not only was the price of goods exorbitant, but the conditions on which the merchants extended credit to the natives were onerous. The entire clan or community was held responsible for the debts of any of its members, while the interest rates frequently reached 100 per cent a year. Much as the Russian administration wished to back enterprising Russian merchants, official reports painted a frightening picture of destitution due to trading practices. When the Chinese began to engage in trade, their methods proved to be even worse. Colonel Popov reported in 1913 that:

[Tuva] has been completely ruined and reduced to a state of pauperism by the colossal exactions of the Chinese authorities and officials on the one hand, and by the unscrupulous practices of the Russian traders on the other hand, and in the last ten years especially by the Chinese tradesmen . . . The Russian tradesmen, coarse and cruel, have not hesitated to extort the last sheep for a box of matches given on credit a few years earlier or to grab the best pastures and hay harvests.[12]

Another road of penetration into Tuva came through the activities of the searchers for gold. They brought back such considerable amounts of gold that Russian Government agencies began to be interested in the natural resources of the region. More important than anything else, however, was the settlement of Russian farmers in Tuva. Since the middle of the nineties, thousands of persons migrated to the little-known territory. By 1914 about 10,000 Russians were residing there as farmers, and the flow, tacitly encouraged by the Russian authorities, continued until 1917. At the time of the civil war in Russia there were about 12,000 Russian residents in Tuva alongside some 60,000 natives. The methods of acquiring land were not precisely in agreement with the standard rules of civil law elsewhere. Since the natives were nomads who changed their pastures from time to time, the Russian immigrants either simply seized vast terrains or else "leased" them for a trifling sum. In 1911, at a conference of high Russian officials of Siberia in Ir-

12. Irkutsk Military District, Report of Col. Viktor Popov, *Uryankhaiski Krai* (1913), pp. 86–87.

kutsk, it was recognized that the legal basis of the Russian settlers' status in Tuva was "half lease, half seizure," and that individual properties acquired in this manner often extended over several square miles.

The Russian merchants and settlers were the bold and insistent vanguard clamoring for the annexation of Tuva by Russia. They were aware that their success was due to the political support given by Russian officialdom as well as to the passivity of China. Appealing to the traditions of Russian empire building, they soon succeeded in arousing interest among Russian officials in the neighboring Siberian provinces. In 1907 engineer Rodevich explored the region for Russia, reporting that "Uryankhai is the point of least resistance on the Russo-Chinese periphery." China tried to respond in a forceful manner but failed. The head of the Chinese administration, the Amban of Kobdo, ordered the immediate expulsion of all Russian colonists and the destruction of their property. The Russian Government immediately intervened, and the order was voided.

Serious dissension existed at the time within the Russian Government over the question of the disposition of Tuva. The aggressive Russian diplomats in Peking advised their government to make use of the weakness of China in order to annex the land immediately. Among the Russian Cabinet members one group was inclined to follow such a course; the opinion was widespread that even from a strictly legal point of view Tuva's status was obscure and that Russia could base her claims to the region on certain international agreements—or rather on the vagueness of their terms —in reference to the disputed territory. Thus it was claimed that the Russo-Chinese treaty of Kiakhta in 1727 was unclear in defining the border line between Russia and China in the vicinity of Tuva; [13] it was asserted that for a certain time Tuvinians had paid tribute to both Russia and China. Up to the publication of the relevant volumes of the secret documents from the official archives in the 1930's, the opinion prevailed, even among serious historians, that Tuva was a forgotten land, a "no man's land," because of misunderstandings in the tracing of the frontier. Bold diplomats and generals

13. It was alleged that the Russo-Chinese commission which had drawn up the border line had assumed that the Sayan Mountain range north of Tuva was identical with the Tannu Ola range in the south; therefore the allegiance of Tuva remained undetermined. I. Levine, *La Mongolie* (Paris, 1937), p. 184.

at the war ministry based their program for the annexation of Tuva on these grounds.

On November 21, 1911, the Tuva problem was discussed at a Cabinet meeting in St. Petersburg. The Ministry of Foreign Affairs refuted the prevailing notion concerning the legal status of Tuva; it quoted the border agreement of 1864—the so-called Chuguchak treaty—which clearly defined the border and recognized the whole of Tuva as a part of China. The government, preoccupied with the situation in southeastern Europe, adopted a cautious policy with regard to China in order not to provoke unnecessary trouble with Britain. A decision was adopted by the Cabinet which did not become known until 1933: "The original diplomatic documents, dating back to the eighteenth century, evidently cannot serve as a solid basis for the defense of our claims that the Uryankhai region belongs to Russia. Likewise, the protocol of 1864 . . . apparently vitiates the possibility of declaring our claims to the Trans-Sayan region." [14]

By virtue of this decision, Russia continued her tacit penetration of Tuva without attempting to effect any change in its legal position. "Silent" Russian activity in Tuva involved the establishment of Russian schools, hospitals, churches, and also the dispatch of some hundred Cossacks into the territory. Small Russian military "guard" units were then stationed at several points beyond the Chinese border.

Events did not come to a head, however, until the crisis occurred that led to the Chinese Revolution in 1911. In the peripheral areas of China the upheaval meant a growth of separatist movements and the eventual actual separation of these areas from China. Outer Mongolia proclaimed its autonomy in 1911–12. The Mongolian princes considered Tuva as legitimately falling within their territory; they even began to recruit soldiers among the Tuvinians.

Now the Russian legation in Peking became insistent. "The political circumstances are auspicious," Shchekin, the Russian chargé d'affaires, wrote from Peking to St. Petersburg, and "Russia's rights are beyond any doubt." Sazonov transmitted this dispatch to the Tsar, adding that in his opinion the annexation of Tuva would be neither justifiable nor opportune. But the Tsar did not share his minister's caution; Nicholas II made a blunt notation on Sa-

14. *International Relations*, Series 3, II, 211 (November 21, 1911).

zonov's report: "I, on the contrary, am in full agreement with the chargé d'affaires in Peking . . . We must proceed to resolve this business in a more active manner, or else we shall never do ourselves any good along the Chinese border." [15]

The Tsar's remarks could not be disregarded; besides, Sazonov faced advocates of the same aggressive policy among his fellow ministers. In 1913 it was decided to appoint a special "border commissioner" for Tuva; he was meant to be the Russian governor of the coveted province. The next step was to be the establishment of a formal Russian protectorate over Tuva. Nor was this step taken without sharp disagreements within the Russian Cabinet.

Outer Mongolia, now detached from China and having been formally proclaimed an autonomous state, claimed jurisdiction over Tuva. Tuva had been under Chinese-Mongolian administrative control, and the people of Tuva—or at least that part which was politically articulate—likewise desired to become a part of the Mongolian nation since both Russia and China had often caused bad blood in the country. Now Russian policy aimed its arrows against the unification of Tuva with Mongolia—a policy formulated in 1913–14 and continued in all its details by the Soviet Government from 1921 on. The reason was that Outer Mongolia, large in territory and better known to the world, had to be recognized as an autonomous organism, while small and obscure Tuva could easily be annexed by Russia.

In 1913 the authorities of two Tuvinian provinces (out of a total of five) were persuaded to appeal to the Russian Tsar to accept these *khoshuns* (provinces) into the Russian Empire. The Governor General of Irkutsk reported, at the time, that he forwarded the petition to the government in St. Petersburg, that he had taken the necessary measures to prevent Tuva from merging with Mongolia. Sazonov again opposed the incorporation of Tuva into the Russian Empire, advocating instead the establishment of a Russian protectorate. After prolonged debates among the cabinet ministers, Sazonov's views prevailed. On April 11, 1914, Tsar Nicholas put his "Agree" on Sazonov's memorandum, but the cautious Sazonov instructed the Siberian authorities not to make public the impending change in Tuva's status. A Russian official, Mintslov, was dispatched to Tuva in April, 1914, having been in-

---

15. *Krasnyi Arkhiv*, XVIII, 96–97.

structed to pose as an archeologist. "Our plan," he later wrote, "consisted of the quiet occupation of the region by Russians and the acquisition of de facto possession." [16]

As a result of the activities of Russian agents, the Amban Gombodorchzhi from Tuva addressed to the Tsar a pledge that Tuva would never seek contact with Mongolia and other powers:

1914, July 4.
Year of Barsa 5 Moon 25 Day

From the Chief Tannu of the Uryankhais of the Khoshuns of Oinar, Salchzhak, Tochzhin, the Amban Gombodorchzhi, in possession of the award of the Order of St. Stanislaus, second degree, and of a gold medal for wearing around the neck from the great Russian State, and in possession of the title and seal of corps commander and a peacock feather from the great State of Taitsin [China]—

WARRANT

In receipt of a written announcement through the chief of border affairs, Saita Tsererin, concerning the most gracious deigning of your Imperial Majesty, Nikolai Alexandrovich, to accept five khoshuns of Uryankhai into the protection of Russia, I, Amban Gombodorchzhi, filled with joy and reverence, have given prayers and henceforth, as a faithful and humble servant, shall have no independent, direct contact with Mongolia and other foreign powers whatsoever. If such contact shall be required, so I oblige myself to conduct all negotiations through the representative of the Russian Government residing in Uryankhai, and to submit to his decision all controversies and misunderstandings which may arise amongst the various khoshuns of Uryankhai. At the same time, I most humbly beg to leave to our Uryankhai population their customs, the Buddhist religion, which they practice, their way of life, self-government, ranks, and nomad camps, permitting no special alterations, which would tend toward a loss of power. [17]

On August 1 the World War began. Now Russia's agents were free to act in Tuva. During the Great War no one outside Russia would care about developments in a far-off corner of central Asia. Firm measures were adopted to hitch Tuva's fate to the Russian chariot. Grigoriev, the first Russian commissar of Tuva, fought

16. *International Relations*, Series 3, II, 210–212, 282; and S. Mintslov, *Sekretnoye Porucheniye*, p. 6.
17. *International Relations*, Series 3, IV, 327.

the Tuvinian trend toward incorporation into Mongolia; he ruled with a "strong hand" until the outbreak of the Revolution in Russia.

In 1915 the application of Russian civil and criminal codes was extended to Tuva. In 1916 the demand of Mongolia for permission for their agents to enter Tuva was turned down by Russia; Cossacks were again dispatched there, and a multitude of arrests among the native population were carried out.[18] Russian immigration and resettlement made considerable progress from 1912 to 1917.

The Revolution in Russia did not immediately affect this state of affairs. The first period of the Revolution was too brief, the government too much preoccupied with the war in Europe and with domestic issues to pay much attention to the problems of Inner Asia. Important events did not begin to occur in Tuva until 1918. Sharing the fate of Outer Mongolia, Tuva was again occupied by Chinese troops and deprived of its extensive autonomy. Chinese control did not last long, though, for early in the twenties the Red Army established Soviet control over the newly created Republic of Tannu Tuva.

BARGA

Barga, in the northwest of Manchuria and bordering on Russia and Outer Mongolia, was another area coveted by Russia and a source of Russo-Chinese conflicts. In some ways resembling the development of Uryankhai (Tuva), Barga occupied a great area (60,000 square miles) but on the eve of the first World War had a population of only 30,000 to 40,000. In the thirties it was estimated at about 70,000, with about half of it Mongolian and about a quarter Chinese; Russian émigrés made up about 10 to 12 per cent of the population.

Just as in Mongolia, a conflict arose in Barga over the immigration of Chinese peasants seeking to divide and occupy the pastures of the Mongolian cattle breeders. This conflict between Chinese agricultural settlers and native cattle drivers was at the root of the general unrest and separatist movements among all the non-Chinese nationalities of North China. In 1906 China began stationing mili-

18. R. Kabo, *Ocherki istorii i ekonomiki Tuvy;* and Korostovets, *op. cit.,* pp. 194 ff.

tary forces in Barga and raised new taxes; and in 1911, on the eve of the Chinese Revolution, Peking ordered the schools in Barga to be conducted in the Chinese language. The nationalist movement all over Mongolia violently reacted to these measures, and while Outer Mongolia then gained autonomy, the local chieftains in Barga requested Peking to remove the Chinese troops and stop the Chinese colonization of their region. When the Chinese Government refused, an uprising ensued, and the local leaders, after ousting the Chinese troops, turned to Russia as the natural protector and supporter in their conflict with Peking.

In the meantime a revolutionary government had replaced the Manchu dynasty; with the backing of Russia, peripheral provinces were attempting to detach themselves from the body politic of China. In May, 1912, Foreign Minister Sazonov ordered his envoy in Peking to warn the Chinese against sending troops "into the regions of interest to us," and in particular to Barga. Simultaneously the Russian Government instructed its special border guards not to permit Chinese troops to enter Hailar, capital of Barga. Actually Russia thus underwrote complete autonomy for Barga from China.

The intentions of Russia went beyond mere autonomy for Barga, however, such as had been conceded to Outer Mongolia. The plan called for the outright annexation of North Manchuria at an appropriate moment; and with it Barga was to be incorporated into the Russian Empire. This is why the Russian Government did not approve of the merger of predominantly Mongol Barga with Outer Mongolia. The Russian program for Barga was outlined by the Russian envoy, Krupensky, in a dispatch to the consul in Hailar:

Barga will share the fate of northern Manchuria [he wrote], and that is why we have not included it in autonomous Mongolia and have consented in principle to the re-establishment of Chinese sovereignty there. However, the latter must take place by virtue of peaceful negotiations in which the Imperial Government will assume the role of middleman. On the other hand, the subjection of Barga [to China] by force of arms would affect Russian interests too much for us to remain indifferent.

Negotiations were conducted early in 1914. Among the demands raised by Russia was the administration of Barga by its own nationals, Russian priority in railway building, and Russia's threat not to recognize any agreement between China and Barga unless concluded with knowledge.

China refused to accept these demands, which would have given Barga complete autonomy. Yet Russian pressure remained strong, and Russian troops were stationed near by. In November, 1915, during the World War, an agreement was signed with China by which Barga obtained considerable autonomy.[19] Barga, the agreement said, was to constitute "a special district of the Chinese Republic," into which immigration of Chinese was, however, to be restricted. According to the agreement, the Chinese Government was to be empowered to send its troops into Barga, but only after advance notice had been given to Russia. By the same accord, Russia acquired priority rights for the construction of railroads in Barga.

For all intents and purposes Barga was on the way to becoming a part of one of the provinces of Siberia. The Russian Revolution interrupted this trend, and during the civil war Chinese troops returned to North Manchuria and reoccupied Barga. A number of Russians fleeing from the Red guerrillas crossed the Amur River and settled in the adjoining area of Barga, right across the frontier. These "White Guardists," as they were called in the Soviet press, for a considerable time remained a thorn in the flesh of the Soviet authorities.

During the 1920's Barga was formally under the rule of Chang Tso-lin, the Manchurian dictator, and later under his son and successor, Chang Hsueh-liang. In 1928 Mongolian cavalry detachments sometimes advanced as far as Hailar. When the armed conflict broke out in 1929 over the Chinese Eastern Railway, it was Mongolians armed with Soviet rifles who occupied Hailar. After the creation of Manchukuo, Barga found itself under Japanese control until in August, 1945, it was occupied by Soviet troops and soon became a part of the large area controlled by the Chinese Communists.

19. *International Relations*, Series 2, XXI, 85; Series 3, I, 72, 232–233, 352, 471–472 (May 29, 1912; January 20, February 6, February 19, March 2, 1914); and *China Year Book, 1921*, pp. 580 ff.

SINKIANG

Ili and the other regions of Sinkiang were, as we have seen, restored to China after 1881, and for some time Russia did not dispute Chinese sovereignty over Sinkiang. Relations between Russia and Sinkiang were largely economic for the following quarter of a century, and the turnover of trade rose to 7 million rubles before the first World War—a high mark under the circumstances.

Nonetheless the Russian Government as well as its consuls in Sinkiang continued to treat the Ili district, occupied by Russia in the seventies, as a potential Russian possession. "Our border patrols who had occupied Kuldja were convinced the region would remain in Russian hands," the Russian consul in Sinkiang reported. Fiodorov, the consul in Kuldja, wrote that "the Ili district is an agricultural country suited for the settlement of a great number of immigrants, and it would be of importance to us if a purely Russian population were to settle here." [20]

Actually the Russian Government did not observe the borderline restrictions too meticulously. Thus, for example, military maneuvers were engaged in on the Chinese side of the Ili region near Kuldja. Immediately after the fall of the monarchy in China, military forces were actually moved into the Altai section of Sinkiang.

In January, 1912, War Minister Sukhomlinov suggested the dispatch of Russian troops to Ili, but this proposal met with opposition from Sazonov, the Foreign Minister. The government decided to follow the course suggested by Sazonov. Only a force of 200 Cossacks was dispatched to Kuldja "in view of the anarchy threatening" there. Soon other Russian troops arrived in the Altai region too. The Russian Government also supported the request of two companies for a mining concession in the Ili district, and Foreign Minister Sazonov suggested a loan to the local administration to the extent of the comparatively large sum of two million rubles.

Peking demanded the withdrawal of Russian forces from various parts of China (including Sinkiang), which had become a sphere

20. *Zapiski zastennovo Kitaya*, p. 109; *Sbornik konsul'skikh donesenii* (1906), p. 376; *Svedeniya turkestanskovo General'-novo Shtaba* (1901); quoted by Fuad Kazak, *Ost-turkistan zwischen den Grossmächten* (Osteuropäische Forschungen, Königsberg, 1937), pp. 64 ff.

of Russia's special interest and in which autonomist movements were thriving with the backing of St. Petersburg. Now the Russian envoy, Krupensky, offered China conditions on which Russia would withdraw.[21] They included: the right of the native population to be governed by their own national authorities (i.e., the withdrawal of the Chinese from the Altai); and the right of Russian citizens to settle and acquire land (which meant Russian colonization in the Altai and Ili). China rejected these terms, but Minister Sazonov wrote his envoy in Peking that Russia saw no need to press for a rapid solution of the issue. At this point he reiterated the formula for Russian expansion in Asia: China must "recognize, with all the ensuing consequences which derive from the geographic propinquity, the close economic ties which have been established between these regions and Russian territory." [22]

This was the time when Britain was anxious to win Russian approval of the formal recognition of Tibet as part of the British sphere of influence, and the Russian envoy to China characteristically proposed agreement with the British demand on condition that northern Sinkiang be recognized as part of the Russian sphere, with Kashgaria, to the south, going to Britain.[23] Only the outbreak of the World War prevented the successful conclusion of the negotiations.

With the outbreak of Revolution in China, Sinkiang attained virtual independence. The frail bonds that still connected it with the government in Peking were further weakened when the revolutionary regime of Yuan Shi-kai failed to provide the usual appropriation for the upkeep of the western province and was unable to supply the military forces required for the internal and external needs of Sinkiang. The new governor of Sinkiang, Yeng Tsenghsin, was appointed by Peking, but he actually enjoyed full freedom in governing his realm; he did so in a most autocratic manner.

Sinkiang's independence meant the absence of military aid from the outside—a circumstance which made it easy for Russia to occupy an area in the north, as we have seen above. However, as soon as the World War broke out, the pressure from Russia ceased, and with the coming of the Russian Revolution, there was no longer

21. *International Relations*, Series 2, XIX[II], 409.
22. *International Relations*, Series 3, IV, 137 (July 6, 1914).
23. *Ibid.*, Series 3, I, 566. Krupensky to Sazonov, March 11, 1914.

any evidence of a Russian threat to Sinkiang's independence. It was because of the combined effect of the two revolutions that Sinkiang, without an army of its own, without foreign alliances, and without any trade of significant proportions, enjoyed an independent existence for the next decade.

TIBET

Tibet, another part of the vast Asiatic vacuum, never loomed large in the Russian designs for a sphere in China. Located far away from the borders of Russia, Tibet tended to gravitate toward British India rather than toward Russia. From time to time, however, its name appeared among the parts of China which St. Petersburg considered to be of especial interest to Russia; whenever the energies and the dynamism of the empire turned east—as, for instance, between 1895 and 1905, and between 1911 and 1913 —the Tibetan issue regularly appeared on the agenda.

In the original though vague Russian projects of the 1890's, the Tsar manifested personal interest in Tibet. There were no Russian diplomatic or consular agents in that country, and it was the Russian consuls in North India who reported occasionally on developments in the adjoining Chinese territory, which was rapidly being permeated by British trade and political influence.

In 1904 a British military mission succeeded in gaining decisive influence on Tibetan politics, and the Dalai Lama, religious leader as well as head of state, was forced to flee and did not return to Lhasa until 1909; he spent one year of his exile in Mongolia, where he conferred with local princes about the chances of separating both Mongolia and Tibet from China. The Dalai Lama conditioned his support of the separatist movement on the attitude of Russia, whose assistance would have been indispensable for the success of the anti-Chinese movement. In March, 1905, the Lama appealed to the Tsar asking him to "assume protection" over Tibet. The Russian Government refused but extended the right of asylum to the high guest.

"Dalai Lama has most definite plans concerning the political unification of Mongolia with Tibet," the Russian consul wrote from Urga. "These two countries, if united, must free themselves from Chinese rule." At that time, however, Russia was in no position to encourage these plans. The war with Japan had just ended in an impressive defeat, and Russia was forced to withdraw its feelers from Tibet. In May, 1906, Foreign Minister Isvolsky wrote to the Tsar that "no plans concerning Tibet should be made." [24]

The following year Britain and Russia concluded a comprehensive agreement defining their spheres in the Near East and central Asia. According to this treaty, Chinese sovereignty over Tibet was reaffirmed by both Russia and Britain; yet Britain acquired a privileged position in Tibet.

For a few years Tibet disappeared from Russia's diplomatic exchanges, while Britain proceeded to further its ties between India and the virtual no man's land to the north. Tibet reappeared in Russo-British negotiations when the disintegration of the Chinese Empire started in 1911, signaling a new Russian campaign for the extension of its sphere of interest in the East. As a result of a punitive Chinese expedition in 1910–11, in which Chinese troops plundered and ransacked Tibet, the Dalai Lama was again compelled to flee. Once more he turned to Russia, begging for help against both China and Britain. "Do not refuse to help us in Tibetan affairs, which have always bordered [*sic*] on Russian affairs," he wrote to a Russian diplomat. His request for aid was promptly turned down. The Russian envoys to India and China hoped, however, that a way would be found to increase Russian influence in Tibet. "Sooner or later," the Russian envoy, Shchekin, wrote home, "the Dalai Lama is bound to learn about the events in Urga [Outer Mongolia has just been separated from China]; he will then contact the Khutukhtu, and these contacts cannot but become interesting for us."

In February, 1912, the Russian consul in Calcutta, Ravelotti, transmitted to the Dalai Lama a reply from the Tsar. While loyally informing the British authorities of his trip across their sphere, he reported to his government in quite a different vein:

The sincerity of our policy in Tibet [Ravelotti wrote] is well known to the Tibetan people, whereas the British intention of annexing Tibet sooner or later to their system of buffer states is no secret either . . . [Therefore] His Majesty's letter, which was a ray of hope for His Holiness, gave him courage and comfort to continue the struggle against the vagaries of fate. The knowledge that the Russian Tsar *does not forget the lot of the people of Tibet* serves as a greater moral sup-

24. *Novyi vostok*, XX–XXI, 39 ff.

port than the 1,000 rupies which the Indian Government pays monthly for the subversion of the spirit of the ruler of Tibet.

In October, 1912, Foreign Secretary Edward Grey met with the Russian Foreign Minister, Sazonov; he suggested an agreement by which Outer Mongolia would be recognized as a part of the Russian, and Tibet as a part of the British sphere. Sazonov refused: he was resolved to demand another *quid pro quo* for Russia if Britain should press for the recognition of Tibet as her own. In the course of the ensuing negotiations the Russian plan became clear. St. Petersburg demanded, in compensation for the recognition of British control over Tibet, British acquiescence in the Russian sphere in North China.

These negotiations and discussions led nowhere, primarily because of the outbreak of the war in Europe in 1914. Tibet disappeared from the list of unsolved Russo-British issues, and after 1917 Tibet did not re-emerge among the territories claimed or demanded by the Soviet Union.[25]

RUSSIA IN CHINA AT THE TIME OF THE REVOLUTION

Writing in 1917 about the international relations of China, Sun Yat-sen, the father of the Chinese Revolution, estimated that the Russian sphere of interest in China, extending over Outer Mongolia, Sinkiang, and North Manchuria, constituted about 42 per cent of the whole of China's territory. British influence extended over Tibet, Szechwan, and the Yangtze Valley—about 28 per cent of China. French influence covered the two southernmost provinces, while the Japanese sphere comprised South Manchuria, the eastern part of Inner Mongolia, Shantung, and Fukien; the French and Japanese spheres each represented over 5 per cent of China's lands.[26]

Russia's 42 per cent was, however, limited mainly to desert areas and arid wastes of Inner Asia (see Map V), whose population made up but 3 to 4 per cent of the people of China. On the eve of the revolution in Russia, it seemed that the time was near when her geopolitical program would be fulfilled—with the Gobi Desert forming the new frontier between Russia and China, and the latter reduced to her old ethnic provinces.

25. Cf. Korostovets, *op. cit.*; Grover Clark, *Tibet, China and Great Britain* (1924).
26. Sun Yat-sen, *China and Japan* (Shanghai, 1941), p. 20.

VI

The Russian Revolution and the Far East

No revolution in history was involved in such a multitude of international problems as was the Russian Revolution of 1917. When it broke out, German and Austrian armies stood deep inside Russia's borders, while Russia herself was tied up with her allies through a number of treaties concerned with the conduct of the common war and the peace aims. During the eight months of its existence, until the Soviet Revolution occurred, the Provisional Government, created in March, 1917, moved from one crisis to another, in each of which problems of foreign policy played an outstanding, sometimes a decisive, role.

The moderate political elements that constituted the first Provisional Government were inclined to consider the great upheaval as an issue of internal policy. In international affairs the government tried to continue the prerevolutionary line based on a firm alliance with England and France and the continuation of the war to the point of final victory. It also tried to keep in force all agreements and treaties, both public and secret, which after the war would have given Russia the right to annex certain German, Austro-Hungarian, and Turkish territories. Pavel Milyukov, the leader of the Constitutional Democrats (Cadets) became Minister of Foreign Affairs. On the whole, he had supported Minister Sazonov's wartime policy; more than once he had tried to popularize the idea that Russia must expand to the west and south after the war.

From the very outset, this policy of the Provisional Government met with strong opposition on the part of the leftist parties. The program was unpopular—a war for the annexation of foreign territories was felt to be an imperialist war; sacrifices and privations for a war of this kind were resented. A great popular movement arose for "a war without annexations and indemnities." The movement developed swiftly and gathered great strength.

The setting up of soviets (councils) was the result of tremendous political activity and enthusiasm in all levels of Russian society. Like the first soviets created during the Revolution of 1905, the new ones were composed mainly of workers' (and soldiers') deputies representing these popular currents. There was essentially nothing undemocratic about a soviet. At first the Petrograd soviet was dominated by the Socialist parties, the Mensheviks and the Social-Revolutionaries. The Bolsheviks (the term "Communist" was not yet in official use) constituted a small minority whose ideas were originally somewhat vague. In its manifesto of March 27, 1917, the Soviet proclaimed its anti-imperialist program with an appeal to all the peoples of the world: "The time has come to begin a determined struggle against the thieving tendencies of the governments . . . Democratic Russia will be no menace to freedom and civilization."

In this manifesto there was a note of strong opposition to the foreign policy of the Provisional Government. Alexander Kerensky, the only man from the "left" included in the first Provisional Government, was also vice-president of the soviet. In one of his first statements as a Minister, Kerensky took issue with the program of his colleague, Pavel Milyukov, and demanded not only independence for Poland and Russian Armenia but also a renunciation of the claim to the Dardanelles and the adjoining area (conceded by Britain to Russia in a secret agreement of 1915); instead, he proposed international control of the Straits. His interview with the correspondent of a London newspaper aroused great interest in England, and the Russian Ambassador in London inquired of Milyukov whether "a reduction of Russian claims is to be expected." Milyukov told the Ambassador to explain that such an interpretation was incorrect; in a note to the Allied Governments of May 1, 1917, Milyukov again stated that the Russian Government was resolved not only to "continue the war until complete victory" but also to "achieve the necessary guarantees," i.e., security against future attacks by territorial acquisitions from the three enemy states. As these terms covered all former Russian territorial claims, Milyukov's statement brought about the first great crisis of the Provisional Government.

On May 15 the Petrograd soviet issued a new appeal in which it stated that "a peace without annexations and indemnities is the program to be agreed upon by the toilers of all nations, belligerent or neutral, to achieve a stable peace." Milyukov had to resign from the government.

In the meantime the popular movement had attained considerable force. Under the leadership of Lenin who had returned to Russia in April, 1917, the Bolshevik party was growing rapidly. It fully supported the movement for "a peace without annexations and indemnities"; it also strongly opposed acquisition of the Dardanelles. The party, however, soon ceased to discuss war programs and began practically to demand peace at any price. Political strikes and street demonstrations occurred one after the other.

The new Provisional Government, formed in May, was more radical than the first; in addition to Kerensky, a few other Socialists were included in it. Accepting the slogan of the soviet, the government said, in its first declaration, on May 18, 1917: "The Provisional Government aims at the speediest conclusion of peace without annexations and indemnities, based on the self-determination of peoples." On June 16, the new Minister of Foreign Affairs, Mikhail Tereshchenko, officially announced to the Allied governments that Russia was renouncing all claims to foreign territories and proposed a conference of the Allied governments to reconsider war aims.

In the meantime the army was in process of disintegration; desertions rose to enormous proportions; officers were frequently mistreated by their own men and new ones were elected. The national economy was nearing a state of collapse. The government's last attempt to save the situation was the July offensive on the German-Austrian front. It ended in a serious defeat. From that time on events took their inevitable course. The strength of the Bolshevik movement increased at a swift tempo. The party now had the support of the bulk of the disintegrating army, anxious to return home. Consequently the point of view of the soviets gradually moved toward the left, and soon the Bolshevik party was in control of the soviets in the most important cities. On November 7, 1917, the Bolshevik party seized power in Petrograd and proclaimed the Soviet state; it dominated the Congress of Soviets, which convened at the same time.

The program of "a peace without annexations and indemnities" was still the main idea of the young Soviet Government. In one of its first decrees, on November 11, 1917, it proposed to all the belligerent nations "immediately to start peace negotiations" and added: "The government considers a just peace to be one without annexations, without the seizure of foreign lands, without the forced inclusion of foreign nationalities, and without indemnities."

Still more outspoken was the message of the Soviet Government of December 17, 1917, (its author was Joseph Stalin), addressed "to all toiling Moslems of Russia and the East":

A republican Russia and her government, the Soviet of People's Commissars, are against the seizure of foreign lands: Constantinople must remain in the possession of the Moslems . . .

. . . The [Russo-British] treaty concerning the division of Persia is null and void. The Persians will have the right freely to determine their fate.

The [inter-Allied] treaty concerning the partition of Turkey is null and void. The Armenians will have the right freely to determine their fate.

In the meantime, the disintegration of the Russian state proceeded at a rapid pace. When the Germans began peace negotiations with the Soviet delegates in Brest-Litovsk, they dealt with an enemy deprived of an army, of administrative machinery, and of rich territories.

NO ANNEXATIONS?

No other Russian party ever went so far as did the Bolsheviks in calling for "self-determination of nations." Lenin's program provided not only for autonomy for every people within the Soviet state, but also for the right of secession; quite a few nationality groups availed themselves of the newly promulgated privilege. On the other hand, no other party strove so hard to establish a great Soviet state. The Bolsheviks felt that while secession of nations and areas from Russia was sometimes inevitable, it was still a backward step and every attempt should be made to prevent the loss of one foot of the soil of the former empire. In the calamitous years 1917–20, the separation of national minorities formerly within the Russian state became an outstanding trend. Lenin was essentially opposed to the separation of the Baltic States or Finland from the Soviet state and more than once local Communist uprisings tried to reunite these areas with Soviet Russia. In his war against Poland in 1920 Lenin's object was to achieve control of that nation in order to keep direct contact with Germany. He openly proclaimed the right of the Soviet state to conduct aggressive wars and opposed those who favored pure "wars of defense" in contrast to "wars of conquest." "These are," he said, "words which lost their meaning long ago, words of petit bourgeois pacifism . . . We would be not only fools but even criminals if we promised never to commit acts which could be considered aggressive in a military-strategic sense."

For a correct understanding of later Soviet policy in general, and in the Far East in particular, it should be borne in mind that the same ideas have been at the core of Stalin's foreign policy, too: in the Constitution, recognition of every nationality's right "freely to determine its way of life" and, at the same time, uncompromising resistance to all efforts at separatism and a constant effort to create a strong Soviet state by all the means available, including war.

Only the people themselves have the right to determine their fate; nobody may interfere forcefully in the life of a people. A nation can organize its affairs as it pleases. It can organize its life on the basis of autonomy. It can enter into a federation with other nations. It has the right to secede completely. The nation is sovereign and all nations are equal.[1]

In Stalin's eyes, however, this sovereignty of nations does not constitute the highest of principles; it can be violated if it blocks the development of the Communist movement or a Communist government.

There are cases [Stalin said in 1923] when the right of self-determination enters into conflict with another, a higher, principle, namely, the right of the working class [i.e. the Communist party] to strengthen its regime once it has achieved power. In such a case—and this must be frankly stated—the right of self-determination cannot and must not serve as a barrier to the realization of the right of the working class to its dictatorship. *The first right must yield to the second.* Such was, for instance, the case in 1920, when we were forced to march on Warsaw in order to defend the power of the working class.[2]

1. Stalin, *Marxism and the National and Colonial Question.*
2. Speech at the Twelfth Congress of the Communist Party.

In fact, the Russo-Polish war of 1920 gave Lenin's government the choice between two principles: either national self-determination or forcible exportation of Soviet rule. The overwhelming majority of Poles, including Polish workers, were definitely opposed to the Soviet regime. The Moscow government, of which Stalin was a member, defied the Anglo-Polish peace offers and ordered the Red Army to proceed against Warsaw and on to Germany. The campaign ended in a Soviet defeat.

Aggrandizement of the Soviet state is the highest of all principles; it overshadows the sovereignty of nations. During the first period of Soviet history, because of the weakness of the new state, it was rather the independence of nations that was stressed in its foreign policy. But even at that time the other tendency was manifest. Both were clearly observable in the relationships with China and Japan.

JAPANESE INTERVENTION

Japan was among those of Russia's allies of the first World War that benefited from the internal and military collapse of the former Russian Empire.

Everything that occurred in the Far East since 1914 seemed to strengthen the growing conviction in Japan that she was chosen by the gods to rule at least a great part of the world. The sequence of unexpected developments was wonderful indeed. In 1914 the German possessions in China fell to Japan. The German Pacific archipelagoes followed. In 1915 China virtually agreed to Japan's having a predominant influence on the conduct of Chinese external affairs. The disintegration of China and the weakness of the rival groups served to strengthen Japan's position. The entry of the United States into the European war left Japan practically unchecked in the Far East. The prosperous condition of her trade and industry gave her the means necessary for a rapid development of her army and navy. Finally, the revolutionary events in Russia and the weakening of Russia's influence in the Far East removed the pressure exerted by the only other great continental power in the adjoining lands.

The collapse of Russia, which was a source of great anxiety to the United States, Britain, and France, was a boon for Japan. If the Russian Far East could, in one way or another, be brought under control, the Japanese possessions could be rounded out by the addition of a long stretch of land and water from Formosa to Kamchatka; it would then not be long before a gigantic Japanese Empire would be able to dominate the continent of Asia as well as the Pacific Ocean.

After the Revolution in Russia there was relative quiet in the international relations of the Far East which lasted for exactly one year. During this year Japan watched the situation carefully, but made no decisive move. In June, 1917, months before the Soviet upheaval, the Russian Provisional Government received reports from Vladivostok of the arrival from Korea of Japanese spies and gendarmes disguised as laborers. A month later the Japanese Minister of Foreign Affairs inquired of the Russian Ambassador concerning possible mining concessions for foreign financial groups in the Russian Far East. After the local soviets started to seize power in the cities of the Far East, the first Japanese naval vessels appeared near Vladivostok. And then, on April 5, 1918, the first Japanese troops landed on Russian territory. They were, however, few in numbers. The invasion was of a tentative nature—Japan wanted to see just how weak Russia was. The Soviet Government made an official protest, but without success. Because of the separate peace which she had signed with Germany and Austria a few weeks earlier, Russia's position was especially unfavorable.

A further act in Japan's carefully prepared campaign in the Russian Far East was the signing of new agreements with China. The first of these, which was concluded on March 3, 1918, called for joint action in Siberia. Two military agreements (May 16, and September 6, 1918) and one naval agreement (May 19, 1918) followed. By their terms Chinese forces were placed under Japanese command for this operation, and the Chinese Eastern Railway was to assist in the transportation of troops.

Relations between the Allies and Russia deteriorated rapidly, and in the summer of 1918 military intervention in Europe was decided upon; Japan's actions in the Far East, however, were contrary to the Allies' policies, especially to those of the United States. By way of a compromise between American opposition to intervention in Siberia and Japan's insistence upon it, the Supreme War Council decided on July 2, 1918, that a joint operation was to take place in which not only the United States and Japan, but China, Great Britain, France, and Czechoslovakia were to participate. The official reasons given for the landing of foreign troops on Russian soil in the Far East were the safeguarding of the free transportation of the Czechoslovak Legion through Siberia to Vladivostok, and protection against possible actions of German and Austrian prisoners of war against the Allies. The latter argument was only a pretext.

The Czechoslovak Legion, formed in Russia and composed of Austro-Hungarian prisoners of war, was, after the Russian-German armistice, the only military force on Russian soil under Allied control; it retained a certain amount of arms and its military discipline was good. At first the Legion had tried to play a political role in Russia by allying itself with the democratic anti-Soviet elements, but later it abstained from taking sides in the civil war; it desired evacuation through the only possible outlet—the Far East.

On August 8, 1918, the Japanese landing began on a large scale, and soon not only the Far East but also the Trans-Baikalian region was occupied by Japan. American troops arrived a week later. Lacking the men and the arms with which to oppose the foreign troops, the local conference of the Communist party decided on August 28 to cease all frontal resistance and to limit its activity to guerrilla warfare. In September, 1918, there was no longer any Soviet local or regional authority left in the Far East. The Communist party was then weak in the Far East; it counted only a few thousand members in the entire area east of the Baikal.

In order properly to understand the situation that existed during the Soviet upheavals in Europe as well as in Asia, it is well to remember that even in 1922, after their victory in the civil war, the Communists constituted only about one half of 1 per cent of the population of central Russia and western Siberia; in the Far East the percentage was only .13 per cent. According to official party statistics there were in 1922, in the area east of the Baikal, about 8,000 party members and 5,000 "candidates" (members in the probation period); in 1918–21 the number was undoubtedly smaller. But these 8,000 to 13,000 men actually controlled the immense country from Irkutsk to the Pacific; they led armies, waged battles, won victories, negotiated treaties, and set up governments.

The civil war which began in 1918 created a barrier between

Moscow and the Far East. The eastern regions of European Russia and the whole of Siberia were controlled by anti-Soviet regimes. The "White" forces fighting the young Red Army were led by generals and officers of the old tsarist army, while the rank and file consisted mainly of mobilized or remobilized peasants from the areas where they were active. They were given a measure of support from Russia's former allies; this help was scant, however, and the armies remained poorly equipped and badly armed.

The government of Adm. Alexander Kolchak, recognized by the powers in November, 1918, as the legitimate Russian Government, became the main force opposing the Red armies. There was no way of dispatching Soviet troops to the Far East. Far Eastern affairs took their own course, while the Soviet Government had recourse only to official protests, diplomatic notes, manifestoes, and to a political campaign inside Russia and abroad. This of course had little effect on the policy of Japan.

The attitude of the Russian population to the Japanese military intervention was strongly negative—far more negative than it was toward the French and British intervention in Europe. There was clear comprehension that neither Britain nor France intended to annex any part of Russian territory, that Japan's aim, on the other hand, was precisely the extension of her empire over eastern Siberia. Among Russia's political parties opinion was divided regarding British-French policy in Russia and even among the leaders of the large Social-Revolutionary party, an influential group was favorably inclined toward the Allied intervention; only the Mensheviks were firmly opposed to it. There was no doubt, however, of the attitude to the Japanese occupation in the Far East. In its opposition to Japan, the Soviet Government had the overwhelming majority of the people behind it.

Russian White armies operated in different parts of eastern Siberia. Admiral Kolchak had his headquarters at Omsk, western Siberia; under him, operating in the east, were Generals Kalmykov, Kappel, Rozanov, Sakharov, and others. In North Manchuria General Horvath controlled the Chinese Eastern Railway. The White troops in Trans-Baikalia were led by Ataman (later General) Semionov, the most important and best known among the White leaders in the Far East. He continued his activities after the collapse of his armies, and throughout the twenties and thirties worked in

close contact with the Japanese. In 1945 he, along with a group
of other White leaders, was arrested during the advance of the
Red Army; after a trial in August, 1946, Semionov was executed.
Great sections of the population fled to China and settled permanently in Manchuria, Peking, and Shanghai, since the civil war
in eastern Siberia was often atrociously cruel.

In 1919 the Siberian railroad to the east of the Baikal was taken
over by an Inter-Allied Railway Commission.

Japanese troops far outnumbered all other Allied forces taken
together. The intervention in fact was a Japanese rather than an
Allied intervention. Japanese industrial and commercial firms expanded into the Russian Far East, Russian ships were taken over by
Japanese shipping houses, power stations and other "concessions"
were acquired by Japanese companies. It was obvious that Japan
intended to stay in the Far East indefinitely and considered the
area as her future protectorate. Unlike the other Allies, Japan did
not actually support the Russian Government which had been
officially recognized; it gave no aid to Admiral Kolchak. On the
contrary, Japan supported the "autonomy" of small pro-Japanese
Russian armies among whom the troops of General Semionov were
the most important. A future strong and united Russia, as advocated
by France and the United States, was not favored by Japan. Her
interests were far better served by a multitude of Russian regimes
with small armies and a succession of struggles.

Early in 1920 the policy of the Allies began to change. The
military intervention, unpopular among the Allied countries, could
not be justified after the signing of the Versailles Treaty. The
blockade of Russia had never been popular. The White armies had
suffered heavy defeats in Siberia. Kolchak's troops disintegrated
completely, and the Admiral himself was captured at Irkutsk and
executed in February, 1920. The evacuation of the Czechoslovaks
had been completed in the meantime. There was no longer any
plausible reason for the presence of Allied troops on Russia's Far
Eastern soil.

Japan did not intend, however, to relinquish her acquisitions.
Because of this attitude a great political and diplomatic warfare
started which lasted for more than two years and ended in Japan's
withdrawal in 1922. Among the Great Powers, Japan's main antagonist in this struggle was the Government of the United States.

THE UNITED STATES IN THE FAR EAST

The American policy in the Far East has been a policy of a "balance of powers" and it is so today. No other American policy in the Far East has, in fact, been possible.

Basically the Far Eastern problem is the relationship between its three great nations—Russia, Japan, and China. Two of them, Russia and Japan, are Great Powers; the third, China, is unable to rival her neighbors in national strength. So long as the two Great Powers are able, even while competing between themselves, to balance one another, check the other's moves, stop the other's advance, no danger threatens the security of the Western Hemisphere. The situation becomes alarming only when one of the countries achieves great superiority over the other, in which case unification of the whole Far East and of the western Pacific under one power becomes a possibility. Such a development would constitute a danger for America's trade as well as for the security of her western shores.

The superiority of one Far Eastern power over the other always becomes evident in China before reaching its next, more dangerous stage. Weak China is the first testing ground of the rivalry between Japan and Russia. Before attacking the strong enemy, an attempt to advance into China discloses the reaction of the rival and demonstrates his potential strength. Russia's drive against Japan inevitably starts on Chinese soil. Japanese drives against Russia begin by attempting to conquer China. The independence of China is the pivot of a balance of powers in the Far East. The United States, interested in maintaining this balance, is set to support the independence of China.

At the beginning of this century, when Russia's force appeared overwhelming and her drive into northern China apparently met with no resistance, the United States supported Japan. Indeed, had Russia been victorious in her drive into northern China in 1900–1903, Korea would easily have fallen to her; isolated Japan might then have been defeated and a great Far Eastern empire, controlled from St. Petersburg, would have emerged to expand, eventually, to the western Pacific. In the war of 1904–5, Japan, with the support of the United States, defeated Russia.

Over a period of eight years (1906–14) therefore, Russia and

Japan, collaborating or competing with one another, actually balanced each other. During this time no real threat appeared to the United States. During the World War, however, Japan's power began to grow while Russia's strength was on the decline. While the war lasted, the United States was not in a strong enough position to turn against Japan; moreover, by the Lansing-Ishii agreement of November, 1917, the United States recognized the existence of Japanese "special interests" in China, using an ambiguous formula according to which "territorial propinquity creates special relations." This convention marked the summit of American concessions to Tokyo. As soon as the war in Europe ended, the rivalry of the two Pacific powers flared up with unprecedented fury. Meantime Russia had collapsed, China was tied down by the "21 demands," and Japan emerged as the only strong power in east Asia. She seemed to be approaching her goals as she moved to control the Russian Far East as well as North China.

The United States policy now turned against Japan. Between 1918 and 1922 the American demand was for evacuation by Japan of the Russian Far East as well as of the newly occupied provinces of northern China. The American invasion of Russia was aimed not so much against that country as against Japan. The aim was to allow Japan no singlehanded control of Siberia, to prevent further Japanese unilateral moves, and to watch and check Japanese policies.

As Japan progressed in her drive to gain permanent control of the whole Far East, American policy stiffened and relations with Japan deteriorated. In 1919 a military conflict between the two powers in the near future appeared possible, even probable. The world press expressed alarm, while naval construction in the United States as well as in Japan proceeded at high speed until 1922. In a long series of diplomatic notes, some of which assumed a sharp tone, the Government of the United States demanded withdrawal of Japanese troops from Russian soil.

Early in 1920, when American troops were withdrawn from Russia, Japan again extended her occupation deeper into Siberia. The United States asked for immediate evacuation of the Japanese, since there was no legal reason for Japan to remain any longer in the Russian Far East. A diplomatic struggle over these issues followed, lasting for several years. In this case the United States acted as a champion of the integrity and independence of "future Russia." Japan insisted upon her right to stay in Siberia. "No other country," she stated in a reply to the United States on March 31, 1920, "is in such proximity to Siberia as is our empire; . . . the state of affairs in Siberia is a menace to general peace in Korea and Manchuria." Using as a pretext the cruelties perpetrated by Bolshevik guerrillas in Nikolayevsk, where many Japanese lost their lives, Japan also occupied northern Sakhalin. Bainbridge Colby, then United States Secretary of State, sent a strong note to Tokyo, in which he emphasized "the right of the Russian people to work out their destiny" and protested against any "encroachment upon Russian territory in the time of Russia's weakness." The diplomatic dispute continued, and irritation mounted. On May 31, 1921, the American note stated in substance:

"The Government of the United States expected that the withdrawal of American troops would be followed by a complete withdrawal of Japanese troops," since the purpose of assisting the Czechs had been fulfilled. Instead, additional territory had been occupied by the Japanese, the civil administration was "lending to the occupation an appearance of permanence and indicating a further encroachment upon Russian political and administrative rights." Possession of Vladivostok, the stationing of troops in Khabarovsk, Nikolayevsk, De Kastri, Mago, Sofisk, and other ports, and the seizure of the Russian part of Sakhalin Island were also noted.

"The Government of the United States can neither now nor hereafter recognize as valid any claims or titles arising out of the present occupation and control, and cannot acquiesce in any action taken by the Government of Japan which might impair existing treaty rights, or the political or territorial integrity of Russia."

The basic concept of the Soviet Government was that of differentiating between capitalist and Soviet states. Britain, France, Germany, the United States, Poland, and Japan were considered capitalist robbers and gangsters, united in their hatred of the first "proletarian state" and animated chiefly by a desire to erase from the earth the government of the social revolution. There exist, however—the theory went—differences and contradictions between the economic and imperialist interests of these powers, for example, between Germany and the Allies; and between Japan and America. The Soviet Government must "make use" of these internal struggles within the capitalist camp. This concept was the leading, even the favorite, idea of Lenin and his party; it has remained the guiding idea in Soviet foreign policy up to the present time.

In the Far East the outstanding fact was the military weakness of the Soviet Government. A fight against the invaders was out of the question for the newly created Red Army, and actually there were no battles with foreign troops during the Allied occupation. A hard war was being fought between Russian armies of different Russian governments, all of these armies being unstable, undisciplined, and poorly equipped. The Soviet Government was aware that it could not wage a war against Japan. Lenin, with complete frankness, stated more than once: "We cannot wage a war against Japan and must do everything in our power to avoid it, for such a war is beyond our strength." [3] Other political expedients were therefore necessary.

Our policy [Lenin stated] is to make use of the divergencies between different imperialist powers in order to make an agreement between them difficult, or, at least, to make it temporarily impossible. This has been the main line of our policy during the last three years.

So long as we have not succeeded in conquering the whole world [Lenin said in another speech in 1920] so long as we remain weaker then the capitalist world in economic and military aspects, we must adhere to the following rule: to make use of divergencies and contradictions among the imperialists . . . We would be even safer if the imperialist powers were to start a war among themselves . . . The capitalist thieves sharpen their knives for use against us; it is our duty to see that their knives are directed against one another.

These ideas, applied to the Far East, led Lenin to expect a military conflict between the United States and Japan.

America and Japan [Lenin said] are on the eve of a war and there is no possibility of preventing this war, in which there will again be 10 million killed and 20 million mutilated. [America and Japan] are going to spring at one another because Japan has quietly worked during the imperialist war and taken almost the whole of China, whose population is

3. December 24, 1920.

400 million . . . The [American] imperialists say, "We are in favor of a republic, we are for democracy, but why did Japan steal from under our nose more than her share?"

Lenin's underlying idea was that France was no better than Germany, and America no better than Japan.[4] But in Lenin's eyes Soviet Russia's only chance of survival was through these mutual conflicts of the capitalist powers. "To make use of" these differences was a favorite term of Lenin's; he felt himself an element alien to this outer capitalist world, a stranger to its internal struggles and intrigues, inferior in wealth and force, but superior in analysis and shrewdness. He was fond of his shrewdness of policy; without admitting it to himself, he attached exaggerated importance to astute and cunning maneuvers.

One attempt to make political gains by means of an astute diversion was Lenin's idea of strengthening the position of the Soviet Government by granting economic concessions to foreign capitalist groups. In Far Eastern affairs this plan was to play a major role. In 1920, when the civil war in the Far East was nearing its end and the Japanese remained as the last foreign army on Russian soil, Lenin conceived the plan of granting extensive economic concessions to the United States in order to create American interests in the Russian Far East and thus deepen the conflict between America and Japan. Kamchatka seemed the most appropriate territory for this purpose. "We shall give America," Lenin said, "a territory for economic use, in a region where we have no naval or military forces. In this way we incite American imperialism against the Japanese bourgeoisie." Lenin met with opposition among the members of his party, but he won the battle and put his program into practice.

In October, 1920, Washington Baker Vanderlip, an American engineer from California, a pioneer and adventurer who had the backing of a group of oil men, went to Moscow in order to negotiate oil concessions in the Russian Far East. In Moscow he was mistaken for a cousin of Frank Vanderlip, a former president of the National City Bank, and was therefore considered an important,

4. Georgi Chicherin, the Foreign Commissar, addressed amazing notes to the government in Washington. For example, on October 24, 1918, he wrote, "We do not want to wage a war with America, although your government has not yet been replaced by a Soviet of People's Commissars and Eugene Debs, whom you keep in jail, has not yet taken your place."

even a semiofficial, personality. He mentioned his connection with Warren G. Harding, the presidential candidate (who was elected while Vanderlip was in Moscow). In his eagerness to gain access to the American capitalists, Lenin personally received him, and the other Soviet leaders conducted prolonged negotiations with him. In a subsequent report to the Soviet Congress, Lenin told his audience that Vanderlip had written a letter to him asking for oil lands in Kamchatka and had promised great political advantages to Russia if the Soviet Government agreed to the American wishes.

We Republicans [Vanderlip wrote] [5] will win in the November elections and in March we shall have our president. Our policy will not repeat the foolish mistakes which brought the United States into European affairs. We shall be concerned only with our own interests. Our American interests are leading us toward a clash with Japan. It is against Japan that we will fight . . . It is not only necessary for us to have oil, but measures must be taken to deprive the enemy of oil supplies. Near Kamchatka there is some bay [?] with oil wells. I guarantee that if you sell us this piece of land our people will be enthusiastic and we shall at once recognize your government. If you do not sell it to us but only grant us a concession, we will not refuse considering it, but I cannot promise such enthusiasm as would make certain the recognition of the Soviet Government.

Lenin commented, "Kamchatka belonged to the former Russian Empire. To whom it belongs now is unknown. Japan controls the Far East and can do as she pleases there. If we cede Kamchatka, which de jure belongs to us, and de facto is in possession of Japan, to America, we can gain. We decided therefore immediately to conclude an agreement with America."

The agreements drawn up by Vanderlip and the Soviet authorities provided for the lease of 400,000 square miles of Russian territory for a period of 60 years; extensive trade schemes provided for the purchase in America by the Soviet Government of goods to the fabulous total value of 3 billion dollars.

When rumors of this transaction reached Japan the first reaction to Vanderlip's successes was irritation—precisely what Lenin wanted. The Foreign Office in Tokyo announced that the Soviet Government was not recognized by the powers and there-

5. Quoted from Lenin's *Works* in which the Vanderlip letter is printed in quotation marks. Lenin seems to have paraphrased the letter.

fore Japan "is in no way bound to take cognizance of any private agreement nor prepared to assent to an act which affects her vital interests." Lenin was satisfied: "Japan says 'we shall not tolerate anything that infringes upon our interests.' All right, you defeat America. We shall not object. We have already set America and Japan one against the other, and in this way an advantage has been gained."

In the meantime the personality of Vanderlip and his bargainings in Moscow began to attract interest in the United States. Soon the whole deal became the laughing stock of the press. The *New York Times* in an editorial said: ". . . It would appear that Lenin 'fell' for those stories [recognition of the Bolshevik government, Vanderlip's own fabulous wealth, and his political importance] with eager credulity. He may know American Socialists and near-anarchists pretty well, but evidently has a lot to learn about American promoters . . ." In a later editorial: "Mr. Vanderlip . . . comes from Los Angeles, a city where long contemplation of the climate has developed the lens of the human eye into a high-power magnifying instrument, and close association with motion picture press agents has induced a carelessness in arithmetic . . ." [6]

The following spring Vanderlip made a second trip to Moscow and again negotiated huge concessions, this time of forests in the Archangel region. The new concession was to extend over 10 million acres of spruce land and its term was to be 50 years. The agreement was never signed. In the meantime Lenin had felt it necessary to explain his blunders in the Vanderlip affair before a party conference:

Although the counterintelligence of our Vecheka [later the GPU and NKVD] is very efficient it unfortunately had not as yet extended to the United States of America, and we did not succeed in establishing the relationship between these Vanderlips. Some say there is no relationship whatsoever [although this Vanderlip] was described to us as a great magnate, received by all kings and ministers with great honors, which circumstance permits the conclusion that his purse is very well filled.

6. *New York Times* editorials, November 1, and 19, 1920.

THE FIRST "FRIENDLY GOVERNMENT"

When the White armies collapsed, early in 1920, the Red Army did not proceed to penetrate deep into Siberia because it was busy in Europe where, in addition to the civil war, a war with Poland was starting. Siberia and the Far East themselves had to take care of the local and provincial administration and to create new forms of government. The parties which, under these conditions, were called upon to organize the large territories were, first, the democratic Socialist parties (Mensheviks and Social-Revolutionaries), and second, the Communists. (Only in the city of Vladivostok, under Japanese occupation, were the "Cadets" still influential.)

The Communists, although, as we have seen, constituting a small minority in Siberia and the Far East, exerted great influence through their armed guerrilla groups. Unlike the Red Army, the guerrillas had no real military discipline and no adequate political leadership. They consisted mainly of young peasant rebels, of fanatics with little comprehension of the internal and external situation, and of audacious adventurers. They risked their lives daily in the fight with the White armies and were themselves in turn often merciless and cruel; more than once Bolshevik tribunals imposed the death sentence on their own guerrillas because of their outrages.

The Bolshevik movement in Siberia and the Far East was at that time far from a united movement. The guerrilla leaders constituted the base of an uncompromising "leftist" Bolshevism, while other elements, mainly prerevolutionary Bolsheviks, belonged to the "right." The struggle of the two factions lasted throughout the whole period of the Japanese occupation and only the persistent interference of the Central Committee in Moscow was able to keep the organization together. The prestige of Lenin and Trotsky among the members of all factions was great.

One of the chief points of disagreement within the Communist party was the creation in 1920 of an "independent" non-Soviet Republic of the Far East. Japanese forces were in control of the eastern regions and were in a position any day to expand their occupation to the west to reach Chita, Irkutsk, even Omsk. No military force would have been able to fight them successfully; the Soviet Government systematically avoided direct contact and battle because the outcome of such a fight was certain. Even less possible would be the functioning of a Soviet civil administration under Japanese military occupation.

In the cities of Irkutsk and Verkhneudinsk, Admiral Kolchak's administration was at first succeeded by a coalition of the two democratic parties, supported by a great majority of the city population as well as the peasants, and, at the beginning, also by the Bolsheviks. These two parties were, however, inferior to the Communists in fighting spirit and in the number of armed groups and guerrillas. The leftist Bolshevik groups wanted a new upheaval which would remove these two parties from power; they expected the Soviet system of government to be extended to Siberia. In this way all of Russia in Asia, with the exception of areas under direct Japanese occupation, would become "sovietized." The democratic local governments were obviously unstable.

Under these conditions the idea emerged of creating in Siberia a "democratic" buffer state which would separate Soviet Russia from the Japanese forces—a second Russian state, formally independent and sovereign, with a purely democratic constitution, without benefit of soviets or nationalized banks and industry. The Japanese would have no formal reason to attack such a government; for the rest of the world, and particularly for the United States, the democratic constitution would serve to attract sympathy.

Alexander Krasnoshchokov (Tobelson), a young Russian who had emigrated with his parents to the United States and had become an American citizen, returned from Chicago and became leader of the rightist faction in the Bolshevik party of the Far East and the main advocate of this plan. His opponents were the impetuous and passionate leaders of the "left" who did not want to listen to anything except outright incorporation into Soviet Russia and immediate suppression of all other parties. In this internal struggle, the "left" had the support of the majority of the Communists of the East. Krasnoshchokov had to appeal to the Central Committee in Moscow. Not until he had presented an approving telegram signed by Lenin and Trotsky was his buffer plan accepted. The plan: the whole of eastern Siberia and even a large area to the west of the Baikal was to constitute an "independent" state.

Krasnoshchokov went to Moscow to discuss the details, but

in his absence guerrilla troops occupied the city of Irkutsk and, contrary to instructions from Moscow, brought about a Soviet revolution. No one dared to expel them and even Lenin's Central Committee accepted the revolution as a fait accompli.

The new buffer republic was proclaimed on April 6, 1920. Its first capital was the city of Verkhneudinsk; later it was moved to Chita. The government was at first constituted as a coalition of the three parties, but in this form it did not last long. The Bolshevik forces soon destroyed the armed groups of the other parties and suppressed their press. The members of the government representing these parties resigned, and the government, headed by Krasnoshchokov, became actually a one-party Communist government.[7]

In an attempt to put an end to the internal struggles inside the Communist party in Siberia, the Central Committee in Moscow issued detailed instructions concerning the Far Eastern Republic. Lenin's authorship of these secret instructions, which were dated August 13, 1920, is obvious, and the instructions are interesting and important, since they were the first setting forth of a scheme of "a friendly government" and of a "democratic" state under Communist leadership without open sovietization and nationalization of property. Twenty-five years later when, in a quite different international situation, the Soviet Government proceeded to create its "sphere" in central and eastern Europe, it had simply to dig out from the archives and to apply these instructions of Lenin's relating to the Far Eastern Republic.

The bourgeois-democratic character of the buffer is purely formal [Lenin's instructions went, and continued] A parliamentary system must not be permitted . . .

Formal abolition of private property is absolutely inadmissible. But by various restrictions (for example, by confiscation of the enterprises belonging to enemies of the people, especially to those who fled abroad; by introduction of state monopoly of grain and raw materials; and by other measures) an intermediary political situation must be created which will be expedient for the needs of Communist guidance.

The Central Committee [of the Communist party in Moscow] will direct the policy of the Far Eastern Republic through a Bureau for the

7. The government consisted of seven members. There was a joke popular at that time in Siberia: "The government is a million: it consists of one Krasnoshchokov and six zeros."

Far East whose members will be appointed from Moscow and which will be directly subordinate to the Central Committee of the party. The city of Chita will be the capital.

By carrying out these instructions, the fiction of a sovereign state was built up. The Far Eastern Government decided to convoke a Constituent Assembly and to elect deputies by universal suffrage. (The Constituent Assembly in Petrograd had been dissolved as an anti-Soviet institution by Lenin's government in January, 1918.) This Constituent Assembly held its first session on February 12, 1921, at Chita, at which the Communist minority group by various means gained the support of the large "peasant party." A constitution for the new state was soon promulgated—the usual democratic constitution, with no mention of Soviets, and political freedoms guaranteed. Outwardly, the new state had all the trimmings of parliamentary democracy and responsible government.

On May 14, 1920, the Soviet Government officially "recognized" the Far Eastern Republic and appointed a diplomatic envoy. The Far Eastern Republic opened a legation in Moscow. "International" treaties between Moscow and Chita were then entered into concerning boundaries, citizenship, railways, navigation, etc. The Moscow government even granted a "foreign loan" to the Far Eastern Republic. A special agreement concerning Kamchatka was concluded whereby the Soviet Government was entitled to grant concessions to capitalist groups in that area of the Far East.

Soviet Russia and the Far Eastern Republic were both controlled, of course, by one and the same government—Lenin's government. While in Russia the Soviet system and Russia's transition to socialism were continuously exalted, in the Far East the slogan was democracy; abolition of private enterprise was officially neither demanded nor proclaimed. In Russia, in accordance with Lenin's instructions, leaders and members of the democratic parties were to be "cautiously [*sic*] kept in prison"; in the Far East they were sometimes invited to take office in the government and actually occupied important positions in the administration. They participated in elections and held meetings. From time to time even democratic newspapers were permitted to appear.

A corresponding difference was apparent between the for-

eign policies of Moscow and Chita. The Soviet Government forcefully denounced all capitalist powers as interventionists, only from
time to time mentioning the differences in their attitude toward
Soviet Russia. In Chita, on the other hand, the government, always
acting on direct instructions from Moscow, stretched out its hand
to the United States, emphasized friendly relations, and promised
a great field for American trade and investments in the Far East
as soon as normal conditions returned. Although it was never officially recognized, it communicated with the United States State Department, it transmitted to Washington reports of its negotiations
with Japan, and urged the United States to greater activity in Far
Eastern affairs. It appeared as though the Far Eastern Republic
were looking for an outright alliance with the United States—in
striking contrast to Moscow's Comintern policy. This was a mas-
terpiece of Lenin's shrewd and hyperrealistic line of action.

The United States State Department was attentive to statements
and reports from Chita. It of course declined to establish diplomatic relations with that government, but sent an unofficial envoy
to the Far Eastern Republic. A delegation of the Far Eastern Republic arrived in Washington in the fall of 1921, when the Conference for the Limitation of Armaments (Washington Conference) convened, although no delegates representing Russia attended the conference.

The Government of Japan gave de facto recognition to the
Far Eastern Republic on July 15, 1920, soon after its creation. It
conducted protracted negotiations with the Republic, in which
the Japanese conditions for the evacuation of their troops was a
major issue.

Japan strove to conduct all negotiations directly, without participation or interference by any other nation. She did not resent
interference of the Soviet Government as much as she did that of
the United States. For the same reason which prompted Japan to
reduce American influence, Chita and Moscow, ready to negotiate
and confer with Japan, hoped to use American pressure to improve
their bargaining position vis-à-vis Japan. They were therefore reluctant to conclude any binding agreement. To them it was obvious
that Japan's strong position would compel them to make far-reach-

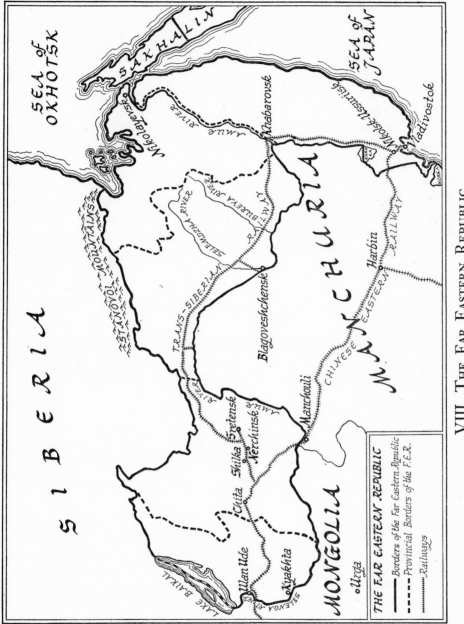

VIII. The Far Eastern Republic

ing concessions and that only the assistance of and pressure by the United States could relieve their difficulties.

When, in July, 1921, President Harding invited the Great Powers to take part in the Washington Conference for discussion of controversial problems affecting the Pacific area, including Japanese occupation of Russian and Chinese territories, the Japanese Government hastened to invite the Far Eastern Republic to a special conference for the settlement of all questions outstanding between them. The conference took place at Dairen, lasting longer than expected—from August 26, 1921, to April 15, 1922; it was interrupted during the Washington Conference. Japan's delegates endeavored to evade a definite pledge concerning the evacuation of their forces from Russian territory by a specific date. Instead they advanced claims of great importance—claims which, were they to be accepted, would have given Japan a privileged position in the Russian Far East and would have made impossible the unification of the Vladivostok area with the rest of Russia. Among Japan's demands were the following: all Russian fortifications on the Pacific coast to be destroyed; Vladivostok to become a purely commercial port, the admittance of naval craft being prohibited; the Far Eastern Republic not to become Communist—in other words, it was to remain permanently separated from Soviet Russia; Japanese citizens to enjoy the same economic rights as Russians even in cases where other nationals were being discriminated against.[8]

The Russian delegates refused to accept these demands; they certainly expected help from the Washington Conference.

When the Washington Conference opened in November, 1921, the Dairen Conference sessions were suspended. Three delegates of the Far Eastern Republic appeared in Washington. Although not admitted to the general conference tables, they worked feverishly to influence public opinion in their favor and they were largely successful in this respect. They published a number of pamphlets describing Japan's operations in the Russian Far East, and the constitution of their state; they made public speeches which on the whole were favorably received due to the general resentment against Japan. They also presented the Far Eastern Republic as a genuine democracy in which all citizens and parties enjoyed liberty

8. *United States Foreign Relations* (1922), II, 843 ff.

within a state that was really sovereign and independent of Soviet Russia. They found many naïve believers.[9]

The Washington Conference took an unfavorable course for the Japanese. Having lost on many issues even the support of their British allies, the Japanese delegates were often forced to yield. Limitation of naval armaments and evacuation of Chinese territory meant a diplomatic defeat for Japan; this was also the meaning of the Japanese pledge to evacuate Russian soil. When at one of the sessions of the conference Secretary of State Charles Evans Hughes pressed the Japanese for a clear-cut statement regarding Russia, Baron Kijuro Shidehara declared, on January 23, 1922: "It is the fixed and settled policy of Japan to respect the territorial integrity of Russia and to observe the principle of nonintervention in the internal affairs of that country, as well as the principle of equal opportunity for the commerce and industry of all nations in every part of the Russian possessions"; he said that Japan did not intend to maintain its troops on Russian soil any longer than necessary.

Following the Washington Conference the delegates of Japan and the Far Eastern Republic resumed their negotiations at Dairen. The Russian delegates felt stronger than before and were now less inclined to make concessions than they had been at the outset. They definitely refused to accept the demands presented by Japan, and the unsuccessful conference dissolved on April 15, 1922.

The Far Eastern Government again appealed to Washington and the State Department once more pressed Tokyo for final action. On June 22, 1922, the Japanese Government informed the United States State Department that the evacuation of the Russian Far East would be completed by October, 1922. This pledge did not, however, apply to Sakhalin Island. Secretary of State Hughes expressed his satisfaction but at the same time demanded the withdrawal of Japanese forces from Sakhalin.

9. In this respect those pro-Soviet Americans who misjudged the Soviet Government and the Far Eastern Republic were the spiritual fathers of American statesmen and writers who, between 1941 and 1946, believed or pretended to believe in "Soviet democracy" and freedom in Russia. The Foreign Policy Association of New York invited one of the Far Eastern delegates, Mr. Boris Skvirsky, to address an Association meeting in March, 1922, at which Skvirsky presented the Far Eastern Republic as a democracy of the Western type, and an American official, C. H. Smith, naïvely claimed that the Russians in the Far Eastern Republic "are determined to have three things established: freedom of speech, private ownership, and representative government . . . The elections were absolutely honestly conducted."

A new conference of Japanese and Far Eastern Republic representatives opened at Changchun on September 4, 1922, for discussion of the Sakhalin question. Japan insisted on permanent far-
reaching privileges connected with economic exploitation of
Sakhalin. In view of the favorable attitude of the United States,
the Soviet Government, which was also represented at the conference, did not deem it necessary to accept Japan's demands, and
the Changchun conference ended without agreement on November 23, 1922.

In the meantime Japan was withdrawing from Russian territory
on the Asiatic mainland. When, on October 25, 1922, the last
Japanese troops left Vladivostok after four and a half years of
military intervention in the affairs of the Russian Far East, the
People's Revolutionary Army of the Far Eastern Republic tri-
umphantly entered the city. A few days later the National Assembly of the Far East decided that the Far Eastern Republic, having served its major purpose, should be dissolved. The fiction of
"real independence" was discarded and on November 19, 1922,
the Soviet Government resolved to incorporate the territories of
the Far East into the RSFSR.

Japan's evacuation of Russian territory was a major Russian
success, but it was also obvious that the victory was due in large part
to the strong support of the United States. Skvirsky, the unofficial
Far Eastern Republic's envoy to the United States, visited the
State Department immediately after Japan's withdrawal and expressed his gratitude for America's aid. "The Russian people," he
said, "appreciate the large part which the friendly interests of the
United States have had in bringing the evacuation about." In
Vladivostok the Soviet military leader, Uborevich, visited the
United States consul and promised friendship, expansion of Soviet-
American trade, and even the right of an American naval vessel to
remain in Vladivostok—all other navies having been invited to
leave immediately.

In Moscow, on the other hand, America's role in the liberation of
the Far East was played down and the success attributed to the Red
Army and to Soviet diplomacy. Lenin dispatched a telegram of
greetings to the Chita government saying that "the Red Army has
made another decisive step toward the final clearance of the territory of the RSFSR and of the Union Republics from foreign

occupants' troops." In his solemn speech on October 31, 1922, he avoided mention of the United States. "The last forces of the White Guardists have been forced out into the sea," he said, adding rather vaguely, "The international situation played a part; . . . a certain measure of credit is also due our diplomacy."

With the dissolution of the pro-American Far Eastern Republic relations between Moscow and Washington took a turn for the worse. As far as the United States was concerned its main object, the weakening of Japan's position on the Asiatic continent, had been achieved. To the Soviet Government, the United States was now merely one of the members of the great imperialist family which had to be fought and destroyed.

PEACE WITH JAPAN

Another two years elapsed before the last of the controversial issues in Soviet-Japanese relations—that of Sakhalin—was settled. In the period 1923–25 Russia was at the peak of her diplomatic successes; she received de jure recognition by one Great Power after another, and the prospects of trade with Russia animated the business world. Japan, weakened as a result of the Washington Conference, and practically isolated, would have to settle the Sakhalin question by agreement with the Soviet Government. The terrible earthquake in December, 1923, made her bargaining position still more difficult.

In unofficial conversations with Adolf Joffe, the Soviet delegate, Japan proposed the payment of 150 million yen for the purchase of Northern Sakhalin. Joffe demanded one billion gold rubles.[10] No agreement was reached. Further negotiations were begun by the Soviet envoy, Lev Karakhan, and the Japanese envoy, Kenkichi Yoshizawa, at Peking, and after a few months of bargaining the Sakhalin question was settled by compromise. Russia had to make important concessions to Japan in order to regain political control of the territory. These concessions remained in force for two decades; they were partially abolished in 1944 and totally abolished after Japan's defeat the following year.

The comprehensive agreement between the Soviet Union and Japan, signed on January 20, 1925, consisted of the main treaty,

10. Louis Fischer, *The Soviets in World Affairs* (London, 1930), II, 554.

two protocols, and a few notes. In the main treaty each party pledged to abstain from interference in the affairs of the other party as well as from acts liable to provoke unrest in the other state; both parties also pledged resumption of trade relations. In accordance with the Treaty of Portsmouth of 1905, Japan's fishery rights were recognized in principle. By the first protocol annexed to the treaty, Japan pledged the evacuation of Northern Sakhalin by the end of May, 1925. The second protocol settled Japan's economic privileges in Sakhalin. She obtained approximately 50 per cent of the oil lands of Sakhalin against payment of the equivalent of 5 to 15 per cent of its yearly output. She further obtained concessions of coal mines against payment of the equivalent of 5 to 8 per cent of their yearly output.

By a secret convention Japan pledged not to ratify a "protocol" of the Great Powers regarding the annexation of the former Russian Province of Bessarabia by Rumania. The Soviet government consistently refused to recognize this transfer of territory, and Japan's support was of considerable value to Litvinov in this connection.[11]

With the signing of this agreement, Soviet-Japanese relations entered a new phase, the political significance of which was apparent since the rapprochement developed simultaneously with the deterioration of Soviet-British and Soviet-American relations. It seemed that there was emerging a Russo-Japanese political combination aimed against Washington and London.

In these months of 1924–25 an anti-British trend in the European policy of the Soviet Government was gaining strength, while collaboration between Russia and Germany was also developing favorably. The new treaty with Japan marked a stage in the evolution of anti-British and anti-American tendencies of Soviet policy in Asia. In China the Russian political line emphasized a program of "liberation from imperialism," meaning, in the first place, liberation from Great Britain and the United States.

The significance of the new treaty was stated by the official *Izvestiya* of January 22, 1925, as follows: "The present treaty with Japan, combined with the recent agreement with China, will strengthen Soviet activities in the Far East and undoubtedly exert

11. Grigori Besedovsky, *Na putyakh k Termidoru* (Paris, 1930–31), II, 13.

considerable influence upon all the powers interested in the Far East . . . The United States and England will be among the first whom it will concern." Georgi Chicherin said, "For Japan the treaty means a secured rear in case of possible complications."

The specter of a great Eurasian alliance stretching from the Rhine to the Pacific and Indo-China, comprising Russia, Germany, China, and Japan, disturbed the political world. This was the appearance of a potential combination which was destined to play a great role in the thirties and forties. The danger was not quite real in the twenties, since the military forces of Germany and Russia, even combined with those of Japan, were not as yet important. The alarm, however, was great.

The Berlin *Lokalanzeiger* printed an alleged secret appendix to the Russo-Japanese treaty containing a military agreement. The Commissariat for Foreign Affairs issued a strong denial stating that "rumors concerning an alliance of the Soviet Union and Japan" were unfounded. The *New York Times* commented editorially on March 9, 1925: "There is no point in minimizing the ultimate political potentialities in the Russo-Japanese understanding. Their immediate importance, however, is in China . . . Some unkind opponent of recognition [of the Soviet Union] might even remind M. Karakhan of Mr. Kipling's refrain: 'Brother, thy tail hangs down behind.' "

Apprehension concerning developments in east Asia was mounting in the United States and England particularly because at that time events in China were taking on a revolutionary character; the nationalist movement, incorporating the Chinese Communists, was growing in force and directing its spiritual weapons against the Great Powers.

VII

Heavy Going in China

All the prerequisites for the best possible relations between Russia and China existed—or so it seemed—after the November Revolution of 1917. The sympathy with China's struggle for independence and the sentiment against the unequal treaties were genuine throughout Russia, and the Soviet Government strongly stressed the "anti-imperialist" trends of its orientation. The misery and humiliations suffered by the people of this great neighbor nation aroused strong emotions during this—the idealistic—period of the Russian Revolution. According to Lenin's concepts, China's status was that of a backward, semicolonial nation, and as such China was considered to be a source of resistance to the "great imperialist powers" of the world and a natural ally of the Soviet Revolution. In this giant uprising against capitalism, the national—although non-Socialist—movements in the backward nations were considered a powerful weapon and the strongest ally of international Communism. In one of its first significant statements, that of January 16, 1918, the Soviet Government, with one eye on China, advocated ". . . a complete break with the barbarous policies of bourgeois civilization, which builds the welfare of the exploiters and a few select chosen nations upon the enslavement of hundreds of millions of toilers in Asia, in the colonies in general, and in the small states."

In a multitude of articles, reviews, and speeches which followed, Soviet leaders affirmed and reiterated their friendly attitude toward China and their readiness to abolish all privileges acquired by old Russia at the expense of the Chinese nation, i.e., annul Russian concessions, cancel the treaties providing for extraterritoriality for Russian citizens in China and consular jurisdiction, renounce Russian territorial acquisitions and claims to the humiliating Boxer indemnities, and so on.

Among the Chinese living in Russia a considerable number were in sympathy with the Communist movement, and three "Congresses of Chinese Workers" were convened during the years of the Russian civil war. At the Third Congress in June, 1920, Mikhail Kalinin himself appeared to greet the convention, and Georgi Chicherin told the members of the Congress that "the Chinese Soviet Republic will be the closest ally of the Russian Republic." The Congress passed a resolution inviting Sun Yat-sen to Moscow and elected a "Central Executive Committee" of Chinese workers living in Russia.

In January, 1922, an international conference of "revolutionary organizations of the Far East" was staged. There were representatives of China, Korea, Japan, India, Java, Mongolia, and the Russian Far East among its 148 delegates. Grigori Zinoviev, the head of the Comintern, and Sen Katayama, veteran leader of Japanese revolutionaries, were among the speakers at this conference.

At the height of the civil war in Russia, the Soviet Foreign Office addressed a note to the Chinese Central Government which, in a sense, contained the entire Soviet program for agreement with China. It summarized the idealistic and anti-imperialist premises of early Bolshevism. This note was of unique historical interest:

. . . We are marching to free the people from the yoke of military force, of foreign money, which is crushing the life and the people of the East, and principally the people of China . . .

The Government of Workers and Peasants has therefore declared null and void all the secret treaties concluded with Japan, China, and the former Allies. The treaties were to enable the Russian Tsarist Government and its allies to enslave the people of the East and principally the people of China . . .

[We promise] to give back to the Chinese people all the power and authority which were obtained by the Government of the Tsar by entering into understandings with Japan and the Allies . . . The Soviet Government has renounced all the conquests made by the Tsarist Government which took away from China Manchuria and other territories. The population of these territories shall decide for themselves to which country they would like to belong . . . The Soviet Government gives up the indemnities payable by China for the insurrection of the Boxers in 1900 . . . No authority or court of law whatever shall be allowed to exist in China except the authority and court of law of the Chinese people.[1]

1. Soviet note of July 25, 1919.

A year later, when the situation in China became more favorable and contact was facilitated through the newly established Far Eastern Republic, a second comprehensive note was sent to China, the Soviet Government again stating:

The Government of the RSFSR declares null and void all treaties concluded with China by the former Governments of Russia, renounces all seizure of Chinese territory and all Russian concessions in China, and restores to China, without compensation and forever, all that had been predatorily seized from her by the Tsar's Government and the Russian bourgeoisie . . . All Russian citizens residing in China shall be subject to all the laws and regulations obtaining in the territory of the Chinese Republic and shall not enjoy any rights of extraterritoriality.

The Government of the RSFSR renounces any payments by China as indemnity for the Boxer uprising.[2]

In the meantime the Second Congress of the Communist International had begun a detailed consideration of the Chinese problem and, under the leadership of Lenin, had formulated the basic conception which held that two forces were the allies of the Soviet Revolution: the revolutionary working class of the Western countries, and the great national movements, comprising different classes of the population, in the colonial and semicolonial states.

The actual developments in Russo-Chinese relations in the first years after the Revolution did not confirm the optimistic expectations. Almost seven years elapsed before the Soviet Government was recognized by China and the enticing propositions became embodied in a treaty. Even after the Russian offers were made part of formal agreements there did not appear the friendliness and durable collaboration that Moscow had hoped for.

Official Soviet historians have attributed this state of affairs during the first seven years after 1917 to the pressure put on China by Japan, England, and the other powers. This is only a half truth. The other reason concerned Soviet policy in regard to China which, itself, despite sympathetic pronouncements, contained the seeds of disagreement.

Special privileges, acquisitions and treaty rights of old Russia in regard to China were of two kinds. The one comprised extrater-

2. Soviet declaration delivered to the Chinese Government, September 27, 1920.

ritoriality, trade privileges, concessions, and the Boxer indemnities. As to these, the Soviet Government was prepared to go to the limit to satisfy all the wishes of nationalist China. The second, however, concerned territorial acquisitions which had made Outer Mongolia and northern Manchuria protectorates of old Russia. These areas had actually been on the verge of formal annexation to Russia, and only a favorable turn in international events had been needed to bring this about. In respect to this second kind of acquisition, the government of the Communist party was much more reluctant to yield than in the matter of the "unequal treaties." It strove to keep under its control as many territories and nationalities as it could, the extent of its control depending on its power and international position. To return these territories to China would be, in the eyes of Moscow, a retreat, a defeat. Under the Soviet regime (so the theory went) these territories would be freed from imperialism, whereas their return to China would be tantamount to their being resubjected to capitalist exploitation by the Great Powers.

Here, for the first time, there became apparent in Soviet policy the trend toward expansion as an instrument of spreading social revolution. While in Europe the weak army of Soviet Russia had to yield and its government was forced to cede territories to Poland and Rumania and reconcile itself to the independence of Finland, it found in central Asia the only region that presented no forceful opposition. The integrity of Bukhara had been guaranteed by Lenin's treaty with Afghanistan, but as the latter was unable to defend her rights by force, Bukhara was annexed to the Soviet Union and disappeared from the map in the twenties. The same disproportion of power existed in connection with Outer Mongolia. It was this Mongolian issue that complicated Soviet-Chinese relations and retarded the conclusion of an agreement which otherwise would have been possible much earlier.

THE MANCHURIAN IMPASSE

In fact the first in a long series of conflicts between the Soviet Government and the Allies of the first World War arose in relation to the Russo-Chinese handling of the Manchurian problem. The situation was both ironical and tragic.

The conflict began in North Manchuria. A soviet, composed of delegates of Russian workers and soldiers stationed in the region, emerged in Harbin, the capital, at the beginning of the Russian Revolution. The Harbin soviet participated in the Russian Soviet congresses and, during the year 1917, evolved in the same manner as did most of the soviets in Russia's big cities—from moderate Socialist to "left." In December, 1917, on general instructions from the Soviet Government, it proceeded to seize power in the region. In Manchuria this meant, first of all, seizure of the Chinese Eastern Railway. The railroad, which dominated the political and economic life of North Manchuria, became the object of a struggle between the local soviet, representing the Russian Soviet Government, and the old Russian directorate under General Horvath. General Horvath was dismissed by the soviet.

It should be noted here that the Chinese Eastern Railway is not merely a means of transportation as are most of the world's railroads. Since its construction, around 1900, it was and still is a political problem and a sensitive barometer to the changing political atmosphere of the Far East. Built on Chinese soil (although far from China's ancient cities), in the vicinity of growing Japan and adjacent to the Japanese sphere of influence in Manchuria, this railroad—the only direct and natural means of transportation between Russia's center and the great port of Vladivostok, and the life line to a new, prospering region with a considerable Russian population—has absorbed all the problems and difficulties of international relations in the extreme Orient. The 50 years' history of the Chinese Eastern Railway is actually the history of the multitude of Far Eastern struggles, problems, and wars.

The Russian envoy to China (who was still recognized by the Peking government), as well as the diplomatic representatives of the Great Powers, protested against the actions of the Harbin soviet; with the consent of the powers, Chinese authorities, for the first time in the history of Manchuria, seized the Russian railroad. The Russian forces were deported back to Russia, and Chinese troops took over. The management of the company was reorganized and Chinese officials were appointed to control it. China subsequently proceeded to take possession of other Russian property, gradually replaced certain Russian authorities in Harbin by Chinese, and even tried to deprive the Russian inhabitants of foreign settlements in China of their treaty privileges. This Chinese policy met with protest on the part of the Great Powers, which, during the military conflict with Soviet Russia in 1918–20, insisted on the maintenance of all of China's treaties with the Allies. Moreover, while the domestic situation in Russia was considered "chaotic," the Great Powers—prompted by anti-Soviet Russian groups and by economic interests at home—often chose to consider themselves the guardians of the interests and privileges of Russia— of a future and "normalized" Russian state. Among these legitimate Russian interests recognized by the Allies were Russian treaty privileges in Manchuria.

Early in 1919 the Allies established a system of temporary control over the Russian railroads of eastern Siberia and Manchuria. Control of the Chinese Eastern Railway was entrusted to China. Meantime, the former Russo-Asiatic Bank, nominal owner of the railway, with the strong support of its French creditors, announced its claims. In the end China had to accept a compromise by which Russians (non-Soviet, of course) were appointed to half the seats on the governing body of the railroad, the rest being Chinese. This organization of the railway's administration became a model for later policy when an agreement was reached between Russia and China.

Now China embarked on a de facto abolition of Russian privileges in China while participating in the united front against the Soviets. In August, 1918, China, along with the other powers, signed the agreement providing for joint military intervention in the Russian Far East. Chinese detachments entered Russian territory and, during the civil war, were located in Vladivostok, Khabarovsk, and on the Trans-Baikal front.

The old Russian envoy, Kudashov, collaborated with the Allies in this policy while systematically protesting China's violations of her former treaties with Russia. Until 1920 the Chinese Government continued regularly to pay to Kudashov the Russian share of the Boxer indemnity payments, while Moscow repeatedly proposed to annul these payments. On August 1, 1920, the indemnity payments were suspended, and on September 23, the Peking government ceased to recognize the diplomatic representatives of pre-Soviet Russia. The stage was set for a quick rapprochement between Russia and China. Moscow's prestige had risen after its victories in the civil war; the Allied intervention had ended, England gave de facto recognition to Soviet Russia early in 1921, and Moscow's statements of policy during 1919 and 1920 made a great impression on Chinese public opinion.

It was somewhat surprising, however, that the constitution of the Far Eastern Republic, adopted in 1920 and approved by Moscow, expressly included the Manchurian "leased territory" as a part of its realm. This claim appeared to be contrary to the previous declarations of the Soviet Government. In 1920 Yurin (Dzevaltovsky), the first Soviet envoy, and a large staff of experts arrived in Peking. Technically Yurin was a delegate of the Far Eastern Republic for trade negotiations, but he was generally and correctly considered a representative of the Soviet Government. He had to fight the influence of Kudashov, the previous envoy, as well as the influence of the Russian residents in China, a great majority of whom were anti-Soviet. He won a partial success: it was in the course of his negotiations that China withdrew her recognition of the old Russian representative. But the real aim of Yurin's mission—mutual recognition by Soviet Russia and China—was not achieved. Nor was it achieved when another Soviet delegate, Paikes, arrived in December, 1921. Nor was it achieved when the renowned Soviet diplomat, Adolf Joffe, came to China in August, 1922. Joffe was given great public ovations, and his official statements were widely acclaimed in China.

While the West [he said] is tossing about from one international conference to another, the East is accumulating strength . . . With hope we watch the growing national consciousness of the many millions of Chinese people, because, in line with the Russian Revolution, the awakening of the Chinese people is a factor of immense historical importance.

Joffe, however, did not obtain the hoped-for recognition and departed for Japan.

He was succeeded by Davtian and then by Lev Karakhan. The latter was well regarded in China since he had signed the widely known notes of 1919 and 1920. On his way to China Karakhan was hailed throughout Manchuria and the northern provinces. Enthusiastic crowds greeted him wherever he went. "If once again foreign hands will interfere in our mutual affairs," he threatened the powers, without naming them, "we must mercilessly cut off their hands." [3] He protested vigorously whenever his country's policy toward China was compared with that of the other powers, even with the United States. When, at a luncheon in his honor, the Chinese Foreign Minister mentioned America, Karakhan retorted:

I decidedly refuse the honor of treading the path of America's policy in China. Russia will never follow the example of America . . . Nothing pleased me more during my recent stay in Harbin than the fact that I saw there a Chinese administration, Chinese laws and the realization of Chinese sovereignty.

To the rising tide of nationalism in China his pronouncements sounded like a battle cry. But for a long time even Karakhan was unable to reach an agreement. The stumbling block was Mongolia.

RECONQUEST OF MONGOLIA

It was not until 1921 that the Red Army entered Outer Mongolia and the struggle over her status began between Soviet Russia and China.

The Russo-Chinese agreement stipulating, on the one hand, the sovereignty of China over Mongolia and, on the other, factual Russian protection and control of Mongol affairs had been in force since 1915. Since the beginning of the Revolution Russia's influence had been diminishing and when she became engulfed in civil war and China became a member of the anti-Soviet coalition, the Peking government quite naturally endeavored to abolish the agreement of 1915 and to regain control of Outer Mongolia. The Mongols hoped under the new circumstances to gain genuine independence from both Russia and China. While they hoped, however, a Chinese army under General Hsu Chow-tseng was preparing to enter Mongolia and to restore it to its former status of a Chinese province. In the fall of 1919 General Hsu with his troops appeared in Urga, the capital, and by means of threats and arrests forced the Mongol Government to request China to abolish the autonomy of Mongolia. The Khutukhtu, presented with an ultimatum, signed a petition as a result of which the President of the Chinese Republic on November 22 proclaimed the reunification of Mongolia with the rest of the country. The old Russian envoys in Urga, as well as

3. Fischer, *op. cit.*, II, 541–542.

the Russian envoy to Peking, demanded maintenance of former Russian rights in Mongolia, but their vigorous protests were, of course, of no avail.

In the meanwhile the Russian civil war had shifted nearer the borders of Mongolia, and certain "White" leaders began to play with the idea, popular among the Mongols, of creating a single great Mongol state comprising not only Outer and Inner Mongolia and the Buryat region of Siberia but the territories of the Tibetans, the Kirghizs, and Kalmyks of central Asia, from the Caspian Sea to Lake Baikal. In February, 1919, at a pan-Mongol congress held in Chita, on Russian soil, a Provisional Government of the future Mongol state was created.[4] Its life was very short. Immediately after its creation Chinese troops began the occupation of Outer Mongolia. The idea of a great Mongol state, however, lived on and became the guiding star of a small White army under Gen. Ungern Sternberg which entered Mongolia in October, 1920. In February, 1921, Ungern captured Urga, the capital, and the Chinese were forced to retreat. For a few months, Ungern was the ruler of Outer Mongolia.

Baron Ungern Sternberg was a former Russian officer of German descent. His native land was in the Baltic provinces of the old Russian Empire which produced a number of exponents of political ideas that bore the seeds of subsequent National Socialism. (Alfred Rosenberg, ideologist of Nazism, was also a native of the Baltic States). Ungern hated democracy, republicanism, political freedom, Communists, Socialists, and Jews. He was cruel in the extreme. The atrocities committed by his troops on his instructions appeared extraordinary even at a time when Russia herself was drowning in the blood and barbarism of the civil war.

Ungern wanted to restore, as autocracies, all the submerged monarchies; Bogdo-Gegen was to regain his throne in Mongolia, the Manchus were to return to Peking, the Hohenzollerns and Romanovs were to be restored in Germany and Russia. The great force that was to achieve these aims was to be an Asiatic power under a new Attila who would create a strong army under the banner of "Asia for the Asiatics" and "march across Europe like the divine wrath." Ungern "geared himself for the role of a new

4. *Novyi vostok*, II, 596–597.

Attila . . . The words 'Bolshevik' and 'Communist' were always accompanied by the phrase 'to be hanged.' " [5]

When Ungern's army entered Urga in February, 1921, massacres on a large scale were perpetrated against Chinese, Russian Jews, and such "reds" as could be found on Mongol soil. Ungern then proclaimed the complete independence of Mongolia from China, and the Khutukhtu was solemnly restored as the supreme ruler of the land. Within a few months Ungern was set for a war against the Red Army in Siberia as well as against the guerrillas of the Far Eastern Republic—a war intended to liberate Russia from Bolshevism. He took the road to Kiakhta and crossed the Russian frontier at the end of May. In the few battles that were fought Ungern was completely defeated. He was taken prisoner by Soviet troops on July 22, and on November 15 he was executed.

Pursuing the remnants of Ungern's armies, the Red detachments entered Mongolia and on July 6, occupied the city of Urga. With their arrival there began a new chapter in the history of Mongolia. Since July, 1921, Outer Mongolia has been under firm Soviet control.

MONGOL "DEMOCRACY"

The methods of Soviet penetration of Outer Mongolia and the technique applied are the more remarkable in that they represent the first instance of extension of Soviet control over a neighboring non-Russian area. All the slogans and devices employed two decades later in other parts of the Eurasian continent were present in this first experiment: propaganda about "friendly government," "higher type" of democracy, "struggle against world imperialism," and actually rule by a small minority, political alliance with Moscow, and military and economic control of the resources of the distant state by the Soviet Government.

Before the Red Army entered Mongolia a conference took place at the Russo-Mongol border town of Kiakhta in March, 1921, under the auspices of a new Mongol party which had been created shortly before—the People's Revolutionary party. The party was a very small one; even officially it did not claim a membership of

5. I. Serebrennikov, *Veliki otkhod* (Harbin, 1936), p. 71.

more than 160. The guiding hand and spirit of Russian Communism were evident in every step of its activities; it was an agency of the Soviet Government.

The party was immediately accepted into the Communist International, and two delegates participated in the Third Congress of the International in July–August, 1921. The party did not call itself Communist—it would seem ridiculous to establish a Soviet or Communist system in a country where neither industry nor railways exist and where the great majority of the population are extremely poor and illiterate herdsmen; nor was it considered possible to establish a Soviet constitution for a nation without a working class.

Practically, however, the party was a segment of the Russian Communist party which had encountered the same backward kind of civilization in certain regions of old Russia, such as Kirghizia, Uzbekia, and Turkmenia. In its program the party did not advocate "socialization of all the means of production," but it called for "political democracy" according to the usual Soviet interpretation —one-party rule, with no opposition tolerated. "It is a bourgeois-democratic system—*of a new type*," with the prospect of avoiding, in its development, the capitalist stage.[6]

At this Kiakhta conference, a "Provisional Revolutionary Government of Mongolia" was set up. On April 10, 1921, the government officially "asked" the Soviet Government for assistance. The assistance was granted, of course, all the details having been prearranged.

The People's Revolutionary party, after it had been established in Mongolia as the pro-Soviet group in power, was paraded before the world as a purely national movement, independent of Russia. The Soviet Army and Soviet officials were kept in the background. During the first three years of its life, the party was cautious in its internal policy, since a difficult diplomatic war was being waged between Russia and China over the fate of Mongolia. As long as that was not definitely determined, the Soviet Government even considered it necessary to keep the Khutukhtu as the nominal head of the state, and the Mongolian People's Revolutionary party therefore proclaimed Mongolia a constitutional monarchy. For two years the party fought popular movements directed against the

6. *Pravda*, April 8, 1936.

new regime; not until 1924 (after China practically gave up her claims to Mongolia) did it proceed to abolish the monarchy and to move to the left, following a great purge in which one of its creators, the commander in chief of its army, and several ministers were executed.

Between 1921 and 1924 the Mongol problem was the chief issue between the Soviet and Chinese Governments. Before the Soviet troops entered Mongolia, Chicherin had sent a reassuring note to China. Russian military units, he said in his note of November 11, 1920, will appear in Chinese territory as "friendly troops who would consider their task fulfilled after the final destruction of White Guardist bands in Mongolia, and the restoration of Chinese sovereignty, and would then immediately leave Chinese territory." [7]

On November 5, 1921, a treaty was concluded between the Soviet Government and the new pro-Soviet regime of Outer Mongolia. It provided for mutual recognition of the two governments; China was not mentioned. The establishment of consulates was provided for, and Russia undertook to construct postal and telephone communication lines in Mongolia—Mongolia obligating herself to cede to Russia such territory as would be needed for the ultimate construction of railroads. An area adjoining Mongolia in the west—called Uryankhai, or Tannu Tuva—and claimed by Mongolia as part of its state, was not acknowledged as such by the Soviet Government. Instead, Tannu Tuva was set up as a separate state and annexed outright to the Soviet Union in 1944. [8]

After the conclusion of the treaty ties between official Mongolia and Russia became closer. Two Russian Communists, Okhtin and Berezin, arrived as the real masters in Urga, and a third, Butin, became financial "adviser" of the Mongol Government. [9] Offices were opened by Soviet economic agencies, such as the Oil Syndicate, the Siberian State Trade, and Wool Purchase agency; the new Mongol Bank depended upon the Soviet State Bank, etc. Soviet military instructors remained in Mongolia even after the rest of the

7. *China Year Book, 1924–1925*, p. 860.
8. In its survey of events of 1922, the People's Commissariat for Foreign Affairs said: "On March 5, the People's Government of the Uryankhai region, between Siberia and northwest Mongolia, notified the Soviet Government of its formation and of the departure of a special delegation for Moscow to establish friendly relations with the RSFSR" (p. 71).
9. I. Levine, *op. cit.*, p. 147.

Soviet troops departed. A secret police, on the Moscow model, was organized in Urga, and from 1922 to 1924 it engaged in unearthing "plots" and suppressing them by the usual methods. Thus, on September 5, 1922, it officially reported a conspiracy of Mongol "reactionaries" who, "after tortures, have admitted their crimes and confessed." [10] Other reports mentioned three counterrevolutionary plots "liquidated" in the years 1922–24.

In order not to complicate the negotiations with China, the text of the treaty with Mongolia was not published. When rumors of the treaty reached Peking, the Chinese Minister asked Paikes, the Soviet envoy, for an explanation. Paikes denied the existence of the treaty. Finally, however, it had to be made public. Irritation against Russian tactics mounted high in Peking. On May 1, 1922, the Chinese Foreign Minister addressed a note to Paikes, in which he said:

According to the recent report of General Li Yuan on the subject of the Russo-Mongolian Treaty, we asked you about this matter when you first arrived in Peking and you replied that it was entirely untrue. However, during a recent conversation with you, I again put the question to you, owing to the recent publication by the papers of the text of the treaty, and you admitted the truth of this report.

The Soviet Government has repeatedly declared to the Chinese Government: that all previous treaties made between the Russian Government and China shall be null and void: that the Soviet Government renounces all encroachments of Chinese territory and all concessions within China, and that the Soviet Government will unconditionally and forever return what has been forcibly seized from China by the former Imperial Russian Government and the bourgeois[ie].

Now the Soviet Government has suddenly gone back on its own word and, secretly and without any right, concluded a treaty with Mongolia. Such action on the part of the Soviet Government is similar to the policy the former Imperial Russian Government assumed toward China.

It must be observed that Mongolia is a part of Chinese territory and as such has long been recognised by all countries. In secretly concluding a treaty with Mongolia, the Soviet Government has not only broken faith with its previous declarations but also violates all principles of justice.

10. Korostovets, *op. cit.*, pp. 330–331.

The Chinese Government finds it difficult to tolerate such an action, and therefore we solemnly lodge a protest with you to the effect that any treaty secretly concluded between the Soviet Government and Mongolia will not be recognised by the Chinese Government.[11]

Thus the Mongol issue became the most important point in dispute between the Soviet and Chinese Governments. In all negotiations conducted by China with the Soviet envoys, "the Russian offers [the official Soviet report read] were turned down by the Chinese Government, which demanded the prior evacuation of Mongolia." The next year's survey melancholically repeated: "Our sympathy for Mongolia was considered by China as an attempt to detach Mongolia from China" (*1923*, p. 99).

While denying the assertion of Wellington Koo that Russia ruled in Mongolia, Comrade Joffe stated that Mongolia was being ruled by local Mongolian authorities, and that Russian forces temporarily remain on Mongolian soil solely in order to prevent making Mongolia once again the staging area for White Guardist forces that are assembled in the Russian Far East and on the territory of China.[12]

A well-known Chinese liberal, Professor Lyu sent an open letter to Joffe in which he said:

During my stay in southern China I read with tremendous interest your energetic protests against the continued occupation of the northern part of Sakhalin Island [by Japan]. I must recognize the propriety of your claims. At the same time I have the honor of reminding you that Russia is committing an exactly similar act in keeping Urga under its control to this day. The city is an absolutely Chinese one, and nonetheless you are occupying it . . . How can Russia hold under its control a part of Chinese territory while it is protesting the Japanese occupation of Sakhalin? [13]

Even in southern China, where pro-Russian sympathies were particularly strong, Soviet policy in Mongolia caused difficulties and aroused protests. If Mongolia is to be independent, why is Russia holding her grip so tight? Is Russia not going the same road as the old tsarist government? The Chinese were accusing Moscow of imperialism; the Soviet leaders retorted by leveling the same

11. *China Year Book, 1923*, p. 680.
12. People's Commissariat of Foreign Affairs, *Mezhdunarodnaya politika RSFSR* (1922), p. 71.
13. *Mezhdunarodnaya Zhizn'* (1923), No. 1, p. 121.

accusation against China: its intention to hold Mongolia under Chinese rule was branded as imperialistic, while Russia's control was considered "liberation."

Moscow was resolved not to return Mongolia to China until China herself should turn pro-Soviet and firmly ally herself with Russia. In this connection Grigori Zinoviev, President of the Third International, stated:

. . . a definitive solution of the Mongolian question will not become possible until the Chinese themselves shall liberate themselves from the yoke of their oppressors, until they chase from their borders the soldiers of foreign imperialist nations, until the revolution shall be victorious in their country.[14]

This Soviet policy had its greatest success with the White émigrés in the Far East and elsewhere, who, seeing in it a return to old tsarist traditions,[15] wholeheartedly applauded it. In Harbin a pro-Soviet group was created among the rightist elements of the emigration under the name *Smena vekh* ("Change of Landmarks"). For the first time (but not the last!) it presented the philosophy of a gradual "evolution" of Russian Communism toward historical traditions, sound nationalism, and imperial expansion. However, those members of the group who thereupon returned to Russia fared badly; their leader, Professor Nikolai Ustryalov, along with a few of his friends "acknowledged his mistakes," "confessed"— and completely vanished from public life.

In all the negotiations with Paikes and Joffe, the Chinese Government returned again and again to the question of Mongolia. The People's Commissariat in Moscow in an official report stated that because of the dissension over Mongolia the long-awaited agreement between the two countries was impossible of achievement. Much as Russia wanted to obtain official recognition from Peking, the actual extension of Russian hegemony over the territory of Mongolia was considered more important than formal recognition by China. Moscow would not sacrifice a real possession for the sake of a diplomatic gain.

In the course of the protracted negotiations with China, the

14. *Novyi vostok*, VIII–IX, 218–219.
15. This was the impression created throughout the world. Professor Alfred Dennis wrote in the *North American Review* (1923), p. 303: "Today Soviet Russia is playing an old game with new cards. The technique of her diplomacy in the Far East is novel, but the policy has much that is familiar."

Soviet Foreign Office also applied a shrewd method which proved quite effective. This was to make use of a certain rivalry that existed between Japan and China (neither of them had as yet settled its relations with Russia, and each was wary lest its rival reach an agreement with Moscow at its expense). China feared that Russia might cede to Japan certain rights to the Harbin-Changchun Railroad, and Japan looked with apprehension at the potential Russo-Chinese combination. In order to increase this nervousness, Joffe went from China to Japan. "Mr. Joffe's visit to Japan occasioned no little uneasiness in Peking . . ." [16] But when Karakhan was appointed to go to China, it was Japan's turn to suspect trouble. In order to prod Japan into an agreement, *Izvestiya* wrote, on August 22, 1923: "Japan displays uneasiness in connection with the resumption of Russo-Chinese negotiations . . . The Russo-Chinese rapprochement may bar to Japan access to the Asiatic mainland." A few days later *Izvestiya* invited the Manchurian ruler, Chang Tso-lin, to break with Japan.

After three years of negotiations, in which the fate of Mongolia was the focal point, the Chinese Government came to the conclusion that it had no forces or means at its disposal with which to restore the status quo ante in Mongolia, and that it had to acquiesce in the actual separation of Mongolia from China. It then reverted to the same construction that had been recognized by both Russia and China before the Revolution: Chinese sovereignty over Mongolia was recognized on paper, while Russia's actual dominance there was acknowledged. On this basis a treaty was finally concluded between Moscow and Peking on May 31, 1924.

With Mongolia eliminated from the Russo-Chinese agenda, the Manchurian problem soon became the bone of contention.

CONFLICTS ABOUT THE LIFE LINE

The Soviet-Chinese treaty of 1924 declared null and void all previous Chinese-Russian agreements. It promised to "replace them by new treaties on the basis of equality, reciprocity, and justice." As for Outer Mongolia, it was agreed that formally "it constitutes a component of the Chinese Republic, and the USSR will respect China's sovereignty." The Chinese Eastern Railway

16. *China Year Book, 1924,* p. 864.

was to be considered a purely commercial enterprise. The local administration in northern Manchuria and in the leased territory was to remain under Chinese jurisdiction. All capitalist concessions in China were renounced by Russia. Finally Russia renounced extraterritorial rights, consular jurisdiction, and its share of the Boxer indemnities. Seven declarations annexed to the main treaty settled other questions in dispute, such as the status of Russian churches in China, buildings, and property rights.

The struggle among the Chinese war lords hit its peak early in the twenties and brought in its wake a high degree of disintegration of China, whose formal government in Peking was helpless and impotent and often fell prey to this or that of the contending generals. In Manchuria, General Chang Tso-lin was absolute dictator, and the autonomy of Manchuria was in fact so great as to amount to complete independence. All the provisions of the Russo-Chinese treaty in regard to Manchuria and the Chinese Eastern Railway could therefore become effective only if acknowledged by the Manchurian dictator. He demanded a renegotiation of terms, then signed the agreement with certain modifications in September, 1924. The new status of the Chinese Eastern Railway was defined as a joint administration by China—actually Manchuria—and Russia on an equal basis. In fact, the agreement provided for equal representation of Russians and Chinese on the board of directors as well as in the several departments and even among the personnel of the railroad. The profits were to be divided equally between Moscow and Mukden. Russia's rights to a 50 per cent share in the railroad were secured for 32 years only; in 1956 China was to succeed to all Russian properties and rights, without payment. China also obtained the right to redeem the railroad before that date at a price to be settled by a special Chinese-Soviet commission. All questions affecting the Chinese Eastern Railway, the agreement said, would be resolved "without the participation of any third party." This was a distinct rebuff by both Russia and China to French and other claims. The Russo-Asiatic Bank lost its case. Foreign investors had to write off considerable sums, and this was a triumph for both Soviet policy and the rising Chinese Nationalist movement.

The harmony resulting from the conclusion of the Mukden agreement was short lived, however. Soon after its signing conflicts arose between the two parties and continued for a period of five years, during which they developed into an armed conflict between China and Russia. The conflicts ended only when Japan invaded Manchuria in 1931 and gave a new slant to the entire problem of the Chinese Eastern Railway.

INDEPENDENT SINKIANG

During the first years after the Russian Revolution trade with Sinkiang decreased considerably; political pressure from the Russian side of the border ceased, the Russian armies in central Asia melted away. Russian influence in Sinkiang all but disappeared.

Now remnants of the defeated and fleeing White armies of General Bakich and Atamans Dutov and Anenkov, crossed into Sinkiang in considerable numbers. It was estimated that some 50,-000 troops thus entered China; the great majority of them soon moved eastward, but about 6,000 remained in Sinkiang during the twenties.[17]

The first agreement between Soviet Russia and Sinkiang was concluded on May 27, 1920. In accordance with the then prevalent trend of abolishing "unjust tsarist treaties," the privileges accorded to Russian tradesmen in 1881 were renounced. The agreement was signed by the Governor of Sinkiang and later approved by Peking. Although technically limited to the Ili district, it was actually applied to all of Sinkiang. It remained in force until October, 1931.[18]

When the great uprisings of the 1920's in Russian Turkestan were quelled, and especially in 1930, when the collective farming experiment there got under way, great numbers of natives of Soviet central Asia began to move into Sinkiang. Unlike the White armies, these Russian "émigrés" belonged to the same ethnic strains as the natives of Sinkiang. At first they managed to move across the border with horses and cattle; later they arrived without any property. The number of these refugees is unknown; it must have amounted to many thousands.

In the meanwhile the Soviet Union was consolidating its central Asian provinces. The formerly vassal states of Khiva and Bukhara

17. I. Serebrennikov, *op. cit.*, pp. 258–262.
18. *China Weekly Review*, February 18, 1939.

were proclaimed People's Republics in 1921; in 1924–25 they ceased to exist as autonomous units and were incorporated into the Soviet Union. By 1925 the former imperial provinces of central Asia were once again firmly in Russia's hands, and now the attention of Moscow was once more drawn to the neighboring Province of Sinkiang. Ten years after the Revolution the drive to the east was resumed.

Soon after the Soviet-Chinese treaty of 1924 was signed, Soviet consulates were opened in Sinkiang, and Chinese consulates in Russia. It was important that the Chinese consuls in adjacent Soviet central Asia were appointed not by the Central Chinese Government but by the provincial administration of Sinkiang. These consuls considered themselves more or less independent of Peking and sometimes assumed attitudes which, under normal conditions, would have been termed disloyal. Thus in December, 1927, after the suppression of the Communist uprising in Canton, Soviet-Chinese relations were severed and the consulates ordered closed. The Sinkiang consular agents, however, published a proclamation to the effect that they were "subordinated to the government of Peking, but only in so far as the actions and instructions of that government are not directed against the interests of western Asia." The Soviet press played up a statement by the Sinkiang Consul General at Semipalatinsk and his secretary, declaring that:

Black reaction in southern China is assuming terrifying proportions . . . The Semipalatinsk consulate has nothing in common with southern China, and therefore cannot assume the responsibility for the current events in southern China. This consulate is subject to western China, which in no way wishes or seeks a disruption of friendship with the USSR . . . The indissolubility and solidity of the friendship of western China with the USSR is fortified by the existence of five of our Chinese consulates of western China in the USSR, namely, in Semipalatinsk, in Zaisan, in Alma-Ata, in Tashkent, and in Andizhan; and the USSR has five consulates in western China, namely, in Urumchi, Chuguchak, Kashgar, Kuldja, and in the Artei region; the interrelations between them being the most friendly and peaceful. These mutual relations and friendship between western China and the USSR must be ceaseless and undying.[19]

19. *Izvestiya*, January 8, 1928.

Two years later Sinkiang again asserted the same measure of independence from China when an armed conflict broke out between China and Russia over the Chinese Eastern Railway. All Chinese consuls in Russia were ordered to close their offices; those of Sinkiang failed to obey and continued to operate as if unaffected by Russo-Chinese relations.

In 1928 Governor Yeng died, after 17 years of autocratic rule, and a new time of troubles began. Early in the thirties the new Turkestan-Siberian Railway was completed, bringing Russia close to Sinkiang's borders. Soviet intervention in the civil war in Sinkiang (1931–34) brought about an upheaval as a result of which the province came under indirect Soviet control. This state of affairs lasted until 1942 when, as a consequence of the Russo-German war, Russian troops and economy were withdrawn from Sinkiang. Soviet influence made itself felt again from 1944 on, growing in step with the increase in Soviet influence throughout east Asia and the disintegration of the Chinese state.

VIII

Kuomintang, Chinese Communism, and Moscow

In 1922–24 the long-cherished hope that a social revolution was developing in Europe and would soon be victorious—that the West would soon join hands with revolutionary Russia—was collapsing. The tide of revolution that began in central Europe in 1918–19 was obviously receding, and the political strikes and uprisings which the Communists had backed were turning into utter failures. The European situation was returning to a modicum of stability. As a consequence of these unfavorable developments in Europe, Moscow had to adopt many a fateful decision on foreign as well as domestic policies.

Gradually China began to advance to the fore as the next probable ally in the great struggle against world-wide imperialism. Were not the devious roads of social revolution leading through Canton rather than through Berlin? If China were to ally herself with Soviet Russia and thus be lost to resurgent "world imperialism"; if her 400 million people should arise against oppression—not only against oppression within China, that is, but above all against oppression by the leviathans of capitalism all over east Asia—then much of what had been lost in Germany and western Europe would be won back for the cause of Moscow.

What was the itinerary of world revolution? Grigori Zinoviev, President of the Communist International, saw a new ray of hope in the East:

After the victory of the Russian Revolution, we all agreed that Germany's turn would be next, after which revolution would make the rounds of all Europe. It is only now that the question is being persistently asked whether this view of the further route of the revolution, as its only possible route, is correct.

Can it be that we are mistaken in appraising this route? We should consider other possibilities . . . The East is moving forward far more resolutely than we expected. England appears to be much more shaken than appeared to us . . . The East with its 900 million population is awakening.[1]

In February, 1926, a special session of the Executive Committee of the Communist International met. Its two-volume report appeared under the title *The Itinerary of the Revolution.* Zinoviev now frankly declared:

At first perhaps we attached our eyes too much to Central Europe. That was the time of our passion for Germany, so to speak. It seemed to us that after Russia, the proletarian revolution must necessarily follow in Germany. At our last plenum in 1925 we were obliged to devote great attention to England, while the prospects of revolution in Germany appeared somewhat more distant . . . Now a new, exceptionally important factor has appeared: *the movement in China,* which is fraught with many surprises.[2]

The announcement of the new "itinerary of the revolution" had the result that an important shift took place in the relations between Russia, on the one hand, and France and England on the other. France had been the most insistent of the enemies of the Soviet Government during the years of the civil war and in the ensuing conflicts between Poland-Rumania and Russia; England never went quite so far as France. During the Allied intervention in Russia, Lloyd George often hesitated in taking action and he never gave full support to Poland in her war against Russia; furthermore, his government was the first among the Great Powers to grant the Soviet regime de facto recognition. Continental France was more fearful of Russian activity in Germany and of the Russian menace to the Balkans than was England.

As attention veered from the West to the East, France began to recede into the background, and the role of England, already great, began to attain enormous proportions in Soviet eyes. In China and in the Far East in general French influence was weak compared to the English. The shift of Soviet attention to the East meant a further deterioration of Soviet relations with England. Even the official recognition of Soviet Russia by England early in 1924 failed to provide more than a few months' change in this state of affairs.

1. *Pravda,* April 1, 1925. Speech of March 25, 1925.
2. Speech of February 20, 1926, at the Sixth Plenary Session of the Executive Committee of the Communist International.

The most pronounced and most consistent trait of Soviet foreign policy has been and is its antagonism toward Britain. This antagonism springs from sources both practical and ideological. In practice Soviet policy encounters Britain on all Russian frontiers from the Balkans around the world to Vladivostok. Each Russian move in Persia, Afghanistan, or China has been met by a British countermove; and British action often turned near Russian victories into defeats. Ideologically, England has always appeared, in the Communist conception, as the incarnation of world capitalism and imperialism. The "struggle against imperialism" has often been understood in Russia as the struggle against the British Empire before anything else. Britain—the cradle of industrial capitalism, investor of millions of pounds in the industries all over the world, conqueror of India and cruel suppressor of popular uprisings, aggressor in the Boer War (still fresh in the memory of the older generation of Communists), nation of enormous riches amassed through exploitation of colonial peoples—aroused hatred. The prototype of the "British gentleman," pictured by Communists as cynical, immoral, cold-blooded, hypocritical, and unscrupulous, the descendant of a long line of pirates and millionaires, disgusted them. The Soviet attitude toward Britain has been not only a matter of realistic calculation but also one involving political emotions.

During these last years the opinion has frequently been voiced in the United States that the negative attitude of the Soviet Government toward the West was a form of distrust and suspicion aroused by the policies of the Allies during the period of military intervention in Russia. This is far from the truth. The Russian attitude toward Britain took shape long before the Revolution. In the case of France—the main instigator of military intervention in Russia—the Soviet government nevertheless found it possible to collaborate and even, in the thirties, to conclude an alliance. But not with England.

Thus, paradoxically, the persistent anti-British attitudes and emotions of Imperial Russia were revived, and all energies were again directed to breaking through the network of Britain's worldwide influence. In the twenties it was aversion to the British Empire rather than sympathy for the peoples of China and India that guided Soviet policy in the Orient, where Communist parties were either nonexistent or extremely weak. There was the hope, however, that revolutionary movements in these countries, even if they did not aim at socialism, would weaken and eventually cause the disintegration of the British Empire. Moscow was not so much interested in the internal effects of the revolutions in these countries as in their external repercussions.

In a resolution drafted by Lenin, the Communist International declared:

England, the stronghold of imperialism, has for a century been suffering from overproduction. Without the possession of extensive colonies, which are so necessary for the marketing of products and also to provide raw materials, the capitalist structure of England would have broken down long ago under its own weight. While it holds hundreds of millions of inhabitants of Asia and Africa in slavery, English imperialism at the same time keeps the British proletariat in subjection to the bourgeoisie . . . The separation of colonies and a proletarian revolution at home will overthrow the capitalist system in Europe. For the achievement of complete success of the world revolution, the co-operation of these two forces is essential.[3]

In 1922 it was Lenin again who wrote:

. . . This is but one episode in the history of the downfall of the international bourgeoisie . . . India and China are seething. They represent more than 700 million men. With the addition of the adjacent homogeneous Asiatic countries, they represent more than half of the world's population . . . The revolutionary movements that are on the rise in India and China are already being drawn into the revolutionary struggle, into the revolutionary movement for an international revolution.[4]

And in December, 1926, the International hopefully stated: "The Chinese Revolution is one of the most important and powerful factors that destroy the stabilization of capitalism . . . The further victories of the Revolutionary Canton Army, supported by wide masses of the Chinese people, will bring about victory over imperialism and independence for China." [5]

The Second Congress of the Communist International stated

3. Second Congress of the Communist International, August 7, 1920. *Stenographic Report* (in Russian), p. 496.
4. Lenin, *Collected Works* (2d Russian ed.), XXVII, 293.
5. Resolution of the Seventh Plenary Session of the Communist International, December 16, 1926.

that "the first step of the revolution in colonial areas must be the overthrow of foreign capitalism." Consequently, "the task of the Communist parties of the Pacific coast region is the conduct of energetic propaganda . . . calling the masses to an active struggle for their national liberation and insisting on their orientation on Soviet Russia." [6]

A complete system of "socialist economy" similar to that of the Soviet Union was out of the question for China. It was conceded that the peasants of China—80 per cent of her population—were a "petty bourgeois" class, and no radical transformation of the agrarian economy was contemplated for the immediate future. Caution and moderation were also considered necessary to facilitate the emergence of a coalition government that would be uncompromisingly opposed to Britain and closely allied with the Soviet Union.

The early twenties was the period when the Soviet Government was striving to gain de jure recognition from great and small nations alike. The relationship between Moscow and Peking was but one chapter in this struggle for recognition. Peking was the site of the official—the only internationally recognized—government of China, whose real strength did not, however, extend beyond a limited territorial area while a war between the Chinese generals was going on. It is for this reason that in the relations between Russia and China, other Chinese governments, personalities, and armies played a more important role than did those of Peking.

There was no Communist party in China in the first years after the Soviet Revolution, and when the party first appeared, around 1921–22, it consisted of a few hundred men without any practical influence. But another revolutionary party existed in China—the Kuomintang—which was neither Communist nor Socialist, which had already played an important role in the Chinese Revolution and which was now prepared to collaborate with the Soviet Government. Yet the policy of the Kuomintang, which was to become the great hope of Soviet activities in the country, was directed against the Peking government from which Moscow desired to obtain recognition.

6. Resolution of the Fourth Congress of the Communist International, December 5, 1922.

DR. SUN AND COMRADE CHIANG KAI-SHEK

In the history of the Chinese Revolution, Sun Yat-sen occupied a position as high as that of Lenin in Russia. An intelligent, stubborn, and hunted revolutionist, he had gone abroad when it became impossible for him to remain in China. He created groups of sympathizers among Chinese emigrants, participated in the Chinese Revolution of 1911–12, and became President pro tempore of the Chinese Republic in 1912. After a short time, however, he was compelled to cede the presidency to Yuan Shi-kai and later had to flee again from China. Not until 1920 did he return to Canton, now hailed as one of the greatest men of China, popular leader and uncompromising revolutionary and anti-imperialist. Father and head of the Kuomintang (literally the Country's People's party), he created the ideology which after his death became the official philosophy of modern China.

A son of southern China, Dr. Sun was animated by a passionate urge to see his nation independent, freed of humiliating treaties and foreign control. In his impressionable early years—the seventies and eighties of the last century—Britain and France were the two powers that had inflicted on China one defeat after another, carved up territories, and imposed unequal treaties. The great port of Hongkong, in the vicinity of Sun's Canton, had been taken over by the British. The French were in Indo-China and had extended their influence into the Chinese Provinces of Kwangsi and Yunnan. Sun Yat-sen witnessed the unfortunate war between China and France in 1885, observed India's fight against Britain, and the Boer War in South Africa. In Sun's native land, Britain annexed lands, prosecuted her trade with great vigor, erected banks and industrial plants. She was the strongest single power on Chinese soil. Sun saw Britain as the mightiest among China's enemies. He often changed his attitude toward other powers, but never his attitude toward Britain. He thus conceived an image of international politics similar to that of Lenin.

While in northern China and Manchuria Japan and Russia were becoming the most important external forces, in southern and central China, England remained in first place. Therefore the Nationalist movement in southern and central China, as soon as it arose, was directed against Britain. For this reason Dr. Sun's party was considered by Moscow as an ally and a source of great hopes.

As far as Japan was concerned, Dr. Sun was rather inclined to take a friendly attitude. To him Japan was living proof that Asiatic nations could rise against and successfully oppose the Western world. He had been delighted to see yellow Japan defeat white Russia. Even China's defeat at the hands of Japan (1894–95) did not substantially change his basic belief that some day Japan would be able to lead the Orient against the Occident. And the Occident was, in the main, Great Britain. This attitude of a great Chinese Nationalist toward Japan can be understood only against his historical background and experience. Japan was gradually rising to the stature of a modern nation, and to a degree she was the pride of the East in its rivalry with the West.

In 1914 Dr. Sun wrote in a letter to Count Okuma, the Japanese Premier:

The governments and peoples of the two countries [China and Japan] will be on much more intimate terms than exist between any other two countries. With China throwing open all her markets for the benefit of Japanese trade and industry, Japan will virtually monopolize the commercial field of her neighbor. China then will strive to free herself from the bondage imposed on her by foreign powers and to revise the unequal treaties, and in order to attain these objectives China will again need Japan's assistance in handling diplomatic questions. If Japan, after China has improved her laws and judicial and prison systems, with Japanese guidance and help, takes the lead in effecting the abolition of extraterritoriality in China, the latter will in turn permit Japanese subjects to settle in the interior, further facilitating the Japanese in China. When China regains her customs autonomy, she will enter into a sort of customs union with Japan, whereby Japanese manufactures imported into China and Chinese raw materials imported into Japan will be mutually exempt from customs duty. In this way the prosperity of Japanese commerce and industry expands with the development of China's national resources.[7]

Dr. Sun's connection with Japan was all the more natural at that time since Japan, opposing the regime of Yuan Shi-kai, supported southern opposition to the Peking government. Dr. Sun therefore rested his hopes on Japan's assistance in his revolutionary

7. Sun Yat-sen, *China and Japan* (Shanghai, 1941). Letter to Count Okuma, dated May 11, 1914. Subsequent quotations are from the same volume.

movement: "What are we expecting from Japan in connection with our revolutionary movement? History shows that France helped America, Great Britain helped Spain, the United States helped Panama, in gaining their independence . . . What is the fear, then, which prevents Japan from going into action?"

Even the "21 demands" and Japan's humiliating policy toward China during the first World War did not dissuade Sun Yat-sen. In 1917 he wrote: "It appears that Japan's aim in China is not necessarily aggressive; her actions have more often than not proved beneficial to China. It is wrong, therefore, to accuse Japan of harboring wild ambitions." And in 1924: "The question remains whether Japan will be the hawk of Western civilization's rule of Might, or the tower of strength of the Orient. This is the choice which lies before the people of Japan."

A few months before his death Dr. Sun repeated his belief in Pan-Asianism, embracing, naturally, a united front of China and Japan: "We advocate Pan-Asianism in order to restore the status of Asia . . . If we want to regain our rights, we must resort to force . . . Should all Asiatic peoples thus unite together and present a united front against the Occidentals, they will win the final victory." [8]

As far as Britain was concerned, Dr. Sun spoke in quite different language. He strongly opposed China's entry into the first World War as Britain's ally against Germany. He saw no reason for antagonism toward Germany, and even less reason to assist the Allies who, to him, had been and remained the great oppressors of the Orient:

England and France have treated their colonial subjects even more cruelly than Germany treats conquered nations, and yet it is said that they have not committed any offense against humanity!

Every year England takes large quantities of foodstuffs for her own consumption from India, where in the last ten years 19,000,000 people have died from starvation . . . What India has produced for herself has been wrested from her by England, with the result that the Indians themselves are starving. Is such action compatible with the principles of humanity?

The British Government, Dr. Sun maintained, was misusing China for British purposes:

8. Speech in Kobe, Japan, November 28, 1924.

For centuries Britain has followed unswervingly a policy of seeking friends among those countries which can be sacrificed in order to satisfy this purpose, and that is why Britain wants her [China] for an ally . . .

If China should join the war, she would sacrifice herself somehow or other for England, and then either Germany or Russia would reap the benefit of China's sacrifice.

In respect to the United States there was no strong animosity, but a great deal of mistrust, expressed in Dr. Sun's statements. He remembered the history of Korea, which was actually ceded to Japan with President Theodore Roosevelt's consent. He did not believe the United States would ever become China's ally against England. The United States therefore seemed unreliable to him:

As America will never antagonize a strong world power [Britain] for the sake of a country in which she has no interest, she cannot be relied upon by China . . . For thousands of years Korea was a tributary state of China. It was the United States that first seduced Korea into separating herself from China . . . Korea perished because it relied upon someone who could not be relied upon.

Thus, Dr. Sun's conceptions seemed strangely parallel to those of the Soviet Government: the same strong animosity toward Britain and the same negative stand toward the United States and France. What, in Moscow's conception, was a struggle between capitalism and Communism, in Sun's teachings appeared as the great fight between Right and Might. To Sun, Oriental civilization was the rule of Right, whereas that of the Occident was the rule of Might.

The war of the future will be between Might and Right. Today Germany is the oppressed nation of Europe. The small and weak nations of Asia (excepting Japan) were all subject to bitter oppression and to all kinds of suffering. They will some day unite with sympathetic fellow sufferers and take the field in a life and death struggle against the oppressive states . . .[9]

Russia, he believed, was then on the side of Right against Might:

At present, Russia is attempting to separate from the white peoples in Europe. Why? Because she insists on the rule of Right and denounces the rule of Might. She advocates the principle of benevolence and jus-

9. Sun Yat-sen, *Principles of Nationalism* (1924).

tice . . . Recent Russian civilization is similar to our ancient civilization. Therefore, she joins with the Orient and separates from the West. The new principles of Russia were considered intolerable by the Europeans.

A vague idea was taking shape in Sun Yat-sen's mind of a great coalition embracing all the nations dominated by the Great Eurasian Powers: Germany, Russia, China,[10] with Japan as a potential adherent.

When the Soviet Government proclaimed a reversal in Russia's policy toward China and came out for complete abolition of unequal treaties, privileges, and "territorial grabs," and when Karakhan addressed one note after another to China calling for collaboration of the two nations against imperialist oppression, Dr. Sun began to wonder whether a new ally had not emerged in his eternal fight for China's national resurrection.

The most important role in this combination would, of course, belong to Russia, which was then considered by Dr. Sun as a nation of Asiatics. Therefore, better relations between Russia and Japan were required. In an interview with a representative of *Jiji*, a Japanese news agency, in November, 1922, he further developed this idea:

If Japan really wants to see Asia ruled by Asiatics, it must develop its relations with Russia.

The Russians are Asiatics. There is Asiatic blood in their veins. Japan must combine with Russia in the defense against the excesses of the Anglo-Saxons.[11]

THE RUSSIAN PERIOD IN THE HISTORY OF THE KUOMINTANG

It would seem that the natural channel for Soviet influence in China would have been the Chinese Communist party. However in the early twenties this party, as we have seen, consisted of a group of only a few hundred men; it was politically negligible. The Kuomintang, on the other hand, was an influential revolutionary

10. Maurice Lewandowsky in *Revue des deux mondes*, April 15, 1926; and Ken-shen Weigh, *Russian-Chinese Diplomacy* (Shanghai, 1928), p. 318.
11. Karl Haushofer, *Japan's Reichserneuerung* (Leipzig, 1930), p. 20. Quoted from the Tokyo *Japan Advertiser*.

organization which dominated an important area and had its leader as president in Canton. But the Kuomintang was an independent party and, from the point of view of Moscow, not completely reliable. For propaganda purposes the little Communist party was sufficient; for a big campaign, at least a combination of the Kuomintang and the Chinese Communists appeared necessary.

This combination was the essence of the Soviet policy of the four-year period from 1923 to 1927, which in the history of the Kuomintang, as well as in that of China at large, can be termed the "Russian period." Great as the influence of Russia's arms and pressure may have been at different moments in the history of the Far East, never before (and never after) was Russian control so extensive and so intensive as during these years. Moreover, the control was willingly accepted by China. Should the friendly government of Canton become master of the whole of China, the potentialities of this control seemed to be enormous.

The Communist-Kuomintang combination was also a prologue to a passionate fight between its two elements in the following two decades. For Russian Communism, to which the Chinese problem was of the utmost importance, it was the initial chapter of the series of dramatic events in the struggle between Trotsky and Stalin.

The idea of a two-party alliance was first publicly discussed at the second conference of the Chinese Communist party in 1922. Subsequently V. Dalin, the delegate of the Russian Communist Youth League, presented to Sun Yat-sen a plan for the incorporation of the Communists into the Kuomintang. Dr. Sun rejected the plan. Indeed, the presence within the Kuomintang of a heterogeneous organism bound by its own discipline and philosophy could not but lead to misunderstandings and friction.

Soon after the 1922 conference an official representative of the Communist International, G. Maring, met with Dr. Sun in Shanghai. Sun was becoming more and more amenable to collaboration with Russia and was seeking an acceptable compromise on Chinese Communism. He declared himself willing to accept into the Kuomintang individual Communists as party members, with the provision, however, that no separate Communist cells should exist within the party. The Communists would nonetheless retain the right to continue as a separate party outside the Kuomintang. It was a dubious solution, especially in view of the tendency of Communists to dominate every organization in which they participate. It was obviously a compromise with an uncertain future. Maring returned to Moscow in September, 1922, and the Soviet Government dispatched Adolf Joffe to China. Joffe had two missions: to conclude a formal treaty of recognition with official China in Peking, and to prepare a far-reaching program of collaboration with Peking's great enemy and rival in Canton, Dr. Sun Yat-sen. Joffe's discussions with Dr. Sun were prolonged and exhaustive. They resulted in a joint statement in which China's goal was proclaimed as neither Communism nor Socialism, but "national independence." The Soviets pledged full assistance in this campaign.

The joint statement, in which the program of a Chinese nationalist war is outlined alongside Soviet promises of moderation in respect to the class struggle in China, said:

Dr. Sun Yat-sen holds that the Communistic order or even the Soviet system cannot actually be introduced into China, because there do not exist here the conditions for the successful establishment or [sic.] either Communism or Sovietism. This view is entirely shared by Mr. Joffe, who is further of opinion that China's paramount and most pressing problem is to achieve national unification and attain full national independence, and regarding this great task, he has assured Dr. Sun Yat-sen that China has the warmest sympathy of the Russian people and can count on the support of Russia.

In order to clarify the situation, Dr. Sun Yat-sen has requested Mr. Joffe for a reaffirmation of the principles defined in the Russian Note to the Chinese Government, dated September 27, 1920. Mr. Joffe has accordingly re-affirmed [sic.] these principles and categorically declared to Dr. Sun Yat-sen that the Russian Government is ready and willing to enter into negotiations with China on the basis of the renunciation by Russia of all the treaties and exactions which the Tsardom imposed on China, including the treaty or treaties and agreements relating to the Chinese Eastern Railway . . .[12]

As a consequence of this agreement between Sun Yat-sen and Adolf Joffe, in 1923 important steps were taken by both sides. Dr. Sun dispatched among others one of his youngest and ablest aides to study in Moscow and to negotiate for Soviet assistance. The student-envoy was Chiang Kai-shek, who left for Russia in

12. *China Year Book, 1924–1925,* p. 863.

July, 1923. When he returned to China six months later, he was assigned to head a new military school for the training of army officers—the so-called Whampoa Academy. The school was not only created on the Soviet model but received financial assistance from the Soviet Government, which advanced three million rubles for its support.[13] Chinese Communists, too, were among the students.

MIKHAIL BORODIN

In return, in September, 1923, Mikhail Borodin was dispatched from Moscow to China as an adviser to the Kuomintang in Canton. "High Adviser" was indeed a modest title for Borodin, who was actually a political and military chief with tremendous power, great financial resources placed at his disposal by the Soviet Government, and a multitude of Russian political and military experts working strictly under his instructions. In the person of Borodin the "Russian period" of the Kuomintang found its most striking expression.

The rise of Mikhail Borodin (Gruzenberg) to world fame was another instance how historical circumstances imparted stature to a man unprepared and unqualified for it. When Borodin, an émigré to the United States, returned to Russia after the Revolution, he was still a modest and prudent man, seeking neither leadership nor adventure. Emotionally he was close to the Mensheviks, though he did not belong to their party. Not until 1921 did he join the Communists. His knowledge of English and Spanish proved decisive for his career. The Comintern needed people versed in foreign languages, and Borodin went to England with false documents as an agent of Zinoviev's International, was arrested and sentenced to six months of hard labor. Then he returned to Moscow, and some time later was dispatched to China, since English was the international language of the Far East. At first he endeavored to reshape everything on the Soviet pattern. His first task was organizational rather than revolutionary: to streamline the Kuomintang organization and its army. The Kuomintang was still a rather loose association, in striking contrast with the continental parties in Europe, especially Borodin's party in Russia. A few influential men were its

13. Fischer, *op. cit.*, II, 640.

leaders; its sympathizers were scattered individuals all over the country. No party discipline, local committees, or party newspapers existed. There was neither party by-laws nor a party program. "The Kuomintang is dead," Borodin said. "It must be revived." [14]

Today it seems a paradox that, upon Soviet-Communist instructions, Borodin did revive the Kuomintang. He drafted the constitution of the Kuomintang, closely copying the by-laws of the Russian Communist party. He was the author of a manifesto of the Kuomintang. Party organs were created in accordance with his suggestions. A Congress of the Kuomintang Party—the first in its existence—was called for January, 1924. Immediately a "purge" was inaugurated: rightist elements of the Kuomintang who opposed any sort of collaboration with the Communists were expelled. Communists were admitted as individuals. (Dr. Sun took pains, however, not to permit Communists to occupy leading positions in his party; thus, a few Communists were included in the Executive Committee, but none became a member of the powerful Kuomintang Secretariat or of the Army General Staff.) Finally, political collaboration with Russia was proclaimed as the only road to China's independence.

Sun Yat-sen intentionally followed Russian models; he fully approved Borodin's program: "In reorganizing the party," he said, "we have Soviet Russia as our model, hoping to achieve a real revolutionary success." The ties with Russia steadily became closer. When the Whampoa Academy was set up Dr. Sun proclaimed: "In founding this Academy, we are following the example of Russia." The armed forces of the Kuomintang were reorganized in accordance with Borodin's suggestions. "Political education" was introduced. Russian military advisers were attached to each Kuomintang army. The chief military authority was the mysterious Russian General Blücher, then known in China as General Galen, and among the commissars and advisers were a number of Chinese Communists. Friction among them and non-Communists caused conflicts which ultimately led to a showdown between the two factions, although this did not occur until three or four years later.

14. Tsui Shu-chin in *Chinese Social and Political Science Review*, XX (Peiping, 1936), 130.

But at this time, 1923–24, Sun's faith in Russia and in Borodin was great. On leaving Canton for northern China, he issued the following instructions: "Comrade Borodin holds opinions similar to mine. In political matters you must accept his opinions. I hope that you will follow him just as you followed me." [15]

Lenin's death occurred a short time after Borodin's arrival in China. The First Congress of the Kuomintang, then in session, adjourned for three days as a token of respect, and Dr. Sun on this occasion wrote:

During the many centuries of human history thousands of leaders and learned men have appeared, preaching beautiful words that were never realized in life. You, Lenin, are an exception. You not only spoke and taught, but translated your words into reality. You have created a new country. You have shown us the road of a common struggle. You have met thousands of obstacles on your road, obstacles that I meet on my road, too. I want to go your way, and even though my enemies oppose it, my people will hail me for it . . . You have died, but in the memory of subjected peoples you will live for ages, you great man! [16]

In the lectures which he delivered in Canton early in 1924, Sun moved still farther to the left and even accepted certain ideas and concepts of Karl Marx, yet this was rather a temporary zigzag in his personal evolution. In another series of lectures delivered a few months later he was critical of Marxism.

Sun Yat-sen died in March, 1925. In his will he again expressed his conviction that only collaboration with Russia could bring about national independence for China. In a letter signed the day before his death, he said:

Taking leave of you, dear comrades, I want to express the hope that the day will soon come when the USSR will welcome in a free and powerful China a friend and ally, and that in the great struggle for the liberation of the subjected peoples of the world, both allies will march toward victory hand in hand.[17]

The Communist International, for its part, honored Sun Yat-sen in a manifesto "to the popular masses of China":

15. *Ibid.*, p. 102. Quoted by Chiang Kai-shek.
16. Quoted by V. Vilenski-Sibiryakov, *Gomindan* (Moscow, 1926), p. 24.
17. Vilenski-Sibiryakov, *op. cit.*, p. 25.

The Communist International appeals to you to close your ranks more tightly around the popular-revolutionary party of the Kuomintang, around the Communist party of China, and to continue the struggle that was begun decades ago by the late leader of the Kuomintang.

The two men who rose to leadership of the Kuomintang after Dr. Sun's death were Chiang Kai-shek and Wang Ching-wei. Wang appeared to stand to the left of Chiang, but both adhered to the maxim of collaboration with Russia. Borodin used to say that "all must obey General Chiang." Chiang, in turn, stated that Dr. Sun had told him, "Borodin's advice is my advice."

The two leaders continued to follow Dr. Sun's policy. Said Chiang Kai-shek: "Our alliance with the Soviet Union, with the world revolution, is actually an alliance with all the revolutionary parties which are fighting in common against the world imperialists, to carry out the world revolution." Wang Ching-wei went even further: "If we wish to fight against the imperialists, we must not turn against the Communists."

Collaboration between Chiang Kai-shek and Borodin was close; Chiang's army was reorganized with Russian money and by Russian instructors. In a series of battles between the Kuomintang Army and armies of other southern Chinese generals, the superiority of the new military organization became evident. In the course of 1925 the territory held by the Canton government was considerably increased.

The program now consisted of expanding Kuomintang control over central and northern China. This ambitious idea animated leaders of both the Kuomintang and Moscow. If the dream came true, China's national aspirations would be realized, and Moscow would gain for a faithful ally a government of a great nation led and advised from Moscow. Chiang Kai-shek seems to have been more impatient to start the big campaign than was the more cautious Borodin. The latter wanted first to see a well-equipped, reorganized army able to fight its northern rivals. It was not until June, 1926, that the campaign started which was commonly referred to as the Northern Expedition. It proved easier and more successful than had been expected in Moscow.

But before Chiang Kai-shek began the campaign an incident occurred that might have resulted in a complete rupture between the Kuomintang and the Chinese and Russian Communists. On March 20, 1926, Chiang Kai-shek took drastic steps to purge his army of some important Communist elements. Neither the Chinese Communist party nor the Russian leaders drew any fundamental conclusions from this move. They continued for another year to recognize Chiang as the leader of the Chinese Revolution and supported him in his domestic and foreign policies.

IX

Trotsky, Stalin, and Chinese Communism

At its very beginning the Chinese Communist party was composed of a group of intellectuals, embittered by the Versailles Treaty, disappointed in the United States, and passionately inspired by the Russian Revolution. Among the group of students who took part in the First Congress of the Chinese Communist Party in the summer of 1921, the leading role fell to Professor Chen Tu-hsiu of Peking University, a man of broad knowledge, who had studied in Japan and Europe. The future leader, Mao Tse-tung, was present, as was Chang Ho-tao, another leader who was expelled from his party in the late thirties. All the delegates together, however, did not represent more than a handful of revolutionary youths; there was no labor movement behind them. They condemned anarchism, but they also rejected an outright affiliation with the Communist International. It was, as was the initial Communism throughout the whole Orient, an idealistic movement of young revolutionaries and sincere, devoted intellectuals prepared to make any sacrifice for their cause; it was not a mass movement.

These characteristics of Chinese Communism continued to be dominant for another three years. Congresses were held almost every year, but until January, 1925, the membership of the party remained below the 1,000 mark. At its Second Congress, in 1922, the party voted to join the Communist International (its membership at that time was 300). Many young Chinese who had gone to Russia to study returned to China and now, in accordance with Soviet policy, the Congress decided upon a program of "self-determination" for outlying provinces, such as Mongolia. The decisive problem, however, was the relationship with the Kuomintang. The Kuomintang was a "bourgeois party," but it was militant and anti-imperialist. Communism from its very outset and in all countries had been exclusive. To stay clear of heterogeneous elements and to fight for political control were first principles laid down by

Lenin for Communists. On the other hand, if the small party were to leave the real struggle to the Kuomintang, the party would have no immediate prospects. No decision was arrived at, and the expectation was that Moscow would give the word.

Negotiations with Sun Yat-sen took place in 1922, and in January, 1923, the Executive Committee of the Communist International in Moscow discussed the problem of "national revolution" in China and decided in favor of "co-ordinated action" between the Kuomintang and the Chinese Communists. It rejected the policy of the Chinese "leftists." The Resolution of the Executive Committee, adopted January 12, 1923, read:

Under present circumstances it is useful to have the members of the Chinese Communist party remain within the Kuomintang. [But] the party must maintain its own organization with a strongly centralized machine . . . On the other hand, the Communist party of China must influence the Kuomintang with the view of uniting its efforts with the efforts of Soviet Russia for a common struggle against European, American, and Japanese imperialism.

The Third Congress of the Chinese Communists, in 1923, accepted these instructions from the Moscow headquarters. However, an important discussion arose concerning the agrarian program. The leftist wing wanted to include in the program a demand for seizure of lands from the landlords. In view of the imminent prospect of coalition with the Kuomintang, however, this demand was abandoned and a less radical program adopted. The party then entered into final negotiations with Dr. Sun and recommended to its members that they take part in Kuomintang organizations. The few hundred Communists became most active in the army, in the Whampoa Academy, and soon also in the trade-unions, which, with the rise of labor unrest in China, were beginning to expand. Chen Tu-hsiu, who was gaining political stature, was in favor of collaboration with the Kuomintang. He wrote: "Co-operation with the revolutionary bourgeoisie . . . is the necessary road for the Chinese proletariat." [1]

Actually the decisions concerning China were made not by the Communist International but by the Politburo of the Russian Communist party. Instructions, money, advisers, and agents were

1. Harold Isaacs, *The Tragedy of the Chinese Revolution* (London, 1938), p. 61.

Russian; the Comintern had but to put its stamp of approval to the Russian decisions. In long sessions, the Russian Politburo discussed the Chinese problem in all its aspects: The Kuomintang and its adviser, Borodin; the Chinese Communists in their activities and relations with the Kuomintang; and, of course, relations between Moscow and the official Peking Government. In Moscow two universities were concerned with Far Eastern affairs: Sun Yat-sen University and the Communist University of the Toilers of the East.

From the very outset, the "opposition" to Stalin—the Russian leftist group of 1923 (Trotsky, Preobrazhensky, Piatakov, and others)—was skeptical as to the desirability of the Chinese Communists joining the Kuomintang. In the main, however, the opposition was inclined to minimize the importance of this question in order not to intensify the strain on their relations with the Stalin-Bukharin faction. Trotsky did not share this "opportunism," and in the Politburo voted against the motion instructing the Chinese Communists to join the Kuomintang.

With Trotsky it was a question of principle. For decades Marxist parties had insisted on the need of a pure workers' party with a clear-cut program of revolutionary socialism and on the principle of class struggle and opposition to any mergers with capitalist, bourgeois, or even obscure populist movements. The Kuomintang was obviously a bourgeois party. For Communists to join it meant that they would have to subordinate their revolutionary policies and demands and their specific methods—general strikes, agrarian uprisings—to the interests of an alien political body. Trotsky wanted to see a completely independent Communist party of China which, he said, would be able to follow a more consistent and more revolutionary policy. He considered any sacrifice of Communism to a treacherous "populism" as treason; it was a deception of the Chinese workers; it was a coalition with the bourgeoisie; it was Menshevism!

Nothing could be more detrimental to the prestige of a Communist leader than a charge of moderation, of collaboration with the bourgeoisie—of Menshevism. Trotsky's accusations, therefore, had the effect of a whip. Stalin took the leadership in the fight against him and developed another concept: unlike Russia and the Western nations, China was fighting for her national independence, and in this fight there was a community of interest between the various classes such as was unknown in the West. The Kuomintang was a coalition of different classes; it was not a pure "bourgeois party." To dissolve the Communist-Kuomintang coalition would be a heavy blow to the Communist cause in China. Trotsky, Stalin maintained, did not want to recognize that revolutions develop in stages, and that the current phase of the Chinese revolution was necessarily characterized by participation of the nonworker classes in the great revolutionary movement. The interests of the Chinese peasantry, he said, are paramount, and Communism is obliged to take them into consideration. Trotsky is a former Menshevik and therefore unable to measure accurately the importance of the peasant movement. In falling back to his old Menshevism, he is betraying the cause of Communism.

In such form and accompanied by hysterical accusations and exaggerations, the discussion developed in the four years until 1927. Everywhere in Russia, party meetings were called to discuss the Chinese problem. Hundreds of resolutions and counterresolutions were adopted. Books were written and published to show the rightness of the respective lines. The mass of historical material concerning the struggle between Trotsky and Stalin on the question of China is often clouded by the scholastic terminology used by both factions. At times, however, the "Stalinites" revealed the real political problem, the anti-British essence of their Chinese policy. "Our *most immediate* perspective and our *most immediate* aim in China [Bukharin affirmed] is the defeat of the imperialist enemy." [2] Trotsky's "exclusiveness," in Bukharin's opinion, endangered the success of this undertaking. Another old Bolshevik and leader of the Comintern, Dmitri Manuilsky expressed the same idea when he attacked British imperialism in China, "English imperialism in China is already a beaten dog . . . The task of the Chinese Revolution is to finish the licking of this mischievous, predatory dog." [3]

Whose policy was more "revolutionary"—Trotsky's or Stalin's? This question appeared to be of enormous importance to both the Russian and the international Communism of the time; moderation —so-called "opportunism"—was the greatest of crimes. Both fac-

2. Seventh Plenary Session of the Executive Committee of the Communist International, Moscow, November, 1926.
3. *Ibid.*

tions claimed to represent the truly revolutionary tendency, and both had convincing arguments. Even today, more than two decades later, it it impossible to say whether Trotsky's policy, radical on the surface, would in practice have meant a more radical solution of the problem. If the Chinese Communist party had renounced its alliance to the Kuomintang and tried to overthrow the government in order to create a Soviet China, it would certainly have remained an orthodox although small group. In so far, however, as such a policy would have endangered the progress of the Kuomintang's nationalist wars, it would have weakened the "anti-imperialist" movement and thus strengthened the position of the foreign powers in China.

What was more important for Russian Communism—the creation of a pure, albeit small, communist movement in China, or the integration of the Orient into a great war against Britain? Both aims were revolutionary. But a choice had to be made. There is no basis for awarding a higher degree of orthodoxy to either alternative. Stalin's policy, at any rate, was in conformity with the traditional trend of merging all possible forces against Britain and her allies in the Orient.

THE REVOLUTIONARY TIDE—1925–1927

The dissensions within the Russian Communist party on Chinese affairs developed into a bitter struggle as soon as a strong popular movement arose in China which appeared to strengthen either of the two contending factions in Moscow.

The labor movement in China was almost nonexistent before 1920; [4] there were no trade-unions, and the first serious strike, in Shanghai, had taken place as recently as 1919. Other strikes followed in 1920–21. A greater momentum developed, especially among the merchant marine in Canton and Hongkong. In May, 1922, the first Conference of Chinese Trade-Unions was held in Canton, and in February, 1923, the first railroad strike on the Peking-Hankow Railroad attracted general attention. There were political overtones in these strikes. The workers were Chinese, and the management was foreign; "anti-foreignism" easily devel-

4. A strike movement of some importance had developed, however, during the Revolution of 1911–12.

oped into "anti-imperialism," and a new field for the activities of Communist intellectuals seemed to open up.

The turning event in these initial stages of the Chinese labor movement was the Shanghai strike of May, 1925, which marked the beginning of a great political revolt. The strike broke out in Japanese-owned textile mills, but everything in China was so charged with "anti-Britishism" that, by a strange paradox, the strike developed into a demonstration against the English in China. The striking workers, accompanied by large crowds of students and youths, marched through the International Settlement, and the clash with British police resulted in killed and wounded among the demonstrators. This event transformed the anti-Japanese economic strike into an anti-British political uprising. In July a similar movement developed in other cities—Hankow, Peking, Nanking. Protest strikes lasted for several months. The "blockade of Hongkong" lasted for 16 months. Passions were aflame. The Communist party rapidly gained thousands of new friends and followers, and the Kuomintang became more revolutionary than ever.

In Moscow hopes rose high. The *Communist International* wrote, in a review of the situation in January, 1926: "England is unable to stop the revolution . . . England is incapable of preventing the growing alliance, political and economic, between the Soviet Union and the peoples of the East." In February, 1926, Dmitri Manuilsky, on a note of triumph, wrote in the same magazine: "The Shanghai events open a new page in human history." Borodin said, "We did not make [the bloody revolt of] May 30, it was made for us." The Shanghai appeal for a boycott of the British sounded to Moscow like the fulfillment of its hopes:

1. Don't work in English homes, stores, or plants;
2. Don't use British banknotes; don't keep your money in accounts in British banks; don't make any transactions through British banks;
3. Don't buy British goods; don't transport Chinese goods on English ships; don't take out insurance in English companies;
4. Don't work on English steamers as crews, mechanics, sailors, etc.;
5. Don't travel on English ships, busses, or trolleys;
6. Don't study in schools founded by the English;
7. Don't hire English lawyers, doctors, engineers, treasurers, etc.;
8. Don't sell Chinese goods to Englishmen! [5]

5. Quoted in *Communist International* (Moscow, July, 1925).

In some public places in China, the Comintern's publication reported with gleeful satisfaction, the old posters reading "Dogs and Chinese not allowed" were replaced by new ones reading "Dogs and Englishmen not allowed." [6]

The situation in China was revolutionary, and the Chinese Communist party was rapidly developing into a serious political force. The flow of new adherents and followers became a flood and the Communist Youth League expanded to considerable proportions. Communist leadership in the rising trade-unions and its activities in certain areas of the peasant movement became a new and important phenomenon in China's political life. Communism was beginning to aspire to political power.

Under these circumstances, Trotsky wanted to follow the Russian example in Shanghai and Canton, that is, immediately to create soviets of workers, expand and revolutionize the agrarian movement against the landlords, and have the Communist party strike for power. Collaboration with the Kuomintang, however, implied a certain amount of moderation: no soviets, no Communist dictatorship, a far-reaching compromise concerning redistribution of land. Trotsky demanded that the Communists leave the Kuomintang. Stalin opposed such radicalism.

Early in 1926 Bubnov, a member of the Stalinist faction in the Russian Central Committee, went to China at the head of a delegation. With his arrival at Canton there occurred the first great clash between Chiang Kai-shek and the Communists mentioned above.[7] Chinese Communist commissars and even some Russian advisers were arrested, Bubnov's guards were disarmed, and many prominent Communists were forced to abandon the high positions they had occupied in the Kuomintang. In order to maintain the established relationship with Chiang, Borodin as well as Bubnov sided with the Kuomintang and accused the purged Communists of having been "too far to the left." Good relations between Moscow and Chiang Kai-shek were re-established immediately, and this was the signal for an all-out attack by Trotsky against Stalin.

The Canton incidents, which to Trotsky were equivalent to a coup d'état by Chiang, were not even mentioned by the Soviet press.

6. *Ibid.*
7. P. 216.

THE KUOMINTANG IN THE COMINTERN

The Kuomintang asked to be admitted into the Communist International; this request was granted in order to achieve complete co-ordination of Russian and Chinese policies in the expected great anti-imperialist campaign; the Kuomintang—how strange it seems today!—became a "sympathizer-member" of the Communist International. Leaders of the Kuomintang became "comrades," Kuomintang delegates attended sessions of the Comintern in Moscow and their speeches were loudly applauded in the headquarters of world Communism. Thus in February, 1926, a high-ranking leader of the Kuomintang, Generalissimo of the Canton army, Hu Hanming (who had been involved in the murder of the Communist leader, Liao Chung-kai, in Canton, and therefore had to leave China, and was persuaded by Borodin to go to Russia) [8] appeared before a session of the Comintern and praised the Soviet Union: "The Kuomintang, in the person of one of its leaders, here for the first time hails the leaders of world revolution. I consider myself your companion in arms, you fighters for world revolution, and I hail the Communist International!" [9]

A few months later, at another session of the Comintern, both the Chinese Communists and the Kuomintang were again represented. The Communist delegate reported on the relative strength of the two parties. According to his report, the Kuomintang had a following of 316,000, of whom only 250,000 were actual members. The rightist Kuomintang faction (which opposed collaboration with the Communists) was estimated to number no more than 30,000. Of the local Kuomintang organizations, 90 per cent, he declared, were under control of Communists and leftist Kuomintang groups. In the summer of 1926 the Communist party of China had a membership of 57,000, but the party was strongly entrenched in the Kuomintang and its army.

Shao Li-tse, Kuomintang delegate to the Comintern, addressing the gathering as "comrades," said: "Sincere, friendly co-operation between the Kuomintang and the Chinese Communist party is the pledge of victory of the national revolution. (Applause) . . . We

8. O. M. Green, *The Story of China's Revolution* (Hutchinson & Company, 1945), p. 80.

9. Sixth Plenary Session of the Executive Committee of the Communist International, Moscow, February, 1926.

must not forget our fundamental purpose, i.e., the complete destruction of imperialism and militarism. I can assure you that the Kuomintang will fulfill this task." [10]

Central China was run by a number of war lords, who competed with each other for power. While Chiang Kai-shek was to strike from the south, Moscow's plans also called for a campaign against central China by the war lord, Feng Yu-hsiang, the so-called "Christian general," in northern China, on whom Moscow placed great hopes. The first contacts with Feng had been made by Adolf Joffe and had later been maintained by Ambassador Karakhan. Feng became the standard-bearer of the pro-Russian orientation in the intricate struggle among the war lords of China. He obtained considerable financial help and arms from Russia. When he was defeated by Marshal Chang Tso-lin he went to Russia "to study the Soviet system and Soviet reality." For about a year he lived in a suburban *dacha* (summer house) near Moscow. In an interview with a *Pravda* correspondent, Feng showered lavish praise on the Communists and the Russian Communist party.[11]

When Feng returned from Moscow to China in September, 1926, a number of war lords were again engaging in a contest for power. In accordance with the Soviet policy of that moment, Feng joined the Kuomintang, and pledged to support Chiang Kai-shek's Northern Expedition to unite China.

Feng's home base was in Inner Mongolia, and there existed certain plans for the unification of that region with Soviet-controlled Outer Mongolia. Copying the political configuration of the Mongolian People's Republic, a National-Revolutionary party had emerged in Inner Mongolia in 1925 and held its first Congress in Kalgan. Its appearance was not without the sponsorship and instigation of Moscow. Delegates from Chinese Inner Mongolia took part in the Fourth Congress of the National-Revolutionary Party of Outer Mongolia in Urga (Ulan-Bator). Damba, Premier of the Mongolian People's Republic, started negotiations with General Feng concerning a future united Mongolian state. The stamp of Soviet approval and initiative was evident on each one of these

10. Seventh Plenary Session of the Executive Committee of the Communist International, November, 1926. *Stenographic Report,* p. 4.
11. *Pravda,* August 19, 1926.

moves.[12] An attempt was even made to create a "Red" detachment within Feng Yu-hsiang's army, and approximately a hundred Russians under Colonel Gushchin were organized; however, they played no role in subsequent events.[13]

In June, 1926, Chiang began his Northern Expedition, assisted by the Communists and his Russian military advisers. The campaign was a triumph. By the end of 1926 Chiang's armies had reached the Yangtze River, and in December, 1926, the government moved northward. It became known as the Wuhan government (after the three cities of Wuchang, Hankow, and Hanyang). Eugene Chen, one of the greatest haters of the British in the Kuomintang, became Foreign Minister. The general attitude of the Wuhan government toward foreigners, and British subjects in particular, led to a considerable migration of the foreigners from their settlements.

Soon the Nationalist armies approached Nanking and Shanghai, and in the spring of 1927 the first phase of the campaign was successfully completed. Not only the south, but also a part of central China was unified under the Nationalist Government. Chiang Kai-shek became the first among the leaders of China, and his party now represented the strongest trend of public opinion.

Meanwhile a conflict between Chiang's Communist and non-Communist followers was brewing in the rear. The Communists claimed to have gained a decisive influence among the trade-unions, whose membership ostensibly totaled 2,800,000, and in the peasant unions, which from a membership of 200,000, in Kwantung alone, had allegedly grown to a total of about 10,000,000; reports reaching Moscow said that in the first months of 1927 the agrarian movement was especially strong in the Provinces of Hunan and Hupeh. In Hupeh, for example, unions of peasants had an aggregate membership of 800,000 which, two months later, had grown to 2,200,-000. In Hunan 5,200,000 peasants were organized into similar unions.[14] (The accuracy of these figures appears doubtful, but the figures serve to show the state of mind among Chinese as well as Russian Communists itching for action.) The Communist weekly

12. Vostokov in *Monde Slave* (1936), II, 297.
13. Serebrennikov, *op. cit.,* p. 254.
14. *Strategiya i Taktika,* pp. 160–161.

reached a circulation of 50,000—a very large circulation, under Chinese conditions. The Communists were actually at the head of a popular revolution, as chaotic and spontaneous as any revolution.

In Moscow Chinese affairs were transferred from the jurisdiction of the Foreign Office, under Chicherin, to a special commission of the Politburo, under Josif Unschlicht; the real power behind this body was Stalin himself.[15] Instructions from Moscow had become outright contradictory. It was difficult for Stalin to satisfy the demands of the "leftists" and at the same time keep up his collaboration with Chiang. The Politburo, for instance, instructed its Chinese friends by wire to put brakes on the agrarian movement, only to reverse itself a short time later and call for an expansion and support of the peasantry's uprising against the landlords. Other instructions from Moscow sometimes went a long way to meet the extremist demands of Chinese Communists. One set of instructions sent to China from Moscow read:

It is necessary to proceed with the arming of workers and peasants, transforming peasant committees into actual organs of power, with armed troops for self-defense, etc . . . The Communist party must not conceal the treacherous and reactionary policy of the rightist members of the Kuomintang.[16]

While these struggles disrupted the rear of Chiang's armies and complicated his conduct of the war, Chiang himself was growing suspicious of the aims of the Communists, especially of those who were firmly entrenched in his army.

The area into which the Nationalist troops had advanced early in 1927 was the main region of British settlements and enterprises and of foreign populations. Shanghai was the most important port of the Far East and the trade of the port was mainly in British hands. Foreign settlements also existed in Nanking, Wuchang, and other places. With the retreat of the armies of Wu Pei-foo and the approach of the revolutionary armies, the situation became dangerous for all foreigners, and especially for the British. Soon the looting, plundering, and violence reached menacing proportions; foreigners were often compelled to leave their homes and flee to the East. General strikes occurred which often developed into a strug-

15. Besedovsky, *op. cit.*, II, 6.
16. Instructions sent from Moscow in February, 1927. Quoted by Stalin in a speech on April 1, 1927.

gle for political power. Discipline in Chiang's army grew lax; the chaos in the cities and the agrarian movements in the army's rear further weakened the command and made military operations more difficult. The left elements of the Kuomintang voiced protests against "Chiang's dictatorial tendencies." Chiang happened to learn the text of a wire which Borodin sent to another Soviet "instructor," Darovsky, according to which the latter was to hinder the rapid advance of Chiang Kai-shek on Shanghai because his successes began to seem dangerous. Chiang had Darovsky arrested.

It was under these circumstances that Chiang determined to make a decisive turn: he broke with the Chinese Communists as well as with his Russian "advisers."

In April, 1927, he ordered the arrest of Communists in Shanghai who had prepared to take over the city's administration. The fight immediately assumed all the aspects of a bloody suppression. Communist organizations as well as the trade-unions led by them were smashed. In the meantime British and American gunboats had reached Nanking and lay down a barrage to aid the escape of British and American nationals.

A few days later, on April 18, Chiang Kai-shek set up a new government in Nanking, in opposition to the leftist Wuhan government in which five Communists occupied ministerial positions and which continued the traditional leftist coalition. Borodin, of course, was the "political adviser" of the Wuhan government. Thus began the struggle between two nationalist governments.

STALIN'S DEFEAT IN CHINA

In Moscow these events struck like a storm out of a clear sky. Except for a few leaders, the public had been led to believe in the firmness of the Kuomintang-Communist coalition in China. The rapid growth achieved by the Communist movement in the distinctly revolutionary climate of China had seemed to foreshadow great success in the immediate future. Early in 1927 Chiang Kai-shek had sent four autographed photographs to Moscow, one each for Stalin, Voroshilov, Rykov, and Trotsky, asking for their photographs in return. All obligingly sent him their photographs—except Trotsky.[17] If there was a certain amount of mistrust con-

17. *Byulleten' Oppozitzii*, No. 28.

cerning Chiang's sincerity, there was also a hope that he could soon be overthrown by a leftist coalition, combining certain leftist elements of the Kuomintang with the Communists, and that thus the Chinese Revolution could attain the "next stage"—the "higher stage"—of its development toward a "workers' and peasants' government."

The excitement in Moscow was great and the factional struggle between Stalinists and Trotskyites hit its peak. Since the fall of 1926 attention had been focused on China. The Politburo of the Communist party and the higher bodies of the Communist International had discussed China in unending sessions. Between November, 1926, and August, 1927, Stalin made no less than seven speeches dealing with Chinese affairs. Now Chiang Kai-shek's "betrayal" upset all plans and expectations and seemed to confirm Trotsky's warnings. With the biting sarcasm of which he was a master, Trotsky was now able to scourge his opponents by recalling their devotion to "Comrade Chiang Kai-shek" and the sacrifices they made in order to keep Chiang at the head of the coalition.

This apparent triumph of Trotsky's only excited greater passion and increased Stalin's rage. The first reaction was to condemn Chiang Kai-shek and to declare him a traitor and an enemy; [18] this was both easy and natural. But what kind of policy could be adopted following the break with him? There was the Wuhan government, which was proceeding along the old political lines, whose armies, however, were small and weak. Obviously the movement on which Moscow had based its hopes was receding. But to avenge the defeat, to punish Chiang Kai-shek, and, last but not least, to demonstrate Trotsky's fallibility, it was decided to consider the developments in China as signs of progress of the revolution: freed of the dead weight of the Kuomintang's right wing, the revolutionary movement could now develop into a Soviet movement in China! The new instructions called for the creation of peasants' soviets, the development of an agrarian revolution, the creation of a great new army, and, above all, the application of a Red Terror. A set of instructions dispatched from Moscow to the

18. On April 14, 1927, the Executive Committee of the Communist International adopted a resolution, reading in part: "With the greatest indignation and with utter hatred for the hangman, we declare Chiang Kai-shek a traitor and an ally of the imperialist bandits, an enemy of the revolutionary Kuomintang, and enemy of the working class and of the Communist International."

Chinese Communists in May, 1927, ordered: "You must no longer simply resort to persuasion. The time has come to act. The rascals must be punished!" [19] The immense disappointment found expression in a recurrence of bloody measures: "Punish the officers who support and maintain contact with Chiang Kai-shek." The fantastic idea of a great Chinese army under Communist military leadership was Stalin's order of May, 1927: "Mobilize some 20,000 Communists, add some 50,000 revolutionary workers and peasants from Hunan and Hupeh; activate a few new corps, utilize the school's cadets for the officers corps and before it is too late, organize your reliable army!" The instructions from Moscow sounded most revolutionary:

Systematically to develop an agrarian revolution in all provinces, including, and in particular, Kwantung, under the slogan "All power to the peasant unions and rural committees." This is the basis for the success of the revolution and of the Kuomintang. This is the foundation of a powerful political and military force that must be developed in China against imperialism and its agents.[20]

Meanwhile all the hopes placed on the Wuhan government and its army proved vain. The Comintern sent a wire to Borodin instructing him to begin the confiscation of landlords' estates; this amounted to a call to revolution against the coalition government. The Communists were obliged to leave, and therewith the whole Wuhan government disintegrated.

On July 7, when Borodin left Wuhan for Russia, the great military-political intervention of Russia in China in effect came to an end. In the almost four years of his activity Borodin had become a towering, almost a legendary, figure behind Chinese policy. In him the hope and the threat of a Russo-Chinese Empire found their strongest expression. His departure from China signified a decisive turn in relations between the two nations, and the completion of the break between the Kuomintang and the Communists.

From then on Moscow relied on the expectation of a great armed popular uprising in China. Instructions called for a purely Soviet revolution. The new call was for "soviets in China." "And who will head the soviets?" Stalin asked in his speech on September 27, 1927, replying: "Of course, the Communists. But Communists will

19. Stalin, *Ob Oppozitsii*, p. 661. In a speech on August 1, 1927.
20. *Ibid.*

no longer participate in the Kuomintang, should a revolutionary Kuomintang again appear."

A new representative of the Comintern, Lominadze, was sent to China. Two other Chinese generals agreed to accept Soviet help in starting a new campaign against Chiang, and in August, 1927, the Politburo in Moscow appropriated two million dollars for this campaign; later, one million Japanese yen were added; all the funds were transferred to China through Japan.[21]

In accordance with this general course the Communists started a general uprising in Canton on December 12, 1927—a revolt that was doomed from the very beginning. After three days the "Canton Commune" was annihilated. It was one of those criminal adventures that marked the road of the Communist International during the twenties. Trotsky's later criticism was convincing:

At the end of 1927, Stalin's faction, frightened by the consequences of its own mistakes, tried to make up at one stroke what it had failed to do over a number of years. Thus the Canton revolt was organized. The leaders continued to labor under the assumption that the revolution was still on the increase. In reality the revolutionary tide had already been replaced by a downward movement. The heroism of the foremost workers of Canton could not prevent the disaster caused by the adventurous spirit of its leaders. The Canton revolt was drowned in blood. The Second Chinese Revolution was definitely crushed. . . . Early in 1928, when the Chinese revolution was at a low point, the Ninth Plenary Session of the Executive Committee of the Communist International proclaimed a course toward an armed uprising in China. The result of this lunacy was the further defeat of the workers, the liquidation of the best revolutionaries, the disintegration of the party, demoralization in the workers' ranks.[22]

China's relations with Moscow were disrupted by the overt participation of Soviet representatives in the Chinese revolts. The first step against official Soviet institutions in China was taken in the north by Marshal Chang Tso-lin. On April 16, 1927, the Soviet embassy in Peking as well as other Soviet offices were searched. Documents allegedly found in these searches were published to demonstrate the terroristic and revolutionary character of Soviet policy in China. Moscow declared the documents forged; this was

21. Besedovsky, *op. cit.*, II, 3.
22. L. Trotsky, "To the Communists of China and of the Whole World," *Byulleten' Oppozitzii* (1930), No. 15–16, pp. 2–3.

doubtlessly true in the case of part of the published material. On October 25, similar action was taken against the Soviet consulate in Shanghai and in December, in Canton. On December 15, 1927, the Chinese Government informed Moscow that all Soviet consulates and trading agencies in China must be closed.

As for internal affairs in Russia, this meant the end of Trotsky. He became impossible since his criticism appeared to have been justified. So long as Soviet policy in China had been successful, contrary to his warnings and demands, Trotsky could be tolerated. He had had no opportunity to demonstrate the superiority of his own policy which no doubt would have been no less disastrous than that of his opponents. He had the advantage of being a critic without responsibility. Now, when everything collapsed, Trotsky could no longer be put up with. His mere presence was a reproach. He was deported to central Asia in November, 1927, never to return to Moscow. Among the reasons for his liquidation, the Chinese affair was one of the most important.

From China's angle, the four-year period of collaboration with the Soviet had been well worth while. In the fight for China's independence, Chinese nationalism made extensive use of Russia's financial and ideological assistance. At the last moment, when closer ties with Moscow and subordination to Soviet policies seemed imminent, the Nationalist movement found the internal strength for a complete reversal of its policy. From these fights Chiang Kai-shek emerged as the leader of Nationalist China.

The defeat in China was of greater significance for Soviet policy than was generally assumed at the time. The fantastic plans for defeating England in China collapsed, while direct Soviet relations with Britain grew worse every day; diplomatic relations between Russia and England were broken off in May, 1927. Again the itinerary of world revolution had to undergo revision, and the deductions made from the new situation pointed toward the strengthening of the Red Army, the collectivization of agriculture, and the development of war industries.

Chinese Communism, crushed in 1927–28, ceased for a time to be a stronghold of Soviet policy. The Comintern blamed the Chinese Communists for its own mistakes and errors. It adopted a number of resolutions setting forth the errors of its Chinese followers:

The leaders of the Chinese Communist party have committed a number of serious errors from the very beginning, errors that seriously retarded the combat preparedness of the revolutionary organizations and—as subsequent developments have shown—were the initial link in a series of opportunistic mistakes which in the end led to political bankruptcy in the top brackets of the Chinese Communist party . . . In this decisive period of the Chinese revolution, the Central Committee of the Chinese Communist Party did not have a single consistent political line . . . It permitted a number of errors to occur, which in their consequences bordered on treason.[23]

The loyal Chinese Communists willingly accepted the blame. Chen Tu-hsiu, after seven years of leadership, resigned.

At the Fifth Party Congress, in August, 1927, at which he was condemned, this outstanding political leader developed an idea which, although rejected at the time, was revived seven years later, and pointed the way to a new important political development: he proposed the transfer of the entire Chinese Communist movement from the Southern provinces, where it had been entrenched during the twenties, to the north, near Soviet Russia.

Said Chen: "The shift of the territorial base of the Chinese Revolution to the Northwestern Provinces will bring it into the vicinity of the Soviet Union, the bulwark of world revolution." Chen was already a convicted figure, and the shortsighted Congress said, in its resolution, that contrary to Chen's views, the "Communist party cannot imagine a more reliable natural base for the revolution than the Shanghai proletariat, the Canton working class, and the revolutionary peasantry of Kwantung, Kiangsi, Hunan, and Hupeh Provinces." [24]

New leaders of Chinese Communism emerged, while old Chen Tu-hsiu moved into the camp of the Communist opposition, the first prominent victim of the internal feuds. The charges now leveled against him were a lack of revolutionary zeal and excessive moderation—in reality advised by Moscow, sometimes against the will of the Chinese Communists themselves. During the next two years Chen Tu-hsiu severely criticized the newly appointed leaders in a number of letters to the Central Committee. He accused them of having failed to understand, after the Canton uprising,

23. *The Comintern before Its Sixth World Congress* (1928), pp. 367–369.
24. Political Resolution of the Fifth Congress of the Chinese Communist Party, August, 1927.

that the Revolution was beaten. "Offensive tactics were adopted—until the Sixth Congress," Chen remembered; in the eyes of the party's leaders "the revolutionary tide was relentlessly rising." Their one and only slogan was "revolt, revolt, and revolt again."

"Whoever permits himself to doubt the propriety of revolt is an opportunist, a deviationist, etc.," Chen Tu-hsiu paraphrased the party's policy. And after the Sixth Congress it again claimed that "the revolution has come back to life."

Reacting violently against these accusations, the Comintern in its letters to its Chinese section and in numerous public pronouncements harped on the "errors and mistakes" of the "rightist faction" led by Chen Tu-hsiu. This campaign continued until Chen was officially expelled from the party in November, 1929. In November, 1932, Chen, denounced to the police by one of his former political friends, was arrested along with ten other members of the opposition. The following year he was sentenced to 13 years in prison. He was pardoned in 1937 and died in 1942.

The other hero of this era, Mikhail Borodin, likewise fell into disfavor. Moscow announced that Borodin was a "deviator." "Borodin has shown himself to be a typical rightist opportunist [wrote the highly official *Revolutionary East*]. On the eve of the Fifth Congress of the Chinese Communist Party he came out with the demand to yield to the imperialists in order not to aggravate them." [25] After his return from China Borodin was given only nonpolitical assignments. For a time he was an official in the paper industry; in the thirties he became the editor of the *Moscow Daily News*, an unimportant Soviet English-language paper and did not advance any further. When Eugene Lyons met him in 1932 he was "an embittered and broken giant." [26] During the Great Purges, in 1937, Borodin was arrested. He was seen at the front in 1942, but he never played any role of importance again.

25. *Revolyutsionnyi vostok* (1932), No. 1, p. 341.
26. Eugene Lyons, *Assignment in Utopia* (New York, 1937), p. 331.

X

The Status Quo in the North (1925-1931)

The treaty of January, 1925, between Russia and Japan was a milestone in Far Eastern relations. It marked the end of the most prolonged conflict which Soviet Russia had in its initial period, and the inauguration of a new and different attitude toward Japan—an attitude which, on the surface at least, was conducive to peace and stability based on the recognition of the status quo.

Japan was the Great Power of the Far East, while Russia shone in Vladivostok, Shanghai, and Canton merely by reflection of her might in Europe. A clash with Japan was certain to end in a Russian defeat: this had been clear since 1905 and even more so after 1917, when the old Russian Army disintegrated and the newly emerging armed forces, still inadequately trained and equipped, were urgently needed in Europe. A war with Japan had to be avoided at all costs. For the Soviet Government, "at all costs" meant that in case of real danger, everything, including the revolution in China or any other country, would have to be sacrificed for the preservation of the nucleus of world Communism—the Soviet Union.

Ten days after the last Japanese detachments had left Soviet soil in accordance with the treaty, the great outburst of the Chinese Revolution occurred in Shanghai; the event inaugurated a two-year period of the most active intervention of Russia in Chinese affairs, an intervention animated by the hope of seeing the Chinese Revolution, under Communist guidance, sweep over the whole of that vast country, eventually engulfing Manchuria and creating a huge Soviet empire in the Far East. It seemed that all the conditions for success had been fulfilled and that the only unknown in the equation was the attitude of Japan. Russia could not risk a conflict with Japan over China, yet its government wanted to lead the Chinese Revolution to victory. This was the crux of Soviet policy in the middle twenties. "Our basic line of policy in the Far East," said Soviet Ambassador Kopp, "is fundamentally a kindling of the Chinese Revolution by all means, its radicalization to the maximum degree possible, and the ejection of the English from China, with the creation of a direct threat to India." [1]

Moscow's policy was thus a dual one: peace with Japan and the kindling of the Chinese Revolution. Was it possible to pursue these two aims simultaneously? Could they be reconciled? Would Japan acquiesce in Soviet control over a revolutionary movement on the Asiatic continent? A new conception of Stalin's was to prove the practicability of this dual policy.

As far as peaceful relations with Japan were concerned, Stalin emphasized in a number of public speeches his determination to observe and follow the terms of the January treaty. In his report to the fourteenth Congress of his party (December, 1925) he said that "some of our adversaries in the West rub their hands," expecting a conflict between the Soviet Union and Japan in connection with the Chinese Revolution. "All this is nonsense, comrades," Stalin commented. In Manchuria, he said, Gen. Chang Tso-lin was having difficulties "because he has based his policy on divergencies, on the expectation of worsening relations between us and Japan."

"We have no interests," Stalin concluded, "leading to an irritation of our relations with Japan. Our interests lead toward a rapprochement of our country with Japan."

The rapprochement advocated by Stalin was not a rapprochement in the usual sense of that word. It involved more watchfulness than friendship, more apprehension than mutuality. The great design behind this Soviet attitude toward Japan was to divert Japan's dynamism against Britain and the United States while securing Japan's rear on the continent. There was no intention in Moscow of concluding a military alliance with Japan. Stalin's policy consisted rather of a series of shrewd maneuvers. The result was a series of conflicts which, however, never reached the stage of war.

Stalin was convinced that the world was heading for a great war between Britain and the United States. In one speech after another and in resolutions of congresses he reiterated and stressed this view, which was so far removed from actual developments. In this future war, he said, Japan's place would be on England's side against the United States; absorbed in preparations for the hard struggle against America, Japan would be in no position to participate militarily in

1. Grigori Besevodsky, *Na putyakh k Temidoru*, II, 26.

developments on the Asiatic mainland or to impede the Russo-Chinese revolutionary offensive.

Stalin was still a newcomer to world politics and was absorbed in factional struggles and intervention in the Chinese Revolution; the Foreign Commissar played a more important role than in the thirties and forties. Georgi Chicherin shared with Stalin the basic concept of great-power relationship: Britain was considered the main enemy of the Soviet Union; next to Britain, the United States was the menace, with France in third place. These were regarded as the major imperialist powers opposing Russia at every step. Germany, defeated, demilitarized, and weakened, was considered a possible asset in this struggle against the "imperialists," and collaboration with the German Government as well as with the Reichswehr flourished during these years.

In this combination of powers, what was Japan's position, as visualized by Stalin and Chicherin? Did she belong to the class of imperialist sharks, always bellicose, aggressive, and intent on devouring nations and territories? Chicherin tried to picture Japan differently; he hoped that she would be compelled by circumstances of international politics to occupy a place in the Far East analogous to that of Germany in Europe. After the Washington Conference of 1922, Chicherin contended, Japan was practically isolated and obliged to withdraw her forces from northern China; she had suffered a heavy blow in the earthquake of 1923; the American Immigration Act of 1924 was a serious insult to Japanese national honor and a setback to her national interests. As a consequence, Chicherin expected a widening gulf between Japan and the United States, a conflict which would give Soviet Russia a free hand in her activities on the Asiatic mainland.

In a way the foreign office of a great nation is similar in its operations to the general staff of a war-waging army. A multitude of reports reach the army's headquarters from all sectors of the front, and it is up to the general staff to digest the abundant material, put all information in its proper place, reject implausible reports, and then draw conclusions for future action. A high level of intelligence and experience and a strong sense of reality are necessary to make efficient military leaders.

The Foreign Commissariat in Moscow has always been in possession of numerous reports of the situation in all parts of the globe. It has had not only the usual reports of its diplomatic and other representatives but also intelligence gathered from thousands of adherents in other nations, often occupying high positions in their governments, who reported on secret moves, preparations, negotiations, and treaties. The headquarters in Moscow must digest this wealth of material and act accordingly; often, however, it approaches the reports with a prefabricated theory and interpretation, drawing erroneous conclusions, and then moving on to a dead end in its policies. A multitude of failures can be ascribed to the lack of preparedness, incompetence, and bad judgment which resulted from the fact that a feeling for world realities was often absent.

Despite obvious and well-known facts to the contrary, Chicherin claimed that Japan was still allied with England, and that both were conspiring against the United States. His misinterpretation of world affairs was ridiculous; the son of a Russian diplomat and a man of broad education, he completely lacked any realism, and in the conduct of the foreign policy of the Soviet Union, managed to pile up an amazing number of out-and-out mistakes. When Britain began to build her naval base at Singapore, for example, it was clear that this move was directed against Japan. Chicherin, however, did not want to believe this, since Britain's forces—according to his and Stalin's ideas—were supposed to be preparing for war against America.

In building a naval and air base at Singapore [Chicherin wrote, concerning Britain] she gladly lets the public imagine that all this is directed against Japan. In fact, however, what points of friction exist between her and Japan? . . . Not Japan but the United States is the power against which the fortifications at Singapore are directed . . . Anglo-American competition—such is, for a long time to come, the basic leitmotiv, as yet faintly audible, of the concert which the bourgeois states are striving to create on the ruins, still smoldering from the recent fire.[2]

Britain's rapprochement with France in the late twenties was also directed against the United States, Chicherin asserted. He envisioned an imminent war in which the United States would face "the huge combination which will, no doubt, be joined by Japan

2. *Mezhdunarodnaya zhizn'* (1925), No. 2, pp. 130–131. The article is signed "Post-Skript"; Chicherin was the author.

and Central and South America." [3] He foresaw that the United States would lose her predominance in the Western Hemisphere, yield the Philippines to Japan and some Caribbean islands to Britain, and have to agree that she would not build a sizable navy.

If that was the situation in the Pacific, if Japan must feverishly prepare for war against the United States, she would not be able to intervene in the Chinese Revolution and stop Soviet assistance to the new movement. With this theory in mind, Lev Karakhan, a man of Chicherin's faction, in Peking, and Mikhail Borodin, in Canton, were conducting a grand policy of "widening the revolution in China."

To reconcile reality with these concepts, Chicherin and his group misinterpreted even overt anti-Russian moves on the part of Japan. Japanese plans for the annexation of Russian territories were received without the usual outburst of wrath and anger. Such plans were regarded rather as subsidiary projects for a war against the United States; it was said that Japan wanted Russia to refuse the United States the use of Russian bases. The next development after this friendly interpretation of Japanese aspirations was usually the thought of promising Japan, by treaty or otherwise, neutrality and nonaggression under all circumstances. On July 24, 1926, for example, the Soviet envoy reported from Tokyo to Moscow, under the classification "Top Secret," that he had received information about a plan of the Japanese General Staff to occupy an area in the Soviet Maritime Province. The dispatch added that in this matter "the divergencies between the Foreign Office and the General Staff were not so great." Such aggressive intentions were interpreted in Moscow merely as "a part of the preparation for the future war against America"! [4] The same attitude was manifest in the protracted negotiations carried on between Moscow and Tokyo concerning railroad construction in Manchuria. Certain Japanese projects, cutting deep into the sphere of the Chinese Eastern Railroad and approaching the Russian border, were aimed directly against Russia. Yet in Moscow this was officially regarded as a "re-

3. *Ibid.* (1928), No. 9–10, pp. 78–81.
4. *The Soviets in China Unmasked* (Shanghai, 1927), p. 48. The book is a collection of material allegedly found in the Soviet embassy in Peking during the raid of April 6, 1927. It contains forged as well as genuine documents. From all indications it is evident that the report from Tokyo quoted above belongs to the latter group.

mote preliminary of the far-sighted Japanese Government to an inevitable Japanese-American war." [5]

LITVINOV AND HIS FACTION

There was, however, in the Foreign Commissariat in Moscow another faction, headed by Maxim Litvinov. The struggle between Litvinov and Chicherin overshadowed the activities of the Commissariat from 1925 to 1930. Unlike Chicherin, who had belonged to the Mensheviks before the Revolution, Litvinov had been a staunch Bolshevik from his early youth. Again unlike Chicherin, Litvinov lacked a formal education. He possessed, however, good horse sense, which was at times more valuable than the complex conceptions put forth by the party and its leading theoreticians. Litvinov was not opposed to great leaps and turns in foreign policy; but he had the ability to discern between the possible and the impossible, between fantasy and reality. The Soviet leadership in the Chinese Revolution, the challenge to the Great Powers in the Far East, the spending of large sums of gold, and the conduct of policy toward Japan with a view to safeguarding Communist influence in China were to Litvinov parts of a perilous adventure which, he said, could not but end in a catastrophe. While Chicherin was acting through confidants, such as Karakhan, Litvinov had on his side the first Soviet envoy to Japan, Victor Kopp, and, in effect, the chargé d'affaires, Grigori Besedovsky, who conducted Soviet affairs in Tokyo in 1926–27.[6]

In his letters to Kopp, quoted by Besedovsky, Litvinov called Karakhan "a rogue and adventurer," a "dull-witted journalist," a "good-for-nothing diplomat," and "Borodin's spittoon." As to Borodin, Litvinov called him a "suspicious character." "Borodin [is] a crook who sprang from the depths of the Chicago Stock Exchange, where he was known as Gruzenberg, [Litvinov said.] In China he behaves like a dictator. He has a code of his own, giving him direct access to the Comintern, which does not think it necessary to expose his intrigues, big or little." [7]

5. *New York Times,* July 21, 1926.
6. At first Besedovsky was considered an adherent of Chicherin's faction, but he soon changed his views on the Far Eastern situation. In 1930, while serving in the Soviet embassy in Paris, he severed all ties with the Soviet Government and never returned to Russia.
7. Grigori Besedovsky, *Revelations of a Soviet Diplomat* (London, 1931), p. 127.

Kopp reciprocated saying that "I shall not be surprised if some-time in the future we shall learn that Borodin was an agent-provoca-teur." The conflict between Kopp and Chicherin-Karakhan be-came so intense that Stalin personally wired a reprimand to Kopp: "Reports have reached me that you speak about Karakhan and the policy he carries out in the sharpest terms. You do not hesitate to call this policy adventurous and Karakhan himself a rascal. Bear in mind that Karakhan is carrying out in China not his personal policy but acts in accordance with the directives of the Politburo." [8]

Kopp was recalled to Moscow in July, 1926. His successor, how-ever, continued the same line. Residing, as they did, in Tokyo, these men were able to realize how fantastic Chicherin's theories were, and they saw that Stalin, by intervening in China, was walking on a razor's edge. In their reports they predicted that Japan would not remain a passive onlooker, and they stressed the danger of a Soviet-Japanese war. In one of his letters to Litvinov, Kopp proposed to reverse Soviet policy and revert to an agreement of prerevolution-ary times, namely, to agree with Japan on a division of spheres of influence, which, according to the secret treaty of 1912, were to be divided along the 116° 16' meridian.[9]

Such plans were discussed in Moscow but rejected by Stalin as contrary to revolutionary Communism. He had little more than irony for these reminders of old-style nationalism.

Would it not be preferable [Stalin ironically asked in a speech in the summer of 1925] to establish "spheres of influence" in China together with the other "leading" powers and to grab some parts of China for our own benefit? This would be both useful and safe . . . Such is the nationalist outlook of the new type, attempting to liquidate the foreign policy of the October Revolution and harboring elements of regenera-tion . . . The source of this danger, the danger of nationalism, must be attributed to the growing bourgeois influence on the party.[10]

Stalin rejected proposals of spheres of interest in China, since his ambitions went much farther than any specific sphere. He saw the Kuomintang conquering and uniting the whole of China under a revolutionary, anti-British regime; and he saw the Kuomintang rapidly falling under the leadership of the Chinese Communists.

8. Besedovsky, *op. cit.* (Russian ed.), II, 39–40.
9. Actually the secret convention of 1912 foresaw a demarcation line along the 116°27' meridian.
10. Stalin, *Voprosy Leninizma* (3d ed. 1926), pp. 289–290.

Chinese Nationalism, coupled with Communist guidance, would have meant a gain much greater than the control of a modest region as a result of a division of China into spheres, as had previously prevailed between Russia and Japan.

During these years—from 1925–31—Japan limited her attention to Manchuria and northern China. At first her policy was not hostile to the revolutionary movements in China, since they created difficulties for Britain. The revolutionary movement began in Canton, in the south, where Japanese economic interests and political ambitions were slight. Sun Yat-sen's activities were regarded with some sympathy in Japan. Even Chiang Kai-shek's military campaigns seemed to represent no threat to Japanese interests so long as they took place in the south. Therefore, the Russian intervention and the growth of Chinese Communism aroused no loud protests on the part of Japan. In 1927 when the British and Americans decided to shell Nanking, where anti-foreign disorders had developed, the Japanese Navy refused to participate. The anti-foreign movement was directed primarily against Britain; twice a boycott of British goods was proclaimed and carried out, and this gave a certain amount of satisfaction to Japan, after the Japanese-British alliance had been severed.

However, the Nationalist movement and the troops of the Kuomintang, going from victory to victory, rolled north and soon advanced into the Northern Provinces, threatening Peking, Tientsin, and even Manchuria. To Japan this meant the end of passivity and complacency. Baron Giichi Tanaka assumed the premiership, replacing the cautious Shidehara and at the same time inaugurating an aggressive policy toward China and Russia. In his first statement of policy Premier Tanaka declared:

"In the matter of Communist activities in China, Japan can hardly remain indifferent . . . I am confident that this stand will be understood by our friendly neighbor, Russia." [11] He repeated this warning a few days later. Then in May he sent troops to the Chinese Province of Shantung. In September, 1927, the Nationalist movement spread to southern Manchuria, where crowds demonstrated in the streets against Japan. In 1928 Japan again massed troops on Chinese soil to prevent Chiang Kai-shek from making contact with

11. *New York Times*, April 22, 1927.

the armies of Manchuria, and a bloody battle took place near Tsinan between Chinese Nationalists and Japanese. As a result, a boycott of Japanese goods was proclaimed in China in 1928. Japan's envoy in Nanking officially protested to Chiang Kai-shek.

Manchuria's independence from China—this cornerstone of Japanese policy in the twenties—seemed threatened. It appeared that the Nationalist tide would engulf the Japanese "sphere," and the Japanese Government now saw itself compelled to find a new policy. A series of conflicts between China and Japan ensued, conflicts in which the Soviet Government was not directly involved, since the break between Stalin and Chiang Kai-shek had already taken place.

Stalin's idea of preventing Japanese intervention in the Sino-Soviet nationalist-revolutionary activities compelled him to seek the conclusion of a nonaggression pact with Tokyo in order to neutralize Japan. One such proposal was made in January, 1926; under the terms of this offer not only the mutual interests of Japan and Russia in Manchuria but also China's sovereignty and borders would be guaranteed by both countries.

The necessity for closer cooperation by Russia, China and Japan [Soviet envoy Kopp declared in Tokyo] as the basis of peaceful relations in the Far East is an axiom . . . Cooperation does not mean an alliance, especially not an alliance directed against others. . . . Russian Far Eastern policies are free of any aggressive tendencies, as the Japanese public must understand. We have no aspirations as to any part of China . . . Certainly every thought of a division of spheres of influence in China must be rejected categorically.[12]

The Japanese Government, however, saw no reason for accepting this plan.

The revolutionary movement was reaching its high point, and Stalin was again preoccupied with the attitude of Japan. He was prepared to go to great lengths and make signal sacrifices to keep Japan out of China.

"The key to the Chinese problem was Tokyo," the acting Soviet envoy to Japan recollects in his memoirs. Stalin set the program in

12. *New York Times*, January 22, 1926.

these terms: "You must at all costs prevent joint intervention of Japan and Britain in case of a further development of the Chinese Revolution. Maneuver as you see fit, but remember that you will be responsible for ultimate success or failure."

"I am not a diplomat," Stalin continued, "and I cannot give you concrete advice. If the [Chinese] Soviets are successful at Peking, in order to assure their safety from intervention, we can give up to the Japanese not only Vladivostok but even Irkutsk." [13]

At the end of 1926 Besedovsky received, in Tokyo, a telegram from Stalin instructing him again to try to conclude a nonaggression pact with Japan. Besedovsky replied that the Japanese Government was not prepared to agree to such a pact at that time, but Stalin urged: "The agreement must be signed at any cost in the shortest possible time." Besedovsky again tried to negotiate with the Foreign Office in Tokyo, but failed completely. Stalin, in a bitter telegram, again insisted that Besedovsky get at least "a Japanese-Soviet protocol containing a mutual guarantee of nonintervention in China." Once more the Japanese declined. And once again Stalin instructed his envoy to suggest a treaty of mutual nonaggression to the Tokyo government; disturbed by Japan's evident reluctance to promise nonaggression, Moscow was ready to grant considerable economic concessions in the Far East. In a prolonged discussion, Kazugi Debuchi remarked: "Besides, I can state on behalf of the Japanese Government that Japan does not intend to attack the Soviet Union." Besedovsky quickly retorted: "The Soviet Union, likewise, does not intend to attack Japan." So strong was Stalin's desire to come to any kind of agreement that he pretended to be satisfied with these verbal exchanges, considering them an adequate nonaggression agreement.

ECONOMIC RELATIONS WITH JAPAN

The economic ties between Japan and Russia were of three different types: first, the usual foreign trade between the two countries; second, the fisheries agreements (this particular problem of Russo-Japanese relations having arisen after 1907); and, third, the so-called "concessions," i.e., Japanese enterprises on Soviet soil.

The foreign trade between Russia and any other country has,

13. Besedovsky, *op. cit.*, II, 18.

under the Soviet system, generally been a fair barometer of political relations. The Moscow government, the only agent in Moscow's commercial dealings with the outer world, has increased or diminished the volume of goods bought and sold abroad in accordance with changes in the political attitude in regard to any particular country.

Relations with Japan gradually improved after the signing of the treaty of 1925. Thereafter foreign trade grew from year to year, reaching its peak between 1929 and 1931, after which it dropped swiftly.[14] The main items of Russian export to Japan were lumber (more than 50 per cent of all exports) and fish (about 25 per cent of them). Russia imported from Japan primarily metal goods and textiles and also a considerable amount of fishing equipment.

More difficult were the negotiations concerning Japanese fishing rights in Russian waters. Fishing rights in the Far East, vital to Japan's food supply, had been granted by the Russian Government in 1907 in accordance with the Treaty of Portsmouth; the agreement was to run for 12 years. In 1919 Admiral Kolchak's regime prolonged these rights. In 1925, when the Soviet and Japanese Governments concluded the Peking treaty, it was agreed that the practices previously established be maintained pending a revision of the basic convention of 1907. Then, at the end of 1925, negotiations began for a new fisheries agreement.

There was no doubt in Moscow that fishing rights had to be conceded to Japan. Basically, however, the Soviet Government as well as the Communist party were emotionally adverse to the granting of such privileges. The very fact that a group of foreign capitalists were entitled to exploit Russian resources aroused antagonism; be-

14.	SOVIET IMPORTS FROM JAPAN	SOVIET EXPORTS TO JAPAN
	(In Millions of Gold Dollars)	
1913	2.5	0.7
1924	1.0	7.0
1925	0.6	5.5
1927	1.8	5.9
1929	4.3	9.2
1931	6.5	10.2
1933	3.8	4.7
1935	5.6	2.8

Russian and Japanese sources differ somewhat on trade statistics. The above data are taken from the *Foreign Commerce Year Books* of the United States Department of Commerce.

sides, it rivaled the young and weak yet growing Russian fishing industry; and finally, such rights in Russian waters gave Japan ample opportunity for espionage, of which Tokyo, no doubt, made extensive use. For all these reasons, the fisheries negotiations between the two governments were drawn out; after the agreement was finally signed, the Soviet side often made use of loopholes to restrict Japanese privileges as much as possible, for example, certain fishing grounds were excluded from foreign use for strategic reasons. A large number of minor conflicts arose in the late twenties and in the thirties, particularly at the time when the expiring agreements had to be renewed.

Before the first Soviet-Japanese fisheries convention was signed, in 1928, a dispute arose about the extent of Russia's territorial waters. While the territorial limit is generally set at three miles offshore, the Soviet Government insisted on a 12-mile limit; thus Japanese fishermen would lose the right of entry to a considerable area of the sea. The conflict developed when the Russians seized Japanese fishing boats outside the three-mile limit but within the 12-mile radius claimed by Russia. Yan Gamarnik, the future general of the Red Army (he committed suicide during the purge of 1937) was at that time head of the Executive Committee in Khabarovsk. He tried to browbeat the Japanese by a display of two small warships; a Japanese minesweeper captured them easily. In the end a secret agreement was concluded between the Soviet Union and Japan, creating, for Japan, the privilege of a three-mile limit on territorial waters.[15] Incidents occurred again later, however, and were particularly numerous in 1929.

The first fisheries convention of the Soviet period was signed in January, 1928, soon after Baron Tanaka, the new Premier, came into office. The agreement was to run for eight years. The leases of fishing grounds to the various companies were to be auctioned, and Soviet state enterprises had obviously to be excluded since they could outbid every competitor. The convention exempted 37 bays and inlets from the auction. According to the new agreement, Japan leased 80 per cent of the fishing grounds in 1928; the rest, with a potential catch of not more than two millions poods,[16] were

15. Besedovsky, *op. cit.*, II, 52–53.
16. A pood—about 36 pounds.

reserved for Soviet fishing agencies. The amounts paid by the Japanese fishing companies for the leases were considerable, reaching
about three million rubles a year (compared with 106,000 rubles at
the outset, in 1908).

In the following years new differences arose when "private"
Russian fishermen began to exhibit a rivalry with the Japanese and
gained fishing areas. The Japanese were certain that these unexpected numbers of "private fishermen" were Soviet puppets. Indeed
the fishing grounds allotted to the Japanese decreased from 80 per
cent in 1928 to 65 per cent in 1929, 54 per cent in 1930, and 50 per
cent in 1931. Japan considered this a Moscow subterfuge and demanded a supplementary convention. Negotiations took place in
1931–32 which led to the agreement (which has never been made
public) of August 13, 1932. *Izvestiya* reported merely that the maximum catch permitted Soviet fishermen had been increased from
two to five million poods, but that, on the other hand, the fishing
lots leased to Japan (with the exception of 60 lots) had been
granted permanently, until the expiration of the basic treaty, without further auction.

Another dispute arose in 1930 concerning the rate of exchange of
payments due from Japan. The Bank of Chosen [Korea] in Vladivostok, a Japanese institution, took advantage of the depreciated
ruble to handle the Japanese payments at a cheaper rate. In 1930 the
Soviet Government proceeded to close down the Bank of Chosen [17]
and demanded payment at the official rate of exchange. After prolonged negotiations it was agreed, in April, 1931, that payments
were to be made at the rate of 32.5 sen for a ruble, as compared with
the official rate of 97 sen.

The foreign concessions granted to Japan in this period were of
two kinds: one was part of the over-all NEP policy of the 1920's,
which facilitated investment of foreign capital in Russia; the other
was composed of the concessions in Northern Sakhalin granted to
Japan in accordance with the basic Soviet-Japanese treaty of 1925.
The first category embraced mainly lumber and gold concessions
in the Far East. A gold mining concession in Kamchatka was
granted in July, 1927; lumber enterprises were active mainly in the
Maritime Province. When the NEP was abolished, in 1928–30,

17. Moscow explained that this was the last private bank on Soviet soil.

and the new policy of industrialization began, these Japanese concessions were abolished along with the other foreign concessions throughout Russia.

The only concessions that remained in the Soviet Union were those on Northern Sakhalin. Japan considered her right to mine coal and drill oil there a matter of the utmost importance; these rights had been stipulated in a political treaty, and the Soviet Government did not attempt to close down the enterprises until the 1940's, when the international situation had radically changed.

The North Sakhalin Petroleum Company and the North Sakhalin Mining Company were established in December, 1925, with a capital of 10 million yen each. They expanded considerably in the subsequent ten years. The oil output of the Japanese concessions rose from 14,000 tons in 1925 to 104,000 in 1928 and 194,000 in 1930. Similarly, the amount of coal mined arose from 850 tons in 1925 to 150,000 tons in 1930.

By the end of the twenties the economic activity of Japan in Russian waters and on Russian soil was at its peak and political relations between the two powers were relatively good.

XI

Armed Conflict in Manchuria

The most important among Soviet-Japanese issues was, of course, the Manchurian problem.

The prerevolutionary agreement dividing Manchuria into Japanese and Russian spheres of influence had been abolished by the Soviet Government in the first days of its existence, along with a number of other secret treaties. During the civil war and prior to the establishment of normal diplomatic relations with China, Russia as a power was virtually absent from Manchuria. Not until the Mukden government of Manchuria approved the Peking treaty of 1924 did Russia return to Harbin and to the Chinese Eastern Railroad.

Japan's policy in Manchuria, on the other hand, was consistent during the two decades after the Russo-Japanese war. Agreement or no agreement, spheres or no spheres, southern Manchuria was in effect increasingly becoming a component of the Japanese Empire, and increasing attention was paid in Tokyo to Manchurian developments. Only the small territory on the Kwantung Peninsula was legally a Japanese possession. This provided Japan with a base for its strong and growing army and a naval base in Port Arthur, while Dairen developed with amazing speed into one of the greatest ports of the Far East. But from Kwantung's ports and cities threads extended deep into southern Manchuria, which in these years was assuming an important role in Asiatic economy and politics. A network of railroads and highways was established; coal mines yielded a steadily increasing output; industry developed at a rapid pace; and the local agriculture served as the basis of an expanding foreign trade. Millions of immigrants, mainly from northern China, swelled Manchuria's population. In all these achievements Manchuria's national resources were, of course, the decisive factors; they were tapped mainly through the investment of Japanese capital. Economically, Tokyo dominated southern Manchuria.

Two principles were pursued by the Japanese Government with regard to southern Manchuria: first, that no other states should deploy extensive economic activity there and in particular that no railroads should be built with foreign capital; and, second, that Manchuria should remain actually independent of the rest of China, whatever their legal relationship. Manchuria's unification with China and its subordination to a government in Peking or Nanking would jeopardize Japan's predominance in southern Manchuria.

Every Japanese Cabinet, regardless of its political affiliation, adhered to these principles. Japan's policy toward China underwent considerable changes; Japan had to withdraw from formerly occupied ports and yield to international pressure—but not in Manchuria. Even nonaggressive cabinets in Tokyo in the middle twenties left no doubt that, so far as southern Manchuria was concerned, they intended to stand up for their "special rights" there by all, even military, means.[1]

When Russia returned to Manchuria in 1924–25, Japan was firmly entrenched in the south. Tokyo gave way to Russia and agreed to tolerate her as the only foreign power operating in northern Manchuria, but making no secret of her determination to fight, if need be, against possible Russian penetration into her exclusive sphere in the south. At that time, however, the Soviet Government had neither the strength nor the intention of expanding deeper into Manchuria, territorially or economically. The Japanese-Soviet collaboration in Manchuria during the following six years was predicated on Soviet acceptance of the two maxims of Japanese policy there. In fact, the Soviet Government was glad to support Japan in her strong opposition to the penetration of any other nation (i.e., Britain and the United States) into Manchuria, since Russia's animosity toward these powers was no less than Japan's. As for the second principle of Japanese policy—the independence of Manchuria from China—this of course did not fit into the long-range programs

1. As early as 1924, Yoshizawa, the Japanese envoy in Peking, told the press that should military operations spread to Manchuria, Japan would move to protect her "special interests" there. Again on May 18, 1928, Shidehara let Peking know that ". . . should the disturbances develop further in the direction of Peking and Tientsin and the situation become so menacing as to threaten the peace and order of Manchuria, the Japanese Government, on their part, may possibly be constrained to take appropriate and effective steps for the maintenance of peace and order in Manchuria." *China Year Book, 1929–1930*, pp. 195–196.

and theories of Communism. In practice, however, this issue could not become acute as long as the Nationalist movement was growing at the other end of China, between Canton and Shanghai. And since 1928, when the Kuomintang armies finally approached the Northern Provinces, the Soviet Government had become a bitter enemy of Chiang Kai-shek and was not disposed to support Chiang's designs for Manchuria in the face of Japanese opposition.

In a sense this was a paradoxical revival of the Russian policy of 1910–16, when Russo-Japanese collaboration in Manchuria was similarly aimed at the elimination of other powers from that province and at the establishment of Manchuria's factual independence from the Central Government of China. The fact, however, that there was now no compact dividing Manchuria between its two neighbors gave Japan the legal and actual possibility of penetrating the north—the former Russian sphere—expanding into regions from which it could jeopardize Soviet interests, and preparing for the eventual expulsion of Russia from Manchuria.

Between 1925 and 1931 Japan was the stronger of the two powers in Manchuria. As mentioned above, the Soviet Government repeatedly tried to protest against Japanese railway construction in Manchuria, particularly in the north. This was, however, of no avail. The Japanese Government insisted on its right to construct railways; at times it countered that the Soviet Union was free to expand its own railways if it chose to do so. There was some irony in this kind of a reply from Tokyo since Russia possessed no capital for investment in Manchuria, and the Sino-Manchurian administration of necessity co-operated with the Japanese and was reluctant to give assistance to the Soviets.

Yet relatively good relations between Japan and Russia prevailed when the liberal government of Shidehara was replaced by the strong-handed regime of Tanaka. On January 21, 1928, Premier Tanaka reported to the Diet that "good-neighbor relations between Japan and the USSR are becoming increasingly friendly." The Soviet-Japanese Society in Tokyo, of which Count Goto was president until 1929, was very active, and its meetings were occasionally attended by Premier Tanaka himself. On the Soviet side Maxim Litvinov as well as Vyacheslav Molotov praised the good relations with Japan between 1929 and 1931.

The "boss" of Manchuria was General Chang Tso-lin. A dictator over his own people and a powerful war lord when facing other Chinese generals, he was weak and helpless in his relations with the two Great Powers operating in his territory. In any dispute between Russia and Japan, Chang was forced to take sides, and his choice was necessarily in favor of the stronger; besides, his strong anti-Communist views made him an antagonist of Soviet Russia. Chang accepted, of course, Japan's plan for Manchuria's actual independence from China. Japan's financial and frequently direct military help were abundantly placed at the disposal of Chang Tso-lin, whose personal wealth grew step by step with Manchuria's development, making him one of the richest men in the Far East.

While southern and central China were the scene of a rising nationalist movement, the situation in the north was for a long time dominated by the continuing conflict between the war lords seeking contact with one or the other of the Great Powers. Approaching from the south, Chiang Kai-shek was the only military leader who dared oppose foreign intervention and raise the banner of nationalism. This was the source of his strength inside China. In the north, however, where Japanese influence was strong, such a nationalist movement was for a long time impossible. The struggle among Chinese generals was often but a veiled conflict between the Great Powers supporting them. Russia entered on the same path as the other powers and found in Feng Yu-hsiang a general willing to co-operate with her in every respect. At times other generals were similarly employed by the Soviet Government in the tangled relations among the Chinese war lords.

In 1924 a conflict was in the offing between Wu Pei-foo (considered pro-British), who dominated Peking and Shantung, and the pro-Japanese Chang Tso-lin. The Soviet Government was only too glad to take part in this struggle in the same indirect way as Japan. Feng Yu-hsiang, supplied and supported by Russia, joined with Chang in a campaign against Wu Pei-foo. The successful drive meant, as far as international relations went, a Soviet-Japanese victory over British influence in northern China.

But Moscow was disappointed by Chang Tso-lin's preference for Japan and tried to break his hold on Manchuria. Despite Litvinov's opposition, Karakhan, the Soviet envoy to China, succeeded in persuading Gen. Kuo Sun-lin to turn against his chief, Chang Tso-lin. The fight of these two war lords was actually a struggle between Russia and Japan. At first the pro-Soviet Kuo Sun-lin achieved a number of victories. At the same time—the end of 1925—Feng Yu-hsiang, supported by Moscow, occupied Tientsin, and it seemed that northern China and Manchuria would fall prey to anti-Japanese generals. In December, when the Japanese dispatched an expeditionary force to assist Chang, Karakhan demanded of Moscow that Soviet troops cross the Manchurian border to give support to the hard-pressed General Kuo. The Politburo discussed Karakhan's request but, foreseeing a clash and possible defeat at the hands of Japan, refused to comply.

Moscow tried to stop Chang by other means than dispatching its army across the border. In December, 1925, the Soviet-appointed General Manager of the Chinese Eastern Railroad, Ivanov, refused to let Chang Tso-lin transport his armies against Kuo Sun-lin on the Chinese Eastern; on the pretext that Chang had failed to pay for previous troop transports, Ivanov demanded payment in advance. Certain of Japanese backing, Chang arrested Ivanov; Moscow presented an ultimatum, and Ivanov was released. Ambassador Karakhan again demanded the entry of Soviet troops into Harbin, and Voroshilov supported his demand in Moscow. Nevertheless it was decided to inquire in Tokyo how Japan would react to the presence of Soviet troops in Manchuria. The Japanese reply was that in such a case Japan would immediately occupy Changchun and send a division of troops to the north, into Harbin. The Politburo decided to refrain from military intervention.

The whole chessboard was a test of strength, ending in a defeat for Moscow. Kuo Sun-lin was completely defeated; General Feng Yu-hsiang left China and went to Moscow; Chang Tso-lin's troops entered Tientsin and, somewhat later, Kalgan, in Inner Mongolia, previously Feng Yu-hsiang's stronghold. The Soviet envoy in Tokyo tried to get rid of Chang Tso-lin by direct negotiations with the Japanese Government, but despite the fact that Chang had few friends in Tokyo, Japan refused to oust him, and Chang Tso-lin enjoyed Japanese assistance for another two years. Moreover in March, 1926, Chang demanded the recall of Ambassador Karakhan, and Moscow was constrained to comply. Karakhan left China in August, 1926.

A SOVIET-CONTROLLED MANCHURIAN RAILROAD

Since the fall of 1924, in accordance with the new agreements, the Chinese Eastern Railway—this backbone of Russian influence in northern Manchuria—was controlled jointly by the Soviet Union and China-Manchuria. A joint administration by two governments, often divided and antagonistic to one another, would have been a source of incidents and clashes under any circumstances.

On the surface the agreements concerning the railroad provided for strict equality of the two partner-nations, China and Russia; and Moscow as well as the Communist International stressed these agreements as proof of the progressive character of Soviet policy toward subjugated nations. At the head of the railway administration was a board composed of five Chinese and five Russians; in addition, the president of the board was required to be a Chinese appointed by Mukden. There were two assistants to the Russian general manager, and here again the statute prescribed that one must be a Russian, the other a Chinese. Likewise, the personnel of the railway administration had to be apportioned equally between Chinese and Russians.

Actually, however, the Soviet Government intended to have full control over the Chinese Eastern. In March, 1926, a commission was appointed by the Politburo to formulate the Soviet policy with regard to this issue. Its members were Voroshilov, Chicherin, and Dzerzhinsky; Trotsky was its chairman. Its resolution asked for "the strict maintenance of the factual control of the line in the hands of the Soviet authorities." [2]

Given the specific aims of Soviet policy in China and the cautious yet shrewd policy of Japan in Manchuria, the Chinese Eastern necessarily became a storm center. More than once the Russian general manager of the railroad was placed under arrest by the Chinese; often property belonging to the line was arbitrarily seized; the tug of war over the division of profits never stopped; the transportation of armed forces was a further source of contention; the solution of dozens of unsolved problems was postponed time and time again. For five years the conflicts grew in intensity, assuming menacing proportions, until they finally culminated in the military

2. This resolution was revealed in part by Trotsky in 1929. *Byulleten' Oppozitsii* (1929), No. 3. Trotsky's basic attitude toward the Chinese Eastern did not differ from Stalin's.

operations of 1929, which were in effect a Sino-Soviet war over the Chinese Eastern Railway.

The Soviet negotiators of the 1924 agreements had proved far superior to their Chinese colleagues, who had not foreseen how their partner would be enabled to dominate the enterprise. The board of ten was unable to reach a decision whenever the two parties disagreed; it therefore did not function at all, and the Chinese president remained a figurehead. In fact, the Russian general manager was the only deciding authority in the great apparatus of the railroad. One of his aides was also a Russian; the Chinese assistant was, of course, unable to oppose them effectively. Distribution of funds therefore was made in accordance with Soviet wishes, and railway rates were set with an eye to Soviet interests. A board of five auditors was established; however, the agreement provided for a majority of Russian members on this important commission which was to check the financial policies of the management. Nor did the agreement stipulate whether Russians or Chinese were to be placed at the head of particular departments. This gave the general manager the opportunity of appointing Soviet citizens whenever he considered it important.

Although under this agreement the Chinese Eastern was now officially considered a purely commercial undertaking, it still possessed all the earmarks of a great-power agency: it ran its own schools, had its own museums, engaged in construction activities, maintained its own river flotilla, and owned land in excess of its actual needs. In its wage policy it pursued strictly propagandistic aims. While the standard of living of Russian workers was low, the Soviet Government attempted to convince the workers abroad that their living conditions improved as soon as the Soviet Union acquired a decisive role. Therefore, wages and salaries on the Chinese Eastern were set at a much higher level than those usual in Manchuria,[3] and this expense seemed unnecessary and exorbitant to the Manchurian Government.

The telephone and telegraph systems of northern Manchuria

3. Karl Radek, highly influential at the time in the Moscow Foreign Office, frankly stated that "for the workers and employees of the Chinese Eastern Railroad working conditions must be created such as to let the Chinese people see and realize the difference between the imperialistic system on Chinese railroads and the system of a workers' and peasants' government." Preface to A. Kantorovich, *Innostrannyi Kapital i zheleznyye dorogi v Kitaye* (Moscow, 1926), p. vii.

likewise were in the hands of the Russian-dominated Chinese Eastern. Finally, Communist cells and clubs were operated in the area of the railroad, and a variety of ties connected them with the Chinese Communists who were being persecuted by the Manchurian Government.

Despite all agreements, propaganda, and the promise to consider the railroad merely as a business enterprise, it still constituted a Russian fortress on Chinese soil. A "sphere of influence" was still in existence, albeit without formal recognition. Gen. Chang Tso-lin, at times cautious, at other times daring—depending on the exigencies of the moment—intervened in the affairs of the railway to curtail its influence. In 1924 he seized lands belonging to the railway. Early in 1925 the Russian manager dismissed those Russian employees of the railway who had not acquired Soviet citizenship; there were a number of capable experts among them. The Chinese authorities protested but were obliged to give in. In December, 1925, when Chang Tso-lin was engaged in a war with Gen. Kuo Sun-lin, the order already mentioned was issued forbidding transportation of troops without payment—an obvious political move directed against General Chang. In February, 1926, the Russian Municipal Council in Harbin (part of the Chinese Eastern) was disbanded. In April, 1926, following the conflicts, Ambassador Karakhan as well as General Manager Ivanov left for Russia; a new Soviet manager was sent to Harbin. In August of that year the schools operated by the Chinese Eastern were charged with Communist propaganda activities and seized. Chang Tso-lin likewise ordered the seizure of the technical school, museum, and library of the Chinese Eastern. In September Chang Tso-lin seized the river flotilla belonging to the Chinese Eastern Railway on the ground that nothing but the railway proper was to be controlled jointly under the Mukden agreement. In December he succeeded in having the so-called educational fund of the railway divided between himself and the Russians. Under Chang's pressure Lashevich, the Soviet manager of the Chinese Eastern Railway, in 1928 consented to having the dividends of the railway divided in accordance with Chinese wishes. (Soon after, Lashevich committed suicide.)

Apart from these political conflicts, strong disagreement marked the activities of the two parties in the management of the railroad. The manager used a Soviet bank to keep the assets of his company, and in this way the considerable profits of the enterprise were used by the Soviet side without any control by China. Workers' wages were equal for Russians and Chinese. As far as the latter were concerned, this was advantageous but quite unusual. The Chinese directors objected to "unnecessary expenses." The number of Russian employees constantly grew so that in 1928–29, the Chinese press asserted, three quarters of the personnel were Russian.

China's desire to acquire full and sole possession of the railroad, although such possession would have been contrary to the existing treaties, was very strong indeed. The Nationalist wave was engulfing all of China; by 1928–29 even the rulers of Manchuria attempted to make themselves independent of all foreign powers, i.e., Japan and Russia. The struggle against Japan was obviously to be a hard one; it seemed, on the other hand, that the Soviet Union would have no adequate forces to resist and might be compelled to give in and to cede the railway to the Manchurian Government.

After the summer of 1927 Chang Tso-lin tried out a policy which was more than difficult—in fact, it was impossible—namely, to oppose *both* Russia and Japan. In September, 1927, anti-Japanese street demonstrations took place in Mukden, and the Japanese Government officially protested against them; Chang Tso-lin had to prohibit all further unfriendly demonstrations against Japan; the incidents, however, continued to multiply. Chang Tso-lin now opposed Japanese railway projects in Manchuria and encouraged the construction of Chinese lines there to defeat the strategic purpose of the Japanese railways. To prevent the imminent contact between the Nationalist armies approaching from the south and the forces of Chang Tso-lin, the Japanese landed in Tsingtao, drove a wedge between the two army groups and, after a bloody battle at Tsinan—the "Tsinan massacre"—forced both parties to stop a campaign which might have led to the unification of China. A few weeks later Chang Tso-lin was killed in a railway accident engineered by the Japanese.

Chang's son, Chang Hsueh-liang, inherited not only the huge fortune of his father, the rule over Manchuria, and the unscrupulous character of his ancestor, but also the pronounced antagonism toward both Russia and Japan. Anti-Japanese feeling in northern

China ran high after the "Tsinan incident." Unlike the developments in 1925, when Chinese Nationalism was almost synonymous with Anglophobia, a popular anti-Japanese movement now began to grow, which eventually led to battle and war. Japan's policy was still the same—its aim was to prevent the unification of China and Manchuria by any means, and to render impossible even a rapprochement between Nanking and Mukden. In July, 1928, the young ruler of Manchuria received an official warning from Tokyo to refrain from merging with the Chinese Government. Chang Hsueh-liang acceded, and the raising of the Kuomintang's banner was postponed for three months. A few months later new anti-Japanese outbursts occurred in Harbin.

The construction of railways in Manchuria was one of the main sources of conflict, along with the growth of Chinese national consciousness and the tendency toward unification. Since 1928 the Manchurian authorities had been trying to hamper the expansion of Japanese railroads and instead to have railways built with Chinese capital in so far as the means were available. Whereas the Soviet Government was unable actively to intervene and oppose this plan, Chang Hsueh-liang tried to oppose or at least to prolong the negotiations. By 1929 a deep gulf was opening between Japan and China over the question of construction of railroads in Manchuria.

At the same time, Chang Hsueh-liang continued his father's policy toward Russia. Late in 1928 the Chinese authorities seized the telephone network operated by the Chinese Eastern. Chang wanted at least a considerable reduction of Soviet prerogatives in the railway administration in Harbin, demanding, for example, the appointment of a Chinese auditor and the liquidation of all enterprises not directly connected with the business of operating the railroad. On December 28, 1928, an order was issued to cease the raising of the flag of the Chinese Eastern—which was a combination of the Chinese and Soviet flags.

It became obvious that China's immediate aim was the taking over of the Chinese Eastern. On December 31, 1928, the United States consul at Harbin reported:

There is much talk regarding the taking over of the entire railway by the Chinese authorities. It is believed that the Japanese officials of the South Manchuria Railway would take active measures to forestall a movement of this sort, which could be used as a precedent against the Japanese line. Perhaps there exists some sort of understanding between the Soviet and Japanese officials in this respect.[4]

This parallelism and affinity of Soviet and Japanese policies was already discernible. It soon assumed great importance and played a crucial role in the conflict of 1929.

At the end of March, 1929, Soviet Consul General Melnikov, in Harbin, visited Chang Hsueh-liang in order to arrive at a new agreement with the Manchurian dictator. Chang declined, however, to make any new agreements without the participation of Chiang Kai-shek's government, which, in turn, was detested in Moscow. The Manchurian leader already considered himself one of the chief representatives of the all-Chinese Nationalist movement.

A few months later, on May 27, 1929, the participants in a conference in the offices of the Soviet consulate in Harbin—both Russian officials and Chinese—were arrested by the Manchurian police, which declared the meeting to have been a conference of the Communist International. The Foreign Office in Moscow reacted with a sharply worded note in which Karakhan stated that since the Chinese authorities did not respect the usages of extraterritoriality with regard to Soviet consulates, the Soviet Government "for its part no longer regards itself bound by these norms with respect to the Chinese representation in Moscow and the Chinese consulates." It was announced by the Chinese that considerable quantities of Communist literature had been found on the raided premises in Harbin, and that the spreading of propaganda was among the functions of the Soviet officials on Manchurian soil. Communist propaganda in this case served as a pretext for the ensuing Chinese attempt to take over the Chinese Eastern Railway.

A few weeks later, early in July, a conference took place in Peking between the chiefs of the Chinese and Manchurian Governments. Chiang Kai-shek as well as Chang Hsueh-liang and a number of Chinese officers, generals, and diplomats, were present. The most important decision reached was to seize the Chinese Eastern, and pertinent instructions went out to the Chinese generals in northern Manchuria. The fact that the decisions were made

4. United States Department of State, *Foreign Relations* (1929), II, 187.

jointly by Nanking and Mukden was kept secret; it became known, however, as soon as the Sino-Soviet conflict erupted.

On July 10, 1929, the Manchurian authorities seized the Chinese Eastern Railway. Yemshanov, the Russian general manager, was removed from his office, and a Chinese was appointed in his stead. The trade-union of railroad workers was banned and various Soviet offices were closed down. On July 13 the Soviet Government presented an ultimatum demanding that "all unilateral acts should be undone" and "the arrested Soviet citizens set free within three days." China rejected the ultimatum. Yemshanov as well as 142 other Soviet employees of the line were ordered expelled from Manchuria. About 1,000 Soviet citizens were arrested and confined in a concentration camp near Harbin, while the Soviet Government likewise proceeded to arrest about 1,000 Chinese citizens ("Chinese merchants," Moscow emphasized). On July 18, a new note from the Soviet Government informed China that Russia was recalling all her agents from the railroad and all her diplomatic and consular representatives in China, that rail communications were suspended, and that the Chinese representatives had been asked to leave the Soviet Union. The note quoted an important statement by Chiang Kai-shek: "Our steps are designed to take the Chinese Eastern Railroad. Our hands contain nothing unusual—we want first to take hold of the Chinese Eastern Railroad, then to take up the discussion of all the questions." On July 17, 1929, Chiang Kai-shek declared that "Red imperialism is more dangerous than the White."

So far no military clashes had occurred. After the sending of these notes, however, popular unrest began to increase. Trains ceased to arrive; troop movements started on both sides of the border. The Sino-Soviet break thus entered an acute stage. After a few weeks armed clashes began; real fighting took place in November. In December China yielded and restored the status quo ante.

Between July and December, 1929, the Soviet-Chinese controversy was the focus of international politics. It was the first war conducted by Russia since 1920, when both the civil war and the war against Poland had ended.

THE OUTBREAK OF WAR WITH CHINA

A war against China was most unwelcome to the Soviet Government. The government was at this time starting its drive for collectivization, which was provoking considerable resistance in rural Russia. The army appeared to be needed in Europe; China was not an imperialist power, but a "subjugated semicolonial nation." Moreover, to fight a weak nation for the privilege of operating a railroad on its territory seemed disgusting to many a Communist at the time. A mere 12 years after the November Revolution, the Communist party still had some remnants of its initial idealism left. What later became a customary and everyday occurrence—as, for example, the forcible seizure of goods and property of a foreign country simply because it was to the advantage of the Soviet Union—was impossible at that time. Lively discussions went on inside the party; every move of the government had to be ideologically justified. The Communist world was still sensitive to criticism from the Socialist parties of Europe, which severely censured the Soviet policy of enforcing its rule in China and its control over the Chinese Eastern by means of armed might. What was the difference, the critics asked, between the classical and the Soviet patterns of imperialism and aggression?

When the Sino-Soviet conflict developed the discordances in Moscow became obvious. There were, of course, those Communist "Nationalists" who simply contended that the Chinese railroad had been built by Russian means (actually it had been constructed chiefly with the proceeds of French loans), and that therefore Moscow must insist on its rights. Others, however, wanted the railway relinquished to China. Others again insisted that, once in Chinese hands, the railroad would soon become the property of some imperialist power.[5]

5. "Voices were heard telling us that the Chinese Eastern Railroad belonged to us, that the Chinese Eastern Railroad was built with the money of the Russian people, etc. And from these supposedly proletarian but actually nationalist conversations the 'leftist' conclusion was drawn that the Red Army must be brought to Harbin. The party refused to take that position. There were still more voices heard to the effect that we must give up the Chinese Eastern Railroad, that the line causes us only unnecessary 'trouble' and difficulties, etc. This point of view was likewise based on incorrect premises. It failed to take account of a detail, namely, that the transfer of the line to Nanking or Mukden would be a concession to imperialism, tantamount to the transfer of the railroad to the imperialists." P. Madyar, in *Bolshevik* (1930), No. 2.

Karl Radek had earlier made known his opinion that "Soviet Russia will uphold the

Among the various reasons advanced in justification of Soviet control of a Chinese railroad, one, which was uppermost in everybody's mind, was not publicly mentioned: the fact that the Chinese Eastern constituted the shortest road between Vladivostok and Siberia and Europe. Such a motive was, however, in conflict with the internationalism still prevalent in Soviet ideology: why should China suffer because of the peculiar configuration of Russia's borders around Manchuria? Moreover, if these geographic and strategic reasons were to justify the possession of a railroad running across foreign soil, the usual polemics against the "imperialist policies" of other powers became unconvincing. The accepted version, therefore, alleged that the Soviet Union was keeping the Chinese Eastern in its possession only so long as there was no Communist government in China; the government in Moscow was merely a custodian of Chinese property which would be turned over to the Chinese people when they reached maturity, when a Communist government would emerge in China. This was the official version:

The Soviet proletariat carries out the administration of the Chinese Eastern Railroad jointly with the Chinese (bourgeois-landowners) Government in the interests of preventing the transfer of the railroad into the hands of the imperialists subjugating China; in the interests of an easier transfer of the railroad into the hands of the Chinese people after the (genuine, and not social-democratic) victory of the national revolution—to the Chinese people which will have done away with the imperialists, their bourgeois-landlord pillars within China proper; and finally in the interests of the defense of the Soviet Union itself—that country which is building socialism—from the threat of invasions on the part of hostile capitalist countries.[6]

This was, however, insufficient for the multitude of critics within the Communist movement. Why then had Lenin returned so much property and so many Russian privileges to Persia? Had it been proper, back in 1917–20, for Soviet Russia to denounce con-

slogan, 'The Chinese Railroad for the Chinese!' with full energy, despite the fact that Soviet Russia is the owner of the Chinese Eastern Railroad and cannot give up this ownership until such time as its relinquishment would be to the benefit of the people and not of Japanese imperialism." Preface to Kantorovich, *op. cit.*

6, *Communist International* (Russian ed. August 31, 1929), p. 46.

cessions and privileges abroad rather than keep them until the day of social revolution?[7]

After Russia had officially ruptured relations with China in mid-July, 1929, the world anticipated strong action by Moscow. To prevent a military conflict which might spread far beyond Manchuria, the powers initiated diplomatic steps in which the relationship of the governments to each other and their mutual antagonisms became eminently clear.

The one group of powers comprised the United States, Britain, and France, which acted together. On July 25 Secretary of State Stimson received the ambassadors of five powers (Britain, France, Italy, Japan, and Germany) and read to them an American proposal for a commission of conciliation. His draft suggested the ap-

7. This confusion lay at the root of a literary falsification committed by the *Communist International* somewhat later when it was decided to give wide publicity to the so-called *Tanaka Memorial*, published in China. This memorial allegedly embodied a report presented by Baron Tanaka to the Emperor of Japan in 1927, as a general outline of Japan's future policies. The authenticity of the document was emphatically denied by Japan. It was indeed a hoax. In blunt language it explained why it was necessary for Japan to crush the United States, fight Russia, control China. Japanese dominion over Manchuria, Mongolia, and the Russian Maritime Provinces was part of the great design. Even if the *Memorial* was an invention, it correctly and realistically outlined the political offensive of Japan during the subsequent two decades.

In 1931, the *Communist International* republished the *Memorial* in all four of the languages in which the magazine was published; soon Communist publishing houses abroad issued it as a pamphlet and distributed it in great numbers. The Comintern would have been embarrassed, however, to reprint two pages from the long *Memorial*, in which Baron Tanaka—or, rather, his adroit Chinese ghost—describes Soviet policy in Manchuria; he pictured it ably and realistically, but made no distinction between Soviet and non-Soviet imperialism in China! The compromising two pages were deleted by the Moscow magazine and did not appear in any of the reprints published abroad under the auspices of the Communist parties. The paragraphs read in part:

"The Russian plans are designed to strengthen the Chinese Eastern Railroad and thereby to extend its imperialist schemes . . . Although the power of Soviet Russia is declining, her ambition in Manchuria and Mongolia has not diminished for a minute. Every step she takes is intended to obstruct our progress and to injure the South Manchuria Railway. We must do our utmost to guard against her influence . . . We should still secretly befriend Russia in order to hamper the growth of Chinese influence. It was largely with this purpose in view that Baron Goto of Kato's cabinet invited Joffe to our country and advocated the resumption of diplomatic relations with Russia. . . . According to a secret declaration of Soviet Russia, although they have no territorial ambition, they cannot help keeping a hand in the Chinese Eastern Railroad on account of the fact that north of the Chinese and Russian boundary the severe cold makes a railroad valueless. Furthermore, as Vladivostok is their only seaport in the Far East, they cannot give up the Chinese Eastern Railroad without losing also their foothold on the Pacific. This makes us feel the more uneasy."

This part of the *Memorial* was censored by Moscow.

(Quoted from the Harper ed. (New York, 1942), pp. 51–53, *passim*.)

pointment of a prominent neutral citizen, acceptable to both China and Russia, as president and general manager of the Chinese Eastern for the duration of the negotiations. The Kellogg-Briand Pact outlawing war as an instrument of national policy had just been signed by all these nations, and also by the Soviet Government; July 24, 1929, had been set by President Hoover as the day for a solemn celebration of the international covenant to outlaw war forever and to settle disputes by peaceful means. Although the Kellogg Pact had not created any machinery for the peaceful settlement of international disputes, Stimson considered that the United States was destined and entitled to take the initiative, despite the fact that the United States had not recognized the Soviet Union.

The reaction to the Stimson proposal was revealing. France, Britain, and Italy were in agreement with Stimson's démarche, and France in particular was prepared to play the part of an intermediary between Washington and Moscow. Germany, on the other hand, was trying to play the east against the west, and vice versa, and often used the heavy weight of Russia in her diplomatic dealings with the Western Powers. Because of these friendly relations with Germany, the *Narkomindel* (Foreign Office) in Moscow requested the *Auswärtiges Amt* to represent its interests in China, and Germany also represented China's interests in Russia. As soon as *Izvestiya* came out strongly against the notion of mediation in the Sino-Soviet conflict, the German Government declined to participate in any collective action of the Great Powers. Unlike Russia and Japan, however, Germany was on good terms with the Nanking government and tried to induce Russia to conduct direct negotiations with Chiang Kai-shek concerning the status of the Chinese Eastern Railway; she failed in this endeavor.

The decisive role belonged to Japan. Everybody, including Moscow, was attentively watching Tokyo's reaction. Japanese forces were stationed in Changchun, at the southern end of the Chinese Eastern and within a few hours of Harbin, capital of northern Manchuria. A considerable Japanese task force was located on Kwantung Peninsula. The well-equipped Japanese divisions were far superior to both the Chinese and Russian forces. But Japan was utterly disinclined to side with Chang against Russia. Whether the Chinese Eastern belonged to the Manchurians or remained in Russian hands was not so crucial as that other question:

whether Manchuria had become an integral part of China and was to be ruled by Chiang Kai-shek from Nanking. Moreover, the ejection of Russia from the Manchurian network of railroads might forecast the beginning of a similar drive against Japanese interests there. For all these reasons, Japan decided to step aside and not to intervene.

"We must drop a hint to China," *Osaka Mainichi* wrote on July 13, 1929, "that we find no justification for the illegal actions by means of which China has seized the railroad." And *Tokyo Asahi* added, "The talk about the bolshevization of Manchuria is nothing more than a pretext for the seizure of the railroad."

TACIT CONSENT OF JAPAN

The prerequisite of a successful Soviet operation was at least tacit consent on the part of Japan. The Japanese Government, aroused by the friction with Chang Hsueh-liang during the preceding year, was prepared to give its tacit approval to the Soviet drive so long as Soviet troops did not penetrate deeply into Manchuria or jeopardize Japan's dominant position there. Moscow fulfilled these two implicit conditions. Russian Ambassador Yurenev visited Shidehara on July 24, and emphasized that "there would be no fighting unless Russia was challenged by the Chinese." [8]

Japan repudiated the attempt of the Great Powers—particularly the United States—to intervene in Manchuria. With an eye on Tokyo, Moscow, too, refrained for four months from sending troops into Manchuria; when it finally sent its army, it did so cautiously and only for a short time. Disregarding the looming clash of interests, the Soviet press during the crisis of 1929 praised Japan and attacked Japan's critics, above all the United States. With great satisfaction the *Communist International* reported the failure of the American Secretary of State in his attempt to mediate in Manchurian affairs: "American imperialism . . . has run into sharp opposition from Japan, which has justly found a threat to its influence in Manchuria in the efforts of the United States of America to put its hand, in some form or other, on the Chinese Eastern Railway." [9]

8. *Foreign Relations* (1929), II, 240–241.
9. *Communist International* (Russian ed. August 31, 1929), p. 43.

Another Soviet publication likewise stated:

Japan has torpedoed the Stimson project of July 25, to hand the conflict over into the hands of a neutral commission, the appointment of a "neutral" foreign administrator for the railroad, etc. . . . Japan desires peace and the settlement of the conflict by means of direct negotiations between the parties concerned, without any participation whatsoever of the Western Powers. From the very outset of the conflict, Japan has been interested in settling the issue directly with Mukden, without the participation of Nanking . . . They have shown no interest whatever in the efforts of the German Government to establish contact between Moscow and Nanking.[10]

Communist parties throughout the world issued appeals opposing the attempts of "greedy American imperialism" to "stretch out its hands to Manchuria"; contrary to historical reality, they depicted the Chinese nationalist movement under Chiang Kai-shek as a mere tool of American capitalism, and they carefully ignored the menace of Japanese supremacy.

This alignment of Soviet Russia with Japan against Manchuria assured the success of Soviet policy. Early in August, by order of Voroshilov, Vasili Blücher was placed in command of Soviet military forces in the Far East—the newly activated "Special Far Eastern Red Army," which was to be organized during subsequent months. Blücher, under the name of Galen, had formerly participated in the operations of the Chinese Nationalists under Borodin and was considered an expert on the Far East as well as an able military commander. In order not to weaken the Soviet armies in Europe, this new army, consisting of two corps, was recruited primarily from among the inhabitants of Siberia. By fall it numbered over 100,000 men; 7,000 GPU troops were assigned to it from Europe. (Before the crisis, the Red Army forces in the Far East had amounted to about 30,000.) Soviet planes and tanks were also placed under Blücher's command.

Unrest in the border areas was steadily mounting; trenches were dug around Manchouli; food and water became scarce; and a number of border raids occurred, for which the Russian press and radio blamed "White Russians" acting with the consent of China.[11]

---

10. *Mirovoye khozyaistvo i mirovaya politika* (1930), No. 2, p. 81.
11. These local clashes were of no military significance: they were committed largely by local inhabitants and soldiers in search of food.

The diplomatic negotiations, which continued in the meanwhile, mainly through German channels, did not bring the parties together. The Chinese, aware of the difficulty of their situation, wanted at least to save face; they agreed to restore the old order if the Soviet Government would recall its chief delegates on the Chinese Eastern and appoint new ones instead. Litvinov, however, insisted on a simple restoration of the status quo. In October China's bargaining power was further weakened when Gen. Feng Yu-hsiang, who in former years had often collaborated with Russia, suddenly launched an offensive against the forces of the Nanking regime, and the ensuing civil war absorbed the attention and energies of the Nationalist Government.

The main objective of Japanese policy was thus achieved: Manchuria was isolated.

In November the Soviet Government decided to take the offensive. A serious battle was fought on November 18, with the Red Army capturing Manchouli and Dalainor, while the Mongolians, advancing from the People's Republic, reached Hailar. The Soviet troops did not remain in Manchuria, however, but cautiously returned to Soviet soil.[12] The next day a heavy air attack was launched over Chinese territory, resulting in an estimated 2,000 casualties. A few days later there was another attack against the border station of Manchouli and Dalainor; considerable damage was inflicted.

The Tokyo government was sure that Russian forces would not penetrate any deeper into or remain in Manchuria: the Japanese Ambassador to the United States told the State Department on November 25 that "he did not believe that the Russians intended to occupy the railway by force; that to do so . . . would bring them to Changchun and right up against the Japanese." The United States was given to understand that "the Japanese would not sit quietly by and see this happen." [13] Secretary Stimson, however, alarmed by the outbreak of actual warfare and prodded by China, on November 26 again proposed to the five powers that they call collectively upon both parties of the conflict to refrain from warlike acts in accordance with the Kellogg Pact. The alignment of the powers was the same as it had been in July. Britain, France, and Italy accepted; Germany refused, and so, of course, did Japan.

12. Fischer, *op. cit.*, II, 800–801.
13. *Foreign Relations* (1929), II, 348–349.

The latter informed Washington in its reply that it had no intention of taking action, either alone or in concert with other nations.

On December 1 Stimson asked all the signatories of the Kellogg Pact to join in collective action in the dispute. The American appeal reached Moscow through the French Ambassador and, as did the notes of other powers, provoked enormous indignation on the part of Litvinov.[14] The Soviet press violently attacked the United States, France, and England for their diplomatic intervention. The official reply from Litvinov to Stimson stated: "The Soviet Union cannot admit the intervention of anyone in the negotiations or in the conflict." [15]

China's military situation was desperate, and there was little hope that international action would yield positive results. On November 27 Tsai Yun-sheng, Manchurian Commissioner for Foreign Affairs, telephoned the former Soviet Consul General Melnikov, who had temporarily taken up residence in Chita, proposing direct negotiations and accepting the Soviet conditions on behalf of both Chang Hsueh-liang for Manchuria and Chiang Kai-shek for China. A meeting, in reality an armistice conference, took place in Nikolsk-Ussuriisk, and on December 3 a protocol was signed, with Soviet representative Simanovsky acting for Russia, and Tsai acting for both the Manchurian and the central Chinese governments. The agreement re-established the status quo ante on the Chinese Eastern. The only concession made by Moscow consisted in the recall of Yemshanov, the former manager of the line, and Eismont, his assistant; Moscow appointed other Soviet citizens to take their place. A peace conference was then convened at Khabarovsk, and the peace protocol was signed there on December 22, 1929.

The main provisions of the "Khabarovsk protocol" were as follows: the re-establishment of the status quo ante on the Chinese Eastern; the reopening of Soviet consulates, trading and other missions in Manchuria. and of Chinese consulates in the Soviet Far East; the release of all arrested Russians in China and vice versa;

14. The worse reception was accorded to the Rumanian note, since Rumania had been in conflict with the Soviet Government, and there were no diplomatic relations between the two countries. Litvinov tore up the Rumanian note and threw it away in the presence of the French Ambassador.

15. *Foreign Relations* (1929), Vol. II.

the withdrawal of armed forces from foreign territory; and the disarming of the so-called "White Russian" formations in Manchuria, as well as the deportation of their leaders. It was further agreed that a Sino-Soviet conference was to be held in Moscow on January 25, 1930, to discuss all outstanding questions. A new Soviet manager for the Chinese Eastern soon arrived who dismissed employees appointed by China during the conflict and reinstated the former personnel.

As far as international repercussions were concerned, the leading Soviet magazine, *Bolshevik*, summed up the lessons of the struggle in these terms:

The most active, the most aggressive proved to be the greedy American imperialism. There cannot be the least doubt now that *the United States was the initiator, the inspirer* of the conflict. Dollar diplomacy pressed Nanking in order to get the Chinese Eastern Railroad into the hands of American capitalism . . . The Kellogg Pact is not only aimed against the Soviet Union but it represents the efforts of American imperialism at hegemony in the imperialist camp.[16]

Since Japanese imperialism, *Bolshevik* continued, opposes the imperialism of the United States, the united front of imperialist powers against the Soviet Union has become impossible of realization.

When the armed conflict in China was over, Maxim Litvinov appeared before the Central Executive Committee to give a public report on foreign affairs. He was bitter against Henry Stimson and the United States in general. He denounced the other Great Powers. He protested against the "unsolicited intervention of peacemakers." He sharply attacked the "Nanking government." As for Japan, Litvinov had this to say: "We are glad to acknowledge a considerable stabilization in our relations with out great Far Eastern neighbor, Japan, and the mutual loyalty observed by both our governments."

PEACE AND FUTILE NEGOTIATIONS

The peace protocol ending the Sino-Soviet conflict provided for negotiations to be conducted in Moscow on all outstanding problems of Soviet-Chinese relations. From these talks the Chinese

16. *Bolshevik* (1930), No. 2, p. 78. Italics in original.

hoped to win certain improvements in their position in the administration of the Chinese Eastern and, above all, to find out under what circumstances the Soviet Government would be prepared to sell the railroad to China. Purchase of the railway seemed to be the only means whereby China could re-establish her sovereignty over northern Manchuria. Other questions concerning political and commercial relations were also on the agenda. Moscow was a reluctant party to these negotiations; it did not seriously contemplate selling the Chinese Eastern to China, and as far as political relations with Chiang Kai-shek were concerned, it had no intention of effecting a reconciliation. During the 19 months between the end of the railroad dispute and the Japanese invasion of Manchuria, no progress whatever was made.

At first the Nanking government, contrary to the position taken by the Manchurian regime, questioned the validity of the Khabarovsk protocol. Nanking declared that Tsai, who had negotiated the protocol as a delegate of both Chinese governments, had acted ultra vires: he had been empowered (Nanking said) to effect a settlement only of the Chinese Eastern dispute and not of other political issues. It took a few months for Nanking to give way. In May, 1930, the Nanking government dispatched a Chinese delegation to Moscow, headed by Mo Teh-hui, the new president of the Chinese Eastern. Five months elapsed before a meeting of the commission was finally convened, on October 12.

By that time new strife among the war lords had broken out in China. Gen. Yen Hsi-shan, assisted by Feng Yu-hsiang, again attacked Chiang Kai-shek's forces. Feng and Yen also accused Chiang of responsibility for the military conflict with Russia, and Moscow was hopefully inclined to delay the negotiations in Moscow until the result of the struggle became evident.

The war of the generals was soon ended. Conferences were then begun between Lev Karakhan and Mo Teh-hui in which Karakhan used dilatory tactics. There followed an acrimonious exchange of notes between Karakhan and Mo Teh-hui in which the Soviet Government accused China, among other things, of giving support to Russian "White Guardists" in Manchuria; China denied this allegation. A second meeting took place in December; subcommittees were appointed, and Mo left for China. He returned three months later, but the numerous commissions produced no results. It was while these negotiations were in progress that Japan struck at Manchuria, bringing an end, virtually, to the Russo-Chinese negotiations; the Chinese mission sped home. Now even this thin thread binding Nanking to Moscow was broken.

XII

The Chinese Soviets

The autumn of 1927 marked a turning point in the history of Chinese Communism as well as of Soviet policy toward China. The triple coalition between Moscow, the Kuomintang, and the Chinese Communists was shattered. Soviet consulates all over China were ordered to close, and Soviet "instructors" were being recalled; the Chinese Communist party, after a few bloody but futile attempts at insurrection, retreated from the principal areas of political life deep into the countryside. A profound disorientation reigned among both the Comintern leadership in Moscow and the Chinese Communists themselves. The ideas and instructions pouring in from Moscow to China were often confused and contradictory, and for a time no definite view on the situation could be formulated.

Thousands of members and sympathizers turned their backs on the Communist cause; many of them joined the Kuomintang; others gave themselves up to the police in order to avoid persecution. Demoralization was severe. And yet a remarkable core of adherents remained, faithful and devoted, prepared to continue the fight under different conditions and by different means.

This solid core of Communists, the nucleus of the future party, discussed the same problems that were debated in Moscow. Who was responsible for the failures, they asked? What was really the meaning of the complete defeat that Chinese Communism had suffered? Was the revolutionary wave over, or was this only a momentary failure that would soon be succeeded by a new tide of triumph? Had it been necessary and proper for the Communists to ally themselves with Chiang Kai-shek in the first place? And had the attitude which Chinese Communism displayed toward the "Chinese bourgeoisie" and its political bodies been a correct one? After all—exalted Communists in Moscow and China inquired— had Trotsky not been right in his pronouncements that Stalin's pro-Kuomintang policy was leading to disaster and that, instead, soviets of workers' and peasants' deputies, after the Russian model, must be established in China to wrest the power of government from the Kuomintang when the revolutionary torrent seemed to be at its crest?

The Chinese Communists no longer received millions of dollars and scores of instructors from Russia; they could no longer use them. Yet Moscow's hold on the affairs of Chinese Communism did not loosen. The destiny of the Chinese section was closely tied up with the course laid down in the "Headquarters of the World Revolution," as the Comintern so proudly called itself.

Numerous resolutions and instructions were issued from Moscow but it was obvious that even the leadership of the Comintern was confused. It could advance no clear formulae or integrated plans. It never acknowledged that anything could have been wrong with its policy of previous years; the Comintern is always right; somebody else must be the scapegoat. The Moscow leadership in presenting the Chinese problem to the Congress of the Comintern in 1928 reprimanded those Chinese Communists who were "reformists" rather than revolutionaries:

. . . An insufficiently sharp political and organizational differentiation and disavowal of the bourgeoisie by the proletariat, the playing down of the most important revolutionary slogans (in particular, that of the agrarian revolution) was the basic error which was committed by the Chinese Communist party in the years 1925–27.[1]

The Sixth Congress of the Comintern devoted much time to the issue of China.[2] Seven speakers addressed the Congress in the name of China; it was noteworthy, however, that the most important speeches were made by Russians in their capacity as delegates of the Chinese party—Vorovsky and Strakhov. The resolutions on Chinese affairs adopted by the Congress instructed the Chinese party to wage a fight for: the overthrow of the Kuomintang and the consolidation of Soviet power in a united China; the confiscation of industrial property belonging to foreigners; expropriation of banks and landlords' estates; alliance with the Soviet Union. When at the end of the Congress a new executive and a new Presidium of the

1. *Strategiya i taktika*, p. 71.
2. Just before it convened, a Congress of the Chinese Communist Party was held in Moscow at which a number of decisions were passed in line with Comintern directives.

Comintern were elected, Strakhov, the Russian delegate from China, was made a member of the Presidium as well as of the eleven-man Political Secretariat, the highest body of the Communist International.

These were the hardest years in the history of Chinese Communism, and yet the movement did not disappear. Groups of devoted members fleeing persecution by the Nationalists, held together, moving from one locality to another. There were almost no workers left in the party; it was officially stated that only 4,000 workers still adhered, and even this figure is in all likelihood exaggerated. The "revolutionary trade-unions," whose number had risen to 734 in 1927, disappeared. The main activity of the remnant party was naturally concentrated on the agrarian problem, since the Communists were at least temporarily compelled to live in rural areas. Wherever possible they tried to carry out an agrarian revolution, driving out or killing the landlords and dividing the land among the peasants. Concerning the agrarian problems it was again the Comintern in Moscow that was looked to for instructions. Fleeing from the cities, the leadership felt comparatively safe in the countryside; they did not go into hiding, however, but organized a new administration there, removed the old officials and temporarily became the political bosses, and established a sort of local government. This peculiar network of Communist states inside the state of the Kuomintang they labeled, not without some exaggeration, soviets—and the first news of the establishment of "soviets in China" had an electrifying effect in Moscow, where the great defeat of the Chinese Revolution had still not been acknowledged. The news came during the session of the Soviet Communist Party's Congress, and Nikolai Bukharin proudly announced:

For the first time in the history of the Chinese peasant movement a soviet power has been created on a peasant base—a power that has begun a genuine war of annihilation against the landlords. They have cut off the heads of about 300 or 400 landlords. (Applause. Voice from the audience: "Too little. Should be more.") The landlords in this area have been physically done away with.[3]

3. Fifteenth Congress of the All-Union Communist Party, *Stenographic Report* (in Russian), p. 604.

This first experiment with Chinese soviets was short-lived indeed. The soviets were suppressed after a few months, and not until 1930 did they reappear.

The agrarian problem was a sore point in Communist policy. A great number of questions arose whenever an agrarian movement began to spread under Communist guidance. Confiscation of landlords' estates was not questioned, but what about the wealthy peasants—in Russia termed kulaks? To deprive the latter of their land would be to provoke a civil war among the peasantry. It was not at all certain whether political conditions in China were auspicious for such a course. But to refrain from infringing upon the holdings of the kulaks was counter to the fundamental emotions and intentions of the Communists—especially of the militant elements. And then the question of how to divide the expropriated lands. To share the land equally among the members of the community would often mean giving land to a peasant who had not the livestock, man power, or tools to cultivate it. On the other hand, to distribute the land in accordance with the economic capacity of each peasant would be to strengthen the strong and enrich the rich, while leaving the weak unaided. And what about collective farming in China? These were precisely the years when the Soviet Union was turning toward universal collectivization. Should not the Chinese agrarian revolution lead directly toward kolkhozes?

To all these questions, uppermost in the thinking of the Chinese Communists, the Executive Committee in Moscow as well as the Chinese Central Committee gave answers—numerous answers that were often overlapping and contradictory. The leading body of Chinese Communism, with the exception of some guerrilla leaders such as Mao Tse-tung and Chu Teh, was slow moving. In Moscow the "leftist" trend prevailed, and the Executive Committee of the Comintern often had occasion to reprimand the Chinese Central Committee and give support to the revolutionary tactics of Mao and Chu Teh, who were to become the Chinese party's leaders.

The Central Committee of the Chinese Party, for example, sent a letter to Mao Tse-tung, censuring him for his revolutionary tactics:

Our general tactical line demands an alliance with the rich peasantry . . . Pursuing the general tactical task—struggle with the class of landlords—it is imperative to conclude an alliance with the rich peasants; it will be an error for you consciously to try and kindle strife with the rich peasants, the kulaks . . .

The Comintern condemned this policy of the Chinese Central Committee and sided with the revolutionary methods of Mao Tse-tung, the future "Stalin of China"; Ho Lung, the leader of the guer-rillas; and others. Addressing its Chinese comrades, the Executive Committee in Moscow wrote:

"Confiscate the landowners' lands, arm the peasants, create soviets!" [4]

During the following years the membership of the Chinese party declined considerably and started to rise again in 1931.[5]

Actually the Chinese Communist party, as a well-knit organiza-tion, existed between 1928 and 1930 only in a small number of Communist-dominated areas; outside of these there were of course groups of sympathizers. Interest in Communist ideology and policy did exist—providing a promise for the future.

4. *Strategiya i taktika,* pp. 240–241, 257–258; and *Communist International* (1929), Nos. 28 and 51.

5. The figures released by the party itself were often inflated, but the trend is ap-parent even in those figures. In 1928 there were only 30,000 members listed, many of them inactive. In Shanghai, the largest industrial and cultural center, for example, there were only 500 party members in January, 1931; in Hupeh Province, about 1,200; in Kiangsi, 3,000; and in the whole of Manchuria, 1,000; together, in these most important areas outside the so-called Soviet regions occupied by the Communists, there were 5,700 Communist party members. In August, 1931, only eight months later, the official figures for the same four regions were 10,300. Two years later, in the fall of 1933, the party had 19,000 members in these regions: Shanghai, 4,000; Kiangsi, 8,000; Hupeh, 4,000; Manchuria, 3,000. *Communist International* (1933), No. 32.

Figures for the over-all party strength in China frequently included the Communist areas, where the party possessed exclusive power and where a persistent and success-ful recruitment of new members was taking place. The party membership, thus cal-culated, amounted to 130,000 in 1930, over 200,000 in 1931, 300,000 in 1932, and 410,600 in 1933. In non-Soviet China, the official reports stressed, the situation was quite un-satisfactory. Of the 300,000 members reported in 1932, for example, the official figures noted 30,000 as residing outside of Soviet China. The following year the membership for non-Soviet China was 60,000; however, at least half of these Communists were in no contact whatsoever with either local or central party organizations. *Strategiya i taktika,* p. 355; G. Erenburg, *Sovetski Kitai* (1934), pp. 121–122; *Communist International* (1934), No. 20, p. 61.

LI LI-SAN

It was in this period that a new personality rose to great influence and power—Li Li-san, the former president of the miners' union, a leader in the general strike of 1925, and, from 1925 to 1927, president of the Chinese Federation of Labor. Li had studied in France, where he had organized the first group of Chinese Communist students. An enthusiast and hothead, Li seemed at first the right man to carry out the change in policy desired by Moscow, and the Executive Committee was glad to have him at the helm in China. But Li went further than the Comintern had intended he should go; he already saw in the making a great popular uprising against Chiang Kai-shek; he counted the millions of workers and peasants of China as his allies, who were only awaiting the call to arms. It was rather difficult to toe the line of the Comintern and to walk the razor's edge between rightist cautiousness and leftist Putschism.[6]

From the point of view of the International, what was even worse than this fiery leftism of Li Li-san was his critical attitude toward instructions and advice from Moscow. Li did not conceal his real feelings; he spoke of the Comintern as badly misinformed; he told his party that the Comintern did not understand the trends in the development of the Chinese revolution; he even went so far as to state that "as soon as the Chinese Communists seize Hankow, we will be able to speak a different language to the Comintern." Nor could Moscow forgive him his speech before the Central Committee of the Chinese Communist Party in September, 1930, in which he declared that "loyalty to the Comintern is one thing; loyalty to the Chinese Revolution is something else." Moscow could never condone lese majesty. It saw insubordination in Li's activities. Therefore Li, having been brought to the fore with Moscow's consent, had to be removed. The Dalburo of the Comintern began a campaign against him, in which Moscow supported its Far Eastern office. The failure of Li's civil war operations (at Changsha) provided a further pretext for action against him.

"The Executive Committee of the Communist International fully approves of the measures taken by the Dalburo against the at-

6. Putschism was then becoming a widely used term in internal Communist polemics. Derived from the German "Putsch," it referred to wild insurrection having no reasonable prospect of success.

titude and steps of Comrade Li Li-san," the Comintern wrote the Chinese party in October, 1930. "The Executive Committee leaves in force all its previous resolutions and directives concerning the Chinese question . . . Comrade Li Li-san has permitted himself to toy with the worn-out theories of all the rightist and leftist renegades of communism." [7]

Upon the insistence of the Dalburo, a plenum of the Central Committee of the Chinese Communist Party was convened. Upon the advice of the Comintern's agent, "Comrade M.," the conference adopted a number of resolutions condemning the "leftist" trend of Li Li-san. But Li still had a large following, especially among the Communist Youth; he remained at the head of the party. Moscow was not satisfied: Li must be deposed. In October the Executive Committee of the International addressed to the Central Committee of its Chinese section an interesting letter in which, in order to demonstrate Li's Putschism, it pictured the Chinese situation in an entirely new light. This time "the great revolutionary upsurge," which it had wished to see in its previous directives, was not referred to, and the somber aspects of the situation were stressed:

There is as yet no Soviet government in China; and to the extent to which there is one, it exists only in resolutions, on paper, not as a real power, as the engineer and leader of the revolting masses. The Soviet regions have not yet been organized. The Soviet power has not been consolidated . . .

The equalization of land holdings, this most important task of the agrarian revolution, has been carried through in but rare instances . . .

We observe premature and erroneous attempts to create collective farms and state farms and to introduce a planned economy.

. . . the fantastic overestimation of the armed forces of the revolution made by Comrade Li Li-san (5 million workers, 30 million peasants, a workers' guard in every town, 5 millions in the youth guard, etc.). It must be pointed out that Comrade Li Li-san absolutely fails to understand that we do not as yet have a real workers' and peasants' red army with a commanding staff of workers, with a strong party backbone.[8]

Finally in January, 1931, an "enlarged plenum of the Central Committee of the Chinese Communist Party," at which a delegate of the Comintern was present, condemned Li Li-san's policy and

7. *Strategiya i taktika*, p. 290.
8. *Strategiya i taktika*, pp. 286–287.

proclaimed him a "half-Trotskyite." He was removed from the Central Committee and had to leave China for Russia.

The Executive Committee of the International in Moscow stated in a resolution that the Comintern "notes with pleasure that the Enlarged Plenary Session of the Central Committee has at last correctly solved the problem and renovated the party's leadership." With satisfaction and pride, the International further stated that these important changes were carried out under the direct guidance of the Executive Committee in Moscow.[9]

For some time there were rumors of Li's having been subjected to punitive measures, and then he was forgotten and his name never appeared in the press until, 15 years later, he suddenly re-emerged, in the wake of the Red Army's advance against the Japanese, at the head of the Chinese Communist forces in Manchuria.

Now the stage was set for Japan's drive into China—an attack which, within a few years, set the entire Orient aflame.

The twenties were a period of comparative quiet both in Europe and in the Far East. In demilitarized Germany a democratic and peaceful evolution seemed secured. In the Far East Japan's aggressiveness of 1918–21 seemed to have been overcome and abandoned. International conflicts rarely burst beyond the confines of diplomacy, and local revolutionary outbreaks and civil wars did not seem to affect the stability of international relations.

The Great Powers appeared to be lulled by a sense of exaggerated international security. Only Moscow foresaw wars in the near future, but Soviet forebodings of a British and French attack on the Soviet Union were obviously unrealistic and were discounted everywhere else. Least of all did Moscow expect grave complications from Japan. Nor were the other Great Powers discerning enough to perceive the clouds gathering over the Far Eastern sky.

The thirties began with Japan's blow in Manchuria and her exit from the League of Nations. Soon Germany and Italy were to follow her example, and within a matter of years local conflicts in Ethiopia, Spain, and North China merged into one great global war.

9. *Ibid.*, pp. 298 ff. How satisfied Moscow was with Li Li-san's removal can be gathered from the tenor of articles in the *Communist International*. In one of the Soviet areas the *Communist International* (1929), No. 25, wrote, "a peasant beat up his wife. She defended herself, telling him, 'You think we're still living in the times of Li Li-san? Now we live according to the line of the Communist International!'"

Sources and Readings

OFFICIAL DOCUMENTS

Germany. Die Grosse Politik der Europäischen Kabinette. Berlin, 1922–27.

Great Britain. British Documents on the Origins of the War. London, 1926–38.

GRIMM, ERWIN. Sbornik dogovorov . . . 1842–1925. Institut Vostokovedeniya, Moscow, 1927.

HERTSLET, EDWARD C. Treaties. London, 1827–1925.

KLYUCHNIKOV, YURI, and A. SABANIN. Mezhdunarodnaya politika noveishevo vremeni. Moscow, 1925–29.

Krasnyi Arkhiv, Vols. V, XIV, XVIII, XX, XXXVII, LII, LXXXII. Moscow, 1925–1939.

MARTENS, FIODOR. Recueil des traités et conventions . . . St. Petersburg, 1874–1909.

Dogovory s Vostokom. St. Petersburg, 1869.

Dokumenty po peregovoram s Yaponiyei 1903–1904 gg. (Crimson Book). St. Petersburg, 1905.

Mezhdunarodnyya otnosheniya v epokhu imperializma (International Relations in the Era of Imperialism). [Documents from the tsarist archives.] Moscow, 1931–1940.

Recueil des traités et documents diplomatiques concernant l'Extrême Orient. St. Petersburg, 1906.

Svod mezhdunarodnykh postanovlenii opredelyayushchikh vzaimnyye otnosheniya mezhdu Rossiyei i Kitayem. St. Petersburg, 1900.

United States, Department of State. Papers Relating to the Foreign Relations of the United States. Washington, 1918–1947.

GENERAL AND BIBLIOGRAPHIC

GOLDER, FRANK A. Russian Expansion on the Pacific. Cleveland, 1914.

KERNER, ROBERT J. Northeast Asia. Berkeley, 1939.

KRAUSSE, ALEXIS. Russia in Asia; a record and a study, 1558–1899. New York, 1899.

LOBANOV-ROSTOVSKY, ANDREI. Russia and Asia. New York, 1933.

POTIOMKIN, VLADIMIR, ed. Istoriya diplomatii, Vols. II–III. Moscow, 1941–45.

SKACHKOV, PIOTR. Bibliografiya Kitaya. Moscow, 1932.

SKRINE, F. H. The Expansion of Russia, 1815–1900. Cambridge, 1903.
SUMNER, B. H. Tsardom and Imperialism. British Academy, Raleigh Lectures, 1940.
SVATIKOV, SERGEI. Rossiya i Sibir'. Prague, 1929.

RUSSIAN POLICY IN THE FAR EAST BEFORE 1917

ASAKAWA, KANICHI. The Russo-Japanese Conflict. Boston, 1904.
AZBELEV, I. P. Yaponiya i Kitai. Moscow, 1895.
BADMAYEV, PIOTR. Za kulisami tsarizma: arkhiv tibetskovo vracha. Leningrad, 1925.
BARSUKOV, IVAN. Graf Nikolai Nikolayevich Muraviev Amurski. Moscow, 1891.
BEVERIDGE, ALBERT J. The Russian Advance. New York, 1904.
BLAND, JOHN O. P. Li Hung-chang. New York, 1917.
BURTSEV, VLADIMIR. Tsar' i vneshnyaya politika. Berlin, 1910.
DENNETT, TYLER. Americans in Eastern Asia. New York, 1922.
——— John Hay. New York, 1933.
——— Roosevelt and the Russo-Japanese War. Garden City, 1925.
FRANKE, OTTO. Die Grossmächte in Ostasien. Braunschweig, 1923.
GODES, MIKHAIL. Probuzhdeniye Azii. Moscow, 1935.
GRISWOLD, A. WHITNEY. The Far Eastern Policy of the United States. New York, 1938.
GURKO, VLADIMIR. Features and Figures of the Past. London, 1939.
HARRISON, E. J. Peace or War East of Baikal. Yokohama, 1910.
HAYASHI, TADASU. Secret Memoirs. New York, 1915.
HOO CHI-TSAI. Les bases conventionelles des relations modernes entre la Chine et la Russie. Paris, 1918.
ISVOLSKY, ALEXANDER. Mémoires. Paris, 1923.
JOSEPH, PHILIP. Foreign Diplomacy in China. London, 1928.
KENNAN, GEORGE. Siberia. New York, 1891.
——— E. H. Harriman. New York, 1922.
KOROSTOVETS, IVAN. Prewar Diplomacy. London, 1920.
——— Von Cinggis Khan zur Sowjetrepublik. Berlin, 1926.
KUROPATKIN, ALEXEI. Russko-kitaiski vopros. St. Petersburg, 1913.
LAMSDORFF, VLADIMIR. Dnevniki. Moscow, 1926–34.
LANGER, WILLIAM L. Diplomacy of Imperialism. New York, 1935.
——— European Alliances and Alignments. New York, 1931.
LANSING, ROBERT. War Memoirs. New York, 1935.
Letters from the Kaiser to the Tsar. New York, 1920.
LIGIN, YURI. Na Dal'nem Vostoke. Moscow, 1913.
MARTIN, RUDOLF. Die Zukunft Russlands und Japans. Berlin, 1905.
Materialy po Amurskomu i Yuzhno-Ussuriiskomu krayu. St. Petersburg, 1882–83.
MORSE, HOSEA B. International Relations of the Chinese Empire. London, 1910–18.

MORSE, HOSEA B. and H. F. MacNair. Far Eastern International Relations. Shanghai, 1928.

MUSKATBLIT, F. Rossiya i Yaponiya na Dal'nem Vostoke. Odessa, 1904.

NOLDE, BORIS E. Vneshnyaya politika. Petrograd, 1915.

Priamurye. Moscow, 1909.

ROSEN, ROMAN. Forty Years of Diplomacy. London, 1922.

SEMIONOV-TYANSHANSKI, ANDREI. Nashi blizhaishiye zadachi na Dal'nem Vostoke. St. Petersburg, 1908.

STANOYEVICH, MILIVOY. Russian Foreign Policy in the East. Oakland, 1916.

STIEVE, FRIEDRICH. Isvolsky and the World War. London, 1926.

STIEVE, F., and GEORGE A. SCHREINER. Graf Benckendorff's diplomatischer Briefwechsel. Berlin, 1928.

TARLE, YEVGENI. Graf S. Yu. Witte. Leningrad, 1927.

TUZHILIN, ALEXANDER. Sovremennyi Kitai. St. Petersburg, 1910.

UKHTOMSKY, ESPER. Iz kitaiskikh pisem. St. Petersburg, 1901.

―――― K sobytiyam v Kitaye. St. Petersburg, 1900.

―――― Puteshestviye na Vostok. St. Petersburg, 1893–97.

ULAR, ALEXANDER. A Russo-Chinese Empire. Westminster, 1904.

VAGTS, ALFRED. Deutschland und die Vereinigten Staaten. New York, 1935.

VOTINOV, ALEXANDER. Yaponski shpionazh v russko-yaponskuyu voinu. Moscow, 1939.

WITTE, SERGEI. Memoirs. Garden City, 1921.

―――― Prolog russko-yaponskoi voiny. (B. Glinsky, ed.) Petrograd, 1916.

ZABRISKIE, EDWARD H. American-Russian Rivalry in the Far East. Philadelphia, 1946.

THE RUSSIAN SPHERE IN EAST ASIA

BARANOV, ALEXEI. Khalkha. Harbin, 1919.

BELL, CHARLES. Tibet, Past and Present. Oxford, 1924.

CLARK, GROVER. Tibet, China, and Great Britain. Peking, 1924.

CLYDE, PAUL H. International Rivalries in Manchuria. Ohio University Press, 1926.

FRITERS, GERALD. International Position of Outer Mongolia. Dijon, 1939.

GRAJDANZEV, ANDREW J. Modern Korea. New York, 1944.

KABO, RAFAIL. Ocherki istorii i ekonomiki Tuvy. Moscow, 1924.

KALLINIKOV, ANATOLI. Revolyutsionnaya Mongoliya. Moscow, 1925.

KAZAK, FUAD. Ostturkistan zwischen den Grossmächten. Königsberg, 1937.

KUSHELEV, YU. Mongoliya i mongol'ski vopros. St. Petersburg, 1912.

LATTIMORE, OWEN. Inner Asian Frontiers of China. New York, 1940.

LEVINE, ISAAC. La Mongolie. Paris, 1937.

MAISKY, IVAN. Sovremennaya Mongoliya. Irkutsk, 1921.

NIKITIN, B. La Mongolie. Paris, 1930.

NORTON, HENRY. The Far Eastern Republic of Siberia. London, 1923.

OLIVER, ROBERT J. Korea. Washington, 1944.

PHILLIPS, G. D. R. Russia, Japan, and Mongolia. London, 1942.

PRICE, ERNEST B. The Russo-Japanese Treaties of 1907–1916 Concerning Manchuria and Mongolia. Baltimore, 1933.

ROMANOV, BORIS A. Rossiya v Mandzhurii. Leningrad, 1928.

SKRINE, CLARMONT P. Chinese Central Asia. London, 1926.

Uryankhaiski Krai. Irkutsk, 1913.

YOUNG, C. WALTER. International Legal Status of Kwantung. Baltimore, 1931.

—— International Relations of Manchuria. Chicago, 1929.

Constitution of the Far Eastern Republic. Vladivostok, 1921.

Far Eastern Republic. Memorandum to the Washington Conference. Washington, 1921.

Foreign Policy Association. The Far Eastern Republic. New York, 1922.

SOVIET POLICY IN THE FAR EAST

BATES, ERNEST S. Soviet Asia. London, 1942.

BELOFF, MAX. Foreign Policy of Soviet Russia, Vol. I. London, 1947.

BESEDOVSKY, GRIGORI. Na putyakh k Temidoru. Paris, 1930–31; Revelations of a Soviet Diplomat (abbrev. trans.). London, 1931.

BUSS, CLAUDE A. War and Diplomacy in Eastern Asia. New York, 1941.

Communist International. Komintern pered 6 vsemirnym kongresom. Moscow, 1928.

—— Strategiya i taktika Kominterna v natsional'no-kolonial'noi revolyutsii na primere Kitaya. Moscow, 1934.

CONOLLY, VIOLET. Soviet Economic Policy in the East. London, 1933.

DOLIVO-DOBROVOL'SKI, B. I. Tikhookeanskaya problema. Moscow, 1924.

FISCHER, LOUIS. The Soviets in World Affairs. London, 1930.

FUSE, KATSUJI. Soviet Policy in the Orient. Peking, 1927.

GRAVES, WILLIAM S. America's Siberian Adventure. New York, 1931.

HELLER, LEV. Natsional'nyye i rabochiye dvizheniya na Tikhom Okeane. Moscow, 1926.

Mezhdunarodnaya politika RSFSR v 1922 godu. Moscow, 1923.

MILYUKOV, PAVEL. La Politique extérieure des Soviets. Paris, 1936.

PASVOLSKY, LEO. Russia in the Far East. New York, 1922.

PAVLOVICH (WELTMAN), MIKHAIL. Bor'ba za Aziyu . . . Moscow, 1923.

REICHBERG, GEORGI. Yaponskaya interventsiya. Moscow, 1935.

SAFAROV, GEORGI. Kolonial'naya revolyutsiya. Moscow, 1921.

SCHEFFER, PAUL. Seven Years in Russia. London, 1931.

SEREBRENNIKOV, IVAN. Veliki otkhod. Harbin, 1936.

STALIN, JOSEF. Marxism and the National and Colonial Question. New York, 1936.

—— O perspektivakh revolyutsii v Kitaye. Moscow, 1926.

—— Ob oppozitsii. Moscow, 1928.

TSELISHCHEV, M. I. Ekonomicheskiye ocherki Dal'nevo Vostoka. Vladivostok, 1925.

United States, Department of State. Papers Relating to the Foreign Rela-

tions of the United States. Russia: 1918 and 1919. Washington, 1931–32, and 1937.
Voprosy kitaiskoi revolyutsii. Leningrad, 1927.

JAPAN

AVARIN, VLADIMIR. Bor'ba za Tikhi Okean. Leningrad, 1947.
BUELL, RAYMOND L. The Washington Conference. New York, 1922.
Communist International. Far Eastern Section. Yaponiya na russkom Dal'nem Vostoke. Moscow, 1922.
GALKOVICH, MOISEI. Soyedinennyye Shtaty i dal'nevostochnaya problema. Moscow, 1928.
HAUSHOFER, KARL. Japan's Reichserneuerung. Berlin, 1930.
MOTYLEV, WOLF. Zarozhdeniye i razvitiye tikhookeanskovo uzla protivo-rechii. Moscow, 1939.
STIMSON, HENRY L. The Far Eastern Crisis. New York, 1936.
––––– On Active Service. New York, 1948.
TAKEUCHI, T. War and Diplomacy in the Japanese Empire. New York, 1935.
VILENSKI-SIBIRYAKOV, VLADIMIR. Sovetskaya Rossiya u beregov Tikhovo Okeana. Moscow, 1923.

CHINA

AMANN, GUSTAV. Chiang Kai-shek. Heidelberg, 1936.
BAU, MINGCHIEN. The Open Door Doctrine. New York, 1923.
BERG, DOROTHY. American Policy and the Chinese Revolution. New York, 1947.
BORODINA, FANYA. V zastenkakh kitaiskikh satrapov. Moscow, 1928.
CLYDE, PAUL H. United States Policy toward China. Durham, 1940.
DEMIDOV, ALEXANDER. Sovremennyi Kitai i Rossiya. Paris, 1931.
ERENBURG, GRIGORI. Sovetski Kitai. Moscow, 1934.
Far Eastern Information Bureau. Documents [on] the Sino-Russian Dispute. Nanking, 1929.
GREEN, OWEN M. The Story of China's Revolution. London, 1945.
HOLCOMBE, ARTHUR N. The Spirit of the Chinese Revolution. New York, 1930.
HSÜ, SHUHSI. China and Her Political Entity. New York, 1926.
ISAACS, HAROLD R. The Tragedy of the Chinese Revolution. London, 1938.
KANTOROVICH, ANATOLI. Amerika v bor'be za Kitai. Moscow, 1935.
LOZOVSKY, A. Rabochii Kitai v 1927 godu. Moscow, 1928.
MIF, PAVEL. Kitaiskaya Kommunisticheskaya Partiya. Moscow, 1932.
MIKHAILOV, M. Chto proiskhodit na KVZhD. Moscow, 1926.
NORTON, HENRY K. China and the Powers. New York, 1927.
POLLARD, ROBERT T. China's Foreign Relations, 1917–1931. New York, 1933.

POWELL, JOHN B. My Twenty-five Years in China. New York, 1945.

ROY, MANABENDRANATH. Revolution und Konterrevolution in China. Berlin, 1930.

SAVVIN, B. P. Vzaimootnosheniya tsarskoi Rossii i SSSR s Kitayem. Moscow, 1930.

SIMON, PAUL. Le Mouvement communiste en Chine. Paris, 1939.

SKALOV, GEORGI. Sobytiya na KVZhD. Moscow, 1929.

SOKOLSKY, GEORGE. The Story of the Chinese Eastern Railway. Shanghai, 1929.

Sovety v Kitaye. Moscow, 1933.

SUN YAT-SEN. San Min Chu I.

——— China and Japan. Shanghai, 1941.

TANG LEANG-LI. The Inner History of the Chinese Revolution. London, 1930.

The Soviets in China Unmasked. Peking, 1927.

TONG, HOLLINGTON K. Facts about the Chinese Eastern Railway. Harbin, 1929.

TROTSKY, LEO. Problems of the Chinese Revolution. New York, 1932.

TSAO LIEN-EN. The Chinese Eastern Railway. Shanghai, 1929.

VILENSKI-SIBIRYAKOV, VLADIMIR. Gomindan. Moscow, 1926.

VOITINSKI, GRIGORI. KVZhD i politika imperialistov v Kitaye. Moscow, 1930.

WEIGH, KEN-SHEN. Russo-Chinese Diplomacy. Shanghai, 1928.

WILLIAM, MAURICE. Sun Yat-sen versus Communism. Baltimore, 1932.

Index